JOINT APPROACHES TO SOCIAL POLICY

JOINT APPROACHES TO SOCIAL POLICY

Rationality and practice

LINDA CHALLIS   SUSAN FULLER
MELANIE HENWOOD   RUDOLF KLEIN
WILLIAM PLOWDEN   ADRIAN WEBB
PETER WHITTINGHAM   GERALD WISTOW

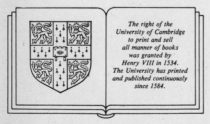

The right of the
University of Cambridge
to print and sell
all manner of books
was granted by
Henry VIII in 1534.
The University has printed
and published continuously
since 1584.

CAMBRIDGE UNIVERSITY PRESS

Cambridge
New York   New Rochelle   Melbourne   Sydney

Published by the Press Syndicate of the University of Cambridge
The Pitt Building, Trumpington Street, Cambridge CB2 1RP
32 East 57th Street, New York, NY 10022, USA
10 Stamford Road, Oakleigh, Melbourne 3166, Australia

© Cambridge University Press 1988

First published 1988

Printed in Great Britain at the University Press, Cambridge

British Library cataloguing in publication data

Klein, Rudolf, 1930–
Joint approaches to social policy.
1. Great Britain – Social policy.
I. Title. II. Plowden, William. III. Webb, Adrian.
361.6′1′0941   HN385.5

Library of Congress cataloguing in publication data

Klein, Rudolf.
Joint approaches to social policy.
Bibliography.
Includes index.
1. Great Britain – Social policy. 2. Central–local
government relations – Great Britain.
I. Plowden, William. II. Webb, Adrian Leonard. III. Title.
HN390.K57 1987   361.6′1′0941   87-13158

ISBN 0 521 30900 X

CE

CONTENTS

BIOGRAPHICAL NOTES

LINDA CHALLIS
Linda Challis is a Lecturer in Social Policy at the Centre for the Analysis of Social Policy at the University of Bath. She has worked in the Personal Social Services in both a practice and research capacity. Her interest in coordination developed as a result of her work on day care for under fives, and from her present research interests in care of elderly people and the relationship between public and private provision. She has been a member of national working parties on aspects of care for both children under five and elderly people, as well as serving as a member of a District Health Authority.

SUSAN FULLER
Susan Fuller is a researcher in the Chief Executive's Department, Cleveland County Council. She obtained a BSc in Political Science at University College of Wales, Aberystwyth in 1978. She subsequently studied for a doctorate in Political Science, which was awarded in 1985. She was a researcher at Loughborough University from 1981 to 1985, working on an evaluation of the government's Opportunities for Volunteering programme, as well as on the study of policy coordination which resulted in the present volume.

MELANIE HENWOOD
Melanie Henwood is a Research Officer at the Family Policy Studies Centre. Her major interests are in the fields of community care; child support; and housing policy and the family life cycle. Her most recent publications, which she co-authored with Malcolm Wicks, are *The Forgotten Army: family care and elderly people* (FPSC 1984), and *Benefit or Burden? the objectives and impact of child support* (FPSC 1986).

RUDOLF KLEIN
Rudolf Klein is a Professor of Social Policy, and Director of the Centre for the Analysis of Social Policy, at the University of Bath. He studied mediaeval history at Oxford, spent 20 years as a journalist and subsequently turned to an academic career. He has edited or written books about public expenditure,

the future of welfare policies and the politics of the National Health Service. His latest book (with Patricia Day) is *Accountabilities*. He is joint editor of *Political Quarterly*.

WILLIAM PLOWDEN
William Plowden is Director-General of the Royal Institute of Public Administration. He has previously worked as a lecturer at the London School of Economics and as a civil servant in the industry and trade departments and in the Central Policy Review Staff. In the latter he was closely involved with the 'Joint Approach to Social Policies' (JASP).

ADRIAN WEBB
After graduating at Birmingham University in 1965, Adrian Webb studied at the London School of Economics (LSE) and was offered a Lectureship in the Department of Social Administration in 1966. During eight years at LSE he taught a wide variety of courses, but specialised in the Personal Social Services. He was appointed Professor of Social Administration at Loughborough University of Technology in 1976, became Head of the Department of Social Sciences in 1981 and Director of the Centre for Research in Social Policy in 1983. He is now Dean of the School of Human and Environmental Studies. He is also a member of the Council of Tribunals. He is author or co-author of ten books and monograph, the latest (with Susan Charles) being *The Economics of Social Policy* (Wheatsheaf).

PETER WHITTINGHAM
Peter Whittingham first trained as a natural scientist before transferring to sociological sciences at Kent University. Prior to joining the Bath research team he was for four years a Research Officer with Lambeth Social Services. He was Head of the Planning, Training and Community Development Unit in the Personal Services Department of the London Borough of Redbridge, and is now Assistant Director with North Yorkshire Social Services.

GERALD WISTOW
Gerald Wistow is co-director of the Centre for Research in Social Policy at Loughborough University of Technology. He has a long standing interest in inter-agency collaboration and has published a number of articles and monographs on joint planning, joint finance and 'care in the community'. He is also the co-author, with Adrian Webb, of three books on the personal social services. His most recent book (with David Hunter) is *Community Care in Britain: Variations on a Theme* (King's Fund 1987).

PREFACE

When we started the research on which this book reports, we thought that we were about to carry out a post-mortem. At the beginning of the eighties, when the Economic and Social Research Council (ESRC) gave us a grant for this work, the landscape was littered with ideas and institutions which had dominated the two previous decades but had seemingly not survived the cold climate of economic retrenchment and ideological change. Gone were the days when Keynesian economic management could be relied upon to make unemployment simply a bad memory. Gone were the days when the Welfare State thrived on the dividends of economic growth. Gone were the days of consensual policy making and corporate institutions. Gone, too, were the days of belief in the pursuit of greater rationality in policy making through the coordination of different policy instruments and agencies.

It was this last casualty of the transformation of the economic, social and intellectual climate which was the subject of our inquiry. The sixties and seventies had spawned a large family of initiatives designed to bring about greater rationality in policy making through coordination. Indeed both central and local government, the health services and the personal services had undergone major reorganisations largely, if not exclusively, designed to make it easier to attack social problems by bringing different strands of policy making to bear on them. And symbolic of this endeavour was the Central Policy Review Staff (CPRS) in Whitehall, designed to cut through the tangle of departmental interests and to bring a rational, synoptic view to the analysis of policy. In turn, it was the CPRS's report *A Joint Framework for Social Policies* (usually known as the 'Joint Approach to Social Policy', or 'JASP') which gave us the working title for our project: 'Whatever happened to JASP?'. For when we started, JASP was dead and the CPRS was clearly dying. And we thought that by taking the problem of social policy coordination as the theme for our undertaking, we would be able to explore some of the problems of modern government: our hope was that, by carrying out such a post-mortem, we would be able to explain why it was that the search for greater rationality in policy making had failed, and what might have saved it. Perhaps the search was doomed from the start; perhaps it was simply carried out too naively, in the expectation that rationality was its own reward. We did not know, but we hoped to find out even at the risk of illuminating only history.

We need not have worried. No sooner had we got the body on the operating table than it showed signs of life. What started as a post-mortem turned out, as we started to write up our findings, to be an inquiry highly relevant for the future of British government. Hardly a day has passed without some new government initiative involving coordination, and this from a government which had forgotten JASP, killed off the CPRS and was committed to a hands-off, market-orientated approach to social policy making. In dealing with the problems of the inner cities, the government set up a task force designed to cut across administrative boundaries. In trying to cope with the issue of law and order, the government exhorted everyone to set up coordinating bodies. In reacting to the problem of child abuse, the government stressed the need for greater coordination between the different agencies involved. In trying to cope with the effects of financial stringency, the government emphasised the importance of coordination between the National Health Service and the Personal Social Services. Coordination has, once again, become a fashionable buzz word.

The trend is evident both within and beyond Whitehall. There have been pleas for the resurrection of the CPRS. And, perhaps most significant of a wider intellectual change, the enthusiasm for coordination also reflects a growing sense of helplessness by single service agencies in the face of social complexity. Doctors and policemen, social workers and teachers are all agreed that what they do is shaped by forces beyond their control. There is a rush, as it were, to disavow responsibility, be it for ill-health or crime, child abuse or illiteracy. And if all such problems reflect multiple causes springing from a complex social environment, then obviously the only way of dealing with them is by coordinating a variety of different agencies in a common enterprise. Once again, then, coordination becomes the key to successful social action.

But if the word itself is once again back in favour, it remains precisely that: a word in search of ways of giving it effective meaning in practice. In government circulars and ministerial policy pronouncements, it is a largely rhetorical invocation of a vague ideal. The centre will prescribe; the periphery will implement. In this respect, little appears to have changed since the last time round, in the seventies, when the concept was last in vogue.

It is because of this that, slightly to our own surprise, our study has considerable relevance for the future. For what we aim to provide in this book, by looking at the practice of coordination at and between all levels of government and a variety of other agencies, is an understanding of what the process actually involves. By taking 'coordination' as problematic, by asking what conditions and incentives are required for it to be a successful recipe for tackling policy problems, we try to generate a series of insights about how to move from policy rhetoric to policy practice. In this, we do not provide a cook-book for policy makers. We do, however, seek to give policy makers – at all levels – some of the conceptual tools needed for thinking about how to make coordination a success. For the central message of our book, to anticipate our final chapter, is that coordination does not just happen because ministers or top civil servants say that it should. It means creating the right kind of framework and providing the right kind of incentives for the individual actors who alone can make it work.

In order to explore these issues, we have been eclectic in our research strategy. We have not only looked at the practice of coordination in a variety of settings, national and local (since by definition any research into coordination must look at the relationship both between central government departments, and between central government and local agencies). We have also tried to combine social anthropology and bureaumetrics. We have sought both to give a picture of how organisational actors in a variety of settings perceive the problems and opportunities of coordination but also to measure the actual outputs or products of coordination (a useful precedent, perhaps, for ministers setting up new coordinating machinery: perhaps they, too, should have such performance indicators to check on the success of their enterprise). In doing so, we open a window not only on the Whitehall village but also on how the inhabitants there perceive their relationship with the lesser tribes in the outlying settlements.

Finally, this study is innovative in another respect as well (although it will be for the reader to judge whether it is a successful innovation). It is itself the product of an exercise in coordination, involving three research teams based in three different institutions (The Royal Institute of Public Administration and the Universities of Bath and Loughborough). It thus illustrates both the costs and benefits of coordination, as well as perhaps the need for an outside body like the ESRC to provide the financial incentives required to make the process work. The costs include, conspicuously, the time involved in bringing three teams together and in exchanging drafts of chapters. In this respect, we found, coordination *is* expensive, and in producing this book we have stretched the patience even of a publisher used to academic dawdlings with deadlines. However, in our own view certainly, the result is a study (to turn to the benefits of coordination) where every argument and assertion has been challenged. The result may not necessarily be more coherent than if it had been by one hand, but it is certainly more rigorous than if any one of us had taken sole responsibility for its production.

For this is a collective book. Individual authors have had a special responsibility for different chapters. So, for example, William Plowden alone is responsible for the chapter telling the story of JASP. Four members of the team – Sue Fuller, Melanie Henwood, Peter Whittingham and Gerald Wistow – were responsible for organising and conducting the local fieldwork, for analysing the materials collected and for writing the relevant chapters (6–10). They also fully participated in planning the book as a whole and drafting other chapters. But coordination did not end with the research. It persisted throughout the long process of writing up the findings and ended with the publication of this book. If coordination can have identifiable, visible and measurable products, then this book is one.

ACKNOWLEDGEMENTS

This book has been made possible by the help and cooperation of a large, but necessarily anonymous, army of people working in central and local government, the National Health Service and voluntary agencies. We are most grateful to them for giving us their time and advice. We only regret that, since one of the conditions of our enterprise was that our sources should not be revealed, we are unable to thank them by name. The orchestration of the work and the typing of successive drafts were tasks shared by a number of secretaries. We would, in particular, like to thank Sylvia Hodges at the University of Bath, and Lorraine Jones, Margaret Millington and Ann Tanner at the University of Loughborough. We would also like to thank the Royal Institute of Public Administration and the Family Policy Studies Centre for providing space and hospitality for the meetings bringing together the three research teams. Finally, we are grateful to Professor Michael Hill and Dr Ellie Scrivens for commenting on an earlier draft of this book.

1 ∽ Rationality – the history of an idea

This is a book about the quest for rationality in policy making. It is about the search for ways of disciplining the anarchy of politics, of devising an organisational architecture of decision making and institutionalising a style of analysis which would allow men to run their collective affairs more efficiently and more effectively. It is about the frustrating pursuit of an elusive vision – the vision of policy making not as the product of the accidents of power but as an ordered process whose every step is guided by the logic of seeking the greatest happiness of the greatest number – which has haunted the minds of men for 150 years or more. It is a quest shaped by the assumption that there is such a thing as rationality in policy making independent of, and indeed opposed to, the rationality of politics. It is an approach which rejects the original sin view of the world in which policy decisions will inevitably reflect the selfish, grasping and narrow interests of social classes or interest groups, in favour of an optimistic, perfectibility of man, view of the world in which improvements in the machinery of decision making can actually lead to better decisions. It is a vision of an administrative City of God, in which appropriately designed institutions and organisations will make mankind if not good, at least rational.

Specifically, this study is concerned with one particular aspect of the quest for rationality in policy making: rationality defined in terms of *coordinating* differing aspects of policy, and so bringing together the various services concerned with the same problems in order to establish a more coherent, consistent and comprehensive grip on the complex, often chaotic reality being addressed by the policy makers. It is a definition of rationality which, conveniently, had its own manifesto: the report of the Central Policy Review Staff entitled *A Joint Framework for Social Policies*[1]. It is this which provided the focus for our research and a helpful starting point for exploring further the vocabulary and ideology of the quest for rationality: the subject of this introductory chapter.

This 1975 report – a Joint Approach to Social Policy (JASP), as it became known – offered both a diagnosis and a prescription. The diagnosis was that 'many of the most intractable problems affect more than one department, and involve central government, local authorities and other bodies'. Information about need and effectiveness was often lacking. So was an 'effective mechanism for determining coherent and consistent priorities'. The incentives to 'increase the efficiency of existing policies' were inadequate. The prescriptions that followed accurately mirrored the diagnosis. The future aim, the document argued, should be: (a) to improve coordination between services as they affect the individual; (b) better analysis of, and policy prescription for, complex problems – especially when they concerned more than one government department; and (c) the development of a collective view among Ministers on priorities as between different programmes, problems and groups.

The birth of JASP is analysed in more detail in chapter 4. For the purposes of this chapter, however, it is enough to draw attention to the concepts which shaped the document and the words used to give them expression. In particular, and most relevantly for the theme of this book, the document shows the way in which the concept of 'coordination' – i.e. the production of 'joint' policies or measures or outputs by different services or agencies – is anchored in the wider vision of rationality in policy making. Thus coordination is seen as the rational response to the complex, untidy sprawl of social problems which do not conform neatly or conveniently to administrative boundaries and responsibilities and to the problem of resource scarcity. It is seen as a way of moving towards a set of *coherent, comprehensive* and *consistent* policies: further key words in the litany of rationality in policy making. Only coordinated policies, defined in terms of their coherence, comprehensiveness and consistency, can then, in turn, lead to *efficiency* and *effectiveness*. Indeed *efficiency* and *effectiveness* appear to be the criteria for judging whether or not rationality is being achieved. The implicit assumption would seem to be that the aim of public policy should be to maximise the output from any given input of resources rather than (say) maximising the number of votes for the party in power or maximising the support for the system of government. From this follows, ineluctably, the emphasis on the crucial importance of information and analysis. Governments, the document argues, need better analysed and monitored information: 'There is clearly a need for a better transdepartmental information base for social policy. This would be an essential tool for regular Ministerial reviews of social policy.' Equally, research was required to 'increase our understanding of the underlying forces at work'.

If rationality required changes in the intellectual processes of policy making, it also demanded equivalent changes in the organisational structure. For in a rational world, the organisational architecture must surely reflect its functions, that is, the promotion of a coordinated – as well as a coherent, consistent, comprehensive and analytical – approach to the production of social policies. So the 1975 document proposed the creation of a new ministerial forum, which would bring together a 'group of senior Ministers' to review priorities and developments across departments. Again, this is discussed more extensively in chapter 4, as are the other specific proposals made in *A Joint Framework for Social Policies*. But what is significant, in the context of our present discussion, is the link between process and structure: stressing rationality in process inevitably leads to demands for a structure which will promote change (and, in turn, may slide into the assumption that changing structures will, in itself, promote the adoption of rational processes).

Lastly, and characteristic of the optimism which tends to sustain and encourage the quest for rationality, the 1975 document had implicit in its analysis a model of institutional behaviour based on cooperation rather than conflict or competition. Its programme of action rested on one key assumption:

that if a 'joint' and more coherent approach to social policies is to have any chance of succeeding, departments and Ministers must be prepared to make some adjustments, whether in priorities, policies, administrative practices, or public expenditure allocations. For example, a study of a problem area might show that short-run remedial measures (department A) were ineffective unless supported by long-run preventive policies (department B); this might require a shift of resources within B, or from A to B, or to B from elsewhere.

In many respects, *A Joint Framework for Social Policies* was very much a document of its time. It came at the end of a decade in which the search for rationality in policy making had been pursued with fervent persistence by successive governments, Labour and Conservative alike. It was a decade in which politics, to caricature only slightly, largely revolved around the competition between the parties to demonstrate their superior ability to deliver the goods of economic growth. It was therefore a period which saw not only a concentration on the improvement of governmental techniques and institutions, but also a stress on cooperation rather than conflict: a hesitant, uneven movement towards the creation of a British version of corporatism, with the creation of new machinery for engaging trade unions, employers and governments in the process of policy making – an attempt to substitute rational dialogue for the clash of power blocks[2,3].

By the time *A Joint Framework for Social Policies* was published, this era was nearing its end. Indeed its fate in part reflected the fact that while it was the intellectual child of the era of economic growth, it was born into a world of stagflation. But its vocabulary and ideology cannot be understood outside this wider context. In turn, if the explanation for the quest for organisational rationality in the decade ending in 1975 is not to be distorted by the special circumstances and preoccupations of those years, it is essential to look at the historical tradition from which it largely drew its ideas and inspiration. While it is not the object of this chapter to provide a history of the search for rationality in policy making in Britain, identifying the broad themes that have informed analysis and action over the past 150 years is an essential safeguard against stumbling into explanations too exclusively anchored in the present day.

FROM BENTHAM ONWARD

'God forbid that any disease of the constitution of a state should be without its remedy', wrote Jeremy Bentham in *A Fragment on Government*[4]. And it is precisely this insistence that it is human minds and human beings that shape institutions, this rejection of the view that it is institutions that shape men and have an independent life and justification of their own, which makes the Benthamite tradition a useful starting point for illustrating the intellectual history of the quest for rationality. This is not to argue that Bentham had no intellectual predecessors, or to imply that there is a direct line of intellectual descent which allows us to link Bentham with the Webbs, and beyond to the Central Policy Review Staff; the search for a rational technique of governance is obviously linked to the rational scientific method of enquiry propounded by Bacon and Pascal[5]. It is rather to identify one particular strand in British political thought – the way in which people thought about the reform of the institutions, structures, organisation and administration of government – without assuming that this was necessarily an intellectually homogeneous, consistent tradition. In a sense what links the often very disparate actors involved is not so much a coherent body of doctrine, which does not exist, but certain off-the-cuff assumptions: a temperamental and intellectual bias.

It is a bias, in the case of Bentham, towards the cheerful assumption that there is no problem of governance which is not susceptible to rational analysis. Only go back to first principles, and it is possible to design legislation and institutions accordingly. Only apply the principle of utility, and we have a yardstick by which to measure all the actions of government:

A measure of government ... may be said to be conformable to or dictated by the principle of utility, when ... the tendency which it has to augment the happiness of the community is greater than any which it has to diminish it.

It is an approach, therefore, which transforms problems of governance from the realm of politics seen as clashing interests, where the outcome will be determined by the balance of organised power, to the realm of technique and analysis. From applying the principle of utility, it is no great leap to trying to base policy making on cost-benefit and similar techniques: equating somewhat brutally and questionably the 'happiness' of the community with its purchasing power[6].

Moreover, it is also an approach which puts the emphasis on giving institutional expression to ideas. Organisations, in the world of Bentham, embody policy aims and, in turn, are designed to promote them. Structure and process reflect and reinforce each other. When Bentham came to give thought to the organisation of government, he expressed his ideas architecturally. Given the need to maintain 'instantaneous intercommunication' between ministers, Bentham proposed the following arrangement:

In the apartment of the Prime Minister, from an apt position within reach of the seat occupied by him, issue thirteen conversation tubes, terminating in corresponding positions contiguous in like manner to the seats of the several ministers in their several apartments. From the apartments of each minister to the apartment of every other minister runs in like manner a conversation tube[7].

Possibly for the first time, but certainly not for the last time, coordination is equated with communication.

The implied antithesis between politics and knowledge, between power and analysis, is one of the recurring themes in nineteenth-century reflections on the problems of government. Consider the following quotation from Henry Taylor's *The Statesman*[8], not one of the most radical documents of its period:

Till the government of the country shall become a nucleus at which the best wisdom in the country contained shall be perpetually forming itself in deposit, it will be, except as regards the shuffling of power from hand to hand and class to class, little better than a government of fetches, shifts, and hand-to-mouth expedients. Till a wise and constant instrumentality at work upon administrative measures (distinguished as they might be from measures of political parties) shall be understood to be essential to the government of a country, that country can be considered to enjoy nothing more than the embryo of a government ...

Taylor's book also adds a new theme to those previously introduced: a theme which, as we shall see, emerges fortissimo in the twentieth century. This is its insistence that good government depends on taking a long-term view. Note Taylor's contempt for 'hand-to-mouth expedients'. Moreover, in a passage introducing the above quotation, he analyses the reasons why this should be so, and they turn out to be remarkably similar to those given for explaining the problems of government in the 1970s: ministerial overload. 'Every day, every hour, has its exigencies, its immediate demands; and he who has hardly time to eat his meals cannot be expected to occupy himself devising good for mankind', wrote Taylor in 1836. So much of the argument that the problems of governance in the twentieth century can be explained solely by the growth in the scale and scope of government activities. And, indeed,

Taylor's recipe for dealing with the problems turns out to be surprisingly modern as well: to set up, within government, a body of men whose special task it would be to 'take thought for the morrow', and to bring together and direct the 'great means and appliances of wisdom which lie scattered through this intellectual country'.

More directly in the Benthamite tradition, Chadwick's career can be seen as the disciple's attempt to translate the prophet's doctrine of rationality in policy making into action[9]. In the outcome, the rationality of politics defeated Chadwick. None of his great projects were fully implemented and he himself was forced into a premature retirement. Yet even though both his great crusades – the reform of the poor laws and the sanitary revolution – failed to reach the promised land, and his hopes remained only partially fulfilled, they offer admirable illustration of the assumptions implicit in, and the intellectual bias of, the rationalist reformer in politics. They are the first of the great nineteenth-century reforms to be based on theory, information and analysis. Chadwick's 1842 Report on the *Sanitary Condition of the Labouring Population of Great Britain*[10] remains a model of analysing a social problem in terms of its geographical and class distribution and the use of what was in effect, if not in name, cost-benefit analysis applied to a social problem. Moreover, Chadwick – true to the spirit of Bentham – institutionalised policy changes in organisational changes: once again, process and structure had to be brought together. His plans were based on the assumption that it would be possible to change the structure in line with its new functions, and that a central inspectorate would supply the information required to whip laggards into line. And, paradoxically, his failure to achieve this transformation – the defeat of administrative rationality by the brute force of local interest groups – remains the best justification of his underlying argument that process and structure cannot be divorced. For it was precisely his failure to achieve the structural changes which help to explain the defeat of his policy intentions and subverted the thrust of the reforms themselves.

Chadwick also had a particular obsession with the reform of local government: not surprisingly perhaps since it had been the 'baleful money interests' and the 'jobocracies' in the boroughs and counties which had frustrated his reforming ambitions. If local government was largely corrupt, he argued, it was because only those who would profit from exploiting the system had an incentive to take part in local government, while the remaining citizens rationally took refuge in apathy. So, concluded Chadwick, the sensible response was to lower the costs of participation for the majority – by paying people to go round to collect votes – and to transfer responsibility for administration from self-interested volunteers to 'properly qualified officers', i.e. salaried experts. The argument used by Chadwick is not only interesting in its own right, for its very modern recognition of participation costs. It also provides a bridge to the next generation of reformers: that strange alliance of Fabians and Liberal Imperialists who set out on *'The Quest for National Efficiency'*[11] at the beginning of the twentieth century. For in so far as this heterogeneous group can be said to have had any unifying faith, it was the belief that the crusade for greater rationality in government would be led by the 'experts'. As Beatrice Webb was to note in her diaries:

We staked our hopes on the organised working-class, served and guided, it is true, by an elite of unassuming experts who would make no claim to superior social status, but would content themselves with exercising the power inherent in superior knowledge and longer administrative experience[12].

The Webbs were, indeed, central characters in the years of critical national self-examination which preceded the outbreak of the 1914 war: years which bear an uncanny similarity to the 1960s and early 1970s, even down to the constant (unfavourable) comparison between the economic performances of Britain, on the one hand, and Germany and Japan on the other. It was a period in which all British institutions of government were critically reviewed, and found wanting when judged by the criterion of 'efficiency'. In 1902 the Webbs founded a short-lived dining club – entitled the 'Co-Efficient Club' – which brought together Haldane, Bertrand Russell, H. G. Wells and Amery, among others. According to Amery, the Co-Efficients were meant to be a 'Brains Trust or General Staff' which would work out the details on which a new 'Party of Efficiency' might appeal to the country.

The search for national efficiency, the view that policy could be divorced from politics, that expert decision making could be independent of interest group power, was a common thread in the rhetoric of the period. One further theme (which was to be taken up again in the 1970s and 1980s) was that government should be more businesslike: the model of managerial rationality in business was frequently invoked. 'After all a State is in essence a great joint stock company with unlimited liability on the part of its shareholders', Lord Rosebery argued in 1900, 'and a business depends on incessant vigilance, on method, on keeping abreast of the time'. Yet another theme, dear to Haldane in particular, was the importance of mobilising the resources of science both for production and for government. In turn, as Searle has argued, 'the claim that governments needed to improve their scientific intelligence service became confused with the belief that politics and public administration could themselves be made an exact science', in which key decisions would lie with 'experts'. The Webbs founded the London School of Economics (LSE) in part because they believed that 'social reconstructions require as much specialised training and sustained study as the building of bridges and railways'. There is a certain logical irony in the fact that the main author of *A*

Joint Framework for Social Policies (and one of the co-authors of this book) was a product of the LSE; and that, moreover, many of the 'social reconstructions' of the 1960s bore the imprint of the LSE influence.

A third theme was the need to bring policy logic into the design of Britain's institutions: that institutions should be shaped not by historical accident but by the functional imperatives inherent in trying to solve certain problems. This was the logic that the Webbs sought to apply to the Poor Law in their 1909 Minority Report[13]. This was an extraordinarily Chadwickian document in its attempt to derive the design of policies and institutions from rationally applied principles. Just as Chadwick derived the recommendations of the Poor Law Report from the principle of less eligibility, so the Webbs based their plan on the 'Principle of Prevention'. The community, through a variety of agencies, would grapple with the principal causes of destitution 'at the incipient stages, when they are just beginning to affect one or other members of a family, long before a family as a whole has sunk into the morass of destitution'. In this crusade, volunteer workers would have a key role: 'the modern relation between the public authority and the voluntary worker is one of systematically organised partnership under expert direction'. In short the Webbs were arguing for a comprehensive, coordinated ('systematic' in their vocabulary) attack on a social problem which would bring together the different strands of public policy and the actions of different social agencies to bear on one particular population group: precisely what the *Joint Framework* was to call for 66 years later.

In the case of the Minority Report, recommendations for organisational structure sprang from the ambition to improve policy outputs. But almost precisely the same themes are evident in what is perhaps the last major intellectual monument to the generation which had embarked on the quest for national efficiency at the start of the twentieth century: the 1918 *Report of the Machinery of Government Committee*[14], largely the joint product of Lord Haldane and Beatrice Webb. Here again, the recommendations flow from a desire to impose a rational unity on an untidy, chaotic world. Better policy outputs will come, the Report assumed, if only the machinery is designed according to the appropriate logical principles and if only policy making is informed by adequate information. However, three specific aspects of the Haldane Report are of particular relevance to the argument of this chapter.

First, there is the emphasis on the role of Cabinet in ensuring 'the continuous co-ordination and delimitation of the activities of the several Departments of State'. The Cabinet is seen not as a loose federation of ministers but – reflecting, as the Report itself makes clear, the wartime experience – as an Executive providing central direction to all government activities. Implicit in this is the prescriptive assumption that Cabinets should pursue coherent and comprehensive social and economic strategies, as distinct from aggregating the demands and policies of individual departments. This is a view which may have become commonplace subsequently but which certainly represented a new definition of the peacetime role of governments in 1918[15].

Second, the Haldane Report canonised the Chadwickian principle of policy flowing from information. 'It appears to us', the Report stated, 'that adequate provision has not been made in the past for the organised acquisition of facts and information, and for the systematic application of thought, as preliminary to the settlement of policy and its subsequent administration'. And while it recognised that the application of information to yield policy prescription was not as simple in 'civil administration' as in the army and the navy – because the 'exact objectives' of policy were more difficult to define – it proposed that 'better provision should be made for enquiry, research and reflection'. Policy analysis – for what is that multihued activity if not 'the organised acquisition of facts and information' and the 'systematic application of thought'? – had arrived in Whitehall.

The third, and last strand, in the Haldane Report was the recommendation for a new, more rigorous principle for distributing functions between government departments. Defining departments according to 'the nature of the service rendered to the community' – rather than according to 'the class of persons dealt with' – would yield a total of ten departments (two fewer than in Bentham's scheme, but otherwise similar in many respects). One advantage of such an arrangement would be that it would encourage the concentration of expertise: 'the acquisition of knowledge and the development of specialised capacity'. One inevitable disadvantage, the Report conceded, was that there might be overlap between departments. 'The work of the Education Department, for example, may incidentally trench on the sphere of Health ... Such incidental overlapping is inevitable, and any difficulties to which it may give rise must in our opinion be met by systematic arrangements for the collaboration of Departments jointly interested in particular spheres of work.' Thus the stress on the importance of coordination – or collaboration – followed logically from the emphasis on functional specialisation. If the organisation of government were to follow the lines of expertise, then special attention would have to be paid to the problems of coordinating different kinds of expertise.

It is no accident that the Haldane Report's celebration of rationality as an organising principle of government came at the end of a world war, and at a time when Lloyd George was heading a coalition government. For not only had the war provided the precise definition of 'national efficiency' which was so conspicuously absent in peacetime – i.e. the ability to mobilise national resources to maximum effect in the pursuit of military objectives – but Lloyd George himself had a congenital bias towards coalition politics. Even before 1914 he had flirted with the idea of trying to set up a coalition government. For the quest for rationality in policy making reflects, as argued earlier, a suspicion of 'normal' politics. Its inbuilt assumption is that there is a rationality over and above the policies produced by the clash of party competition, and that there is a way of rationally defining the national interest independent of selfish group or class interests.

The point emerges clearly when we consider the ideas of one of the key figures linking the debates about public policy in the inter-war period, from 1918 to 1939, and in the 1960s: Harold Macmillan. It was Macmillan who, as Prime Minister from 1957 to 1963, instigated many of the changes in government which provided the background to such documents as *A Joint Framework*. But it was the young Macmillan who sketched out much of the underlying ideology in the 1930s when, as a leading member of the heterodox movement of rebellion against the conventional wisdom of monetarist economics, he set out his ideas for a planned economy in *The Middle Way* published in 1938[16]. In a chapter entitled '*Coordination*' he sketched out the institutional devices for achieving the 'harmonious' coordination of the nation's economic policies: in particular, the creation of a National Economic Council which, 'with all the facts before it' would formulate 'a comprehensive plan for general guidance' in pursuit of a 'common aim' and a 'single national policy'. Here then, we find all our thematic key words and concepts: the stress on collecting facts, the need for comprehensive policies, the invocation of 'coordination', the identification of rationality with planning and the underlying assumption that it was possible rationally to devise policies which would be harmonious (and therefore, by implication, politically acceptable) because in the national interest in a curious conflation of Benthamism and corporatism. They will provide the leitmotifs in the next section, where we consider the more immediate background to the publication of *A Joint Framework*.

RATIONAL POLICIES FROM RATIONAL INSTITUTIONS

The second world war, like the first, gave new impetus to the concept of rationality as the pursuit of well-defined national goals which cut across party lines, interest groups and class conflicts, and which could be pursued by coalition governments. It broadened the experience of planning in general, left a legacy of consensus about the desirability of social planning and created, in government itself, an infrastructure of planning machinery which to a large extent survived the war period itself[17].

In particular, the plans worked out during the period of the wartime

coalition government, and subsequently carried out by the Labour administration, created a framework for social policy that set up the expectations
which lay behind the attempts of the seventies to turn the aspirations of the
original architects of the Welfare State into a reality. For the paradox is that
it was precisely the discovery that the original architects had not succeeded
in their aims – that the seemingly coherent, comprehensive and consistent
schemes for providing universal income maintenance, welfare and health
programmes had not, for example, eliminated poverty – which inspired the
return to the drawing board in the sixties and seventies. Each attempt to plug
gaps in the existing schemes or to add new programmes in response to the
discovery of new needs added to the complexity of the original design. In
turn, greater complexity generated new demands for improving coordination. In this respect, *A Joint Framework* can be seen as the culmination of a
long trend.

The wartime experience also left a legacy of criticism. If the war helped to
consolidate an ideology of planning – in which every reverse or failure was
attributed not to problems inherent in the nature of comprehensive planning
but to the lack of comprehensiveness or consistence – it also bequeathed an
intellectual critique. For example, in his reflections on his experience at the
Ministry of Aircraft Productions, Ely Devons identified what he saw as some
of the fundamental dilemmas of planning[18]. Every attempt at planning, he
argued, revealed two problems:

First, the need to split up the field to be covered so that each administrative unit can
deal efficiently with its own sector; and second, the need to secure that the actions of
these separate units all fit into the general plan. But the implication of these principles always leads to conflict. For the first requires delegation and devolution, so that
plans can be manageable and realistic; and the second requires centralisation, so that
plans can be co-ordinated.

This conflict between devolution and centralisation appeared at every stage of the
administrative hierarchy. At each level the co-ordinators regarded the plans of the
individual sectors as futile and wasteful, because they took no account of what was
happening elsewhere; and those in charge of individual sectors regarded the plans of
the co-ordinators as theoretical, academic and unrelated to the real facts of the situation ... The supreme co-ordinators struggled for more centralisation, the planners
within each department for more to be left to their discretion. But inside each department, the planners, who argued for delegation when dealing with the central organs
of Government, argued for centralisation of decisions inside their own departments.

The wartime experience also produced a philosophic critique of the whole
concept of rational planning. The advocates of planning, argued Hayek,
asserted that 'the increasing difficulty of obtaining a coherent picture of the
complete economic process makes it indispensable that things should be coordinated by some central agency if social life is not to dissolve in chaos'[19].
But this, Hayek maintained, was the reverse of the truth:

There would be no difficulty about efficient control or planning were conditions so simple that a single person or board could effectively survey all the relevant facts. It is only as the factors which have to be taken into account become so numerous that it is impossible to gain a synoptic view of them, that decentralisation becomes imperative. But once decentralisation is necessary, the problem of co-ordination arises, a co-ordination which leaves the separate agencies free to adjust their activities to the facts which only they can know, and yet brings about a mutual adjustment of their respective plans.

In short, the attempt to pursue rational policies – in the sense of attempting a comprehensive, coordinated drive to preconceived objectives – was in itself profoundly irrational. The quest for Chadwick's 'perfect knowledge' was a snare and a delusion. Or, as Popper put it, 'The holistic planner overlooks the fact that it is easy to centralise power but impossible to centralise all that knowledge which is distributed over many individual minds, and whose centralisation would be necessary for the wise wielding of centralised power'[20].

In the fifties, what might be called the sceptical view of planning prevailed. Policy rationality was defined in terms of policy limitation. The emphasis was on cutting back the role of government and substituting the rationality of the market for the rationality of either policy or politics (setting out in a minor key, a theme which was to emerge again in the major key in the eighties). But towards the end of the decade, with the accession of Macmillan to the premiership, it is possible to note the re-emergence of the quest for national efficiency. On the one hand, the post-war consensus about the Welfare State, the general improvement in living standards and the maintenance of full employment seemed to make traditional party ideologies increasingly irrelevant. On the other hand, although Britain's growth rates were reasonably high by historical standards, they were disappointingly low when compared to the performance of her industrial competitors – Germany and Japan, once again, among them. Not surprisingly, therefore, the politics of ideological confrontation yielded to the politics of institutional reform. If the real question facing the voters was which party would deliver the goods of economic growth more bountifully, then it was not surprising that much of the currency of political debate turned out to be technical proposals for increasing the efficiency of government.

But given that the achievement of efficiency was in everybody's interest – that it represented precisely the kind of uncontentious 'common aim' which would allow governments to set 'a single national policy', in Macmillan's words – it was still necessary to devise the institutional framework which would allow the 'harmonious' organisation of different interests in the common pursuit. And Macmillan as Prime Minister from 1957 to 1963 did attempt to give institutional expression to his vision of the thirties. Although nothing like the original, grand design emerged, Macmillan's premiership did mark the attempt to create a corporate structure which would bring both sides of industry together in a dialogue with the government in the framework of a set of National Development Councils[21]. It was a development which, however fitfully and sporadically, was pursued by successive Labour and Conservative governments until 1979, as the different administrations sought to win national support for various types of incomes policy or 'social contracts'. These developments are not, in detail, central to the arguments of this chapter. However, they form an essential backcloth to the attempts to promote rationality in government. For these developments were based on the implicit assumption that political consensus made it possible to seek technical, i.e., institutional, organisational and administrative, solutions to Britain's social and economic problems. It was no accident that as people celebrated the end of ideology (possibly prematurely) they were also celebrating the birth of rationality in policy making (perhaps prematurely too).

The new public philosophy of the sixties and seventies was first expounded in the Plowden Report on the Control of Public Expenditure in 1961[22]. From this Report stemmed the new system of public expenditure control[23,24] based on a rolling five-year programme with the spending plans expressed in terms of the input of real resources, which was to survive until the economic crisis of the mid-seventies undermined its optimistic assumption that it was possible to plan ahead on expectations of economic growth[25]. But, more relevant to the argument of this chapter, the Plowden Report's specific recommendations for public expenditure planning were based on a more general view of how there could be more rationality in the policy making process. A rational approach to public expenditure planning meant, the Report argued, that the spending plans of individual departments should not be treated in a 'piecemeal' fashion, but should be brought together so that Ministers collectively could look at 'public expenditure as a whole'. The aim should be, the Report stressed, to ensure long-term stability in the planning of individual expenditure programmes, since 'chopping and changing in Government expenditure policy is frustrating to efficiency and economy in the running of the public services'. Furthermore, the Report emphasised, there was a need for more sophisticated analytical techniques: 'the developments envisaged in this Report will inevitably call for wider application of mathematical techniques, statistics and accounts, to problems of public expenditure'. Finally, management techniques would have to be employed on a wider scale in order to improve 'the technical efficiency with which large operations of administration are carried out'. So here are set out the main themes for the next 15 years. Some are familiar: such as the emphasis on taking a comprehensive, rather than piecemeal, view of problems, on the use of statistics and on trying to avoid 'chopping and changing' (the last being the complaint of all administrators from the time of Henry Taylor onward). But we also have some new themes (or, perhaps more accurately, old ideas dressed up in a new vocabulary) with the invocation of *managerial* efficiency. All, however, can be traced through a succession of inquiries, White Papers and institutional changes.

The most ambitious, but also the most short-lived, attempt to achieve rationality in planning was the Labour government's 1965 National Plan[26] produced by a new ministry, the Department of Economic Affairs, charged with the coordination of economic and industrial policies. There was, effectively, an attempt to extend the methods of the Plowden Report to the economy as a whole. 'Both Government and industry have to plan several years ahead and it is desirable to co-ordinate the forward estimates of both', the Plan argued. Its approach reveals one of the basic dilemmas of pursuing rationality in policy making. To the extent that planning is partial, so what may be crucial factors will be left out of the equation. But to the extent that planning seeks to be comprehensive, so the problems of control are compounded. While the government could logically argue in the National Plan that public expenditure planning could not be planned in isolation from the development of the economy, it could only gamble on the hope that setting out coordinated targets for both sectors would also yield coordinated outputs. It was a gamble which it lost.

But although the 1965 National Plan had no successors, the public philosophy epitomised by the Plowden Report lived on. Its influence can, for example, be seen in the Report of the Committee on the Civil Service, the Fulton Report[27]. This was a document which would have gladdened the hearts of Chadwick and the Webbs. The Committee denounced what it considered to be the lack of professionalism of the civil service. Government in the twentieth century, the Report argued, called for technical expertise which the civil servants largely lacked. Additionally, the structure of government departments should be designed so as to promote efficiency. Wherever possible departments should be broken up into 'accountable units of management'. Finally, each department should have its own 'Planning Unit' responsible for 'major long-term policy-planning', staffed by men and women who should be 'trained in, and have the capacity to use, relevant techniques of quantitative analysis'. However, the Fulton Report also acknowledged that:

Many of the problems handled by Planning Units will have implications extending beyond the boundaries of a single department. These units may therefore need a measure of central direction if the merging problems of the country are to be tackled systematically and comprehensively and on the basis of common major hypotheses.

Many of the recommendations of the Fulton Committee were never implemented. But its enthusiasm for new techniques – its lyrical invocation of a civil service capable of using statistical and other tools of analysis – accurately reflected the mood of Whitehall: the sense of mission as traditional problems were attacked with the new techniques of rational analysis. The newly created civil service departments, whose birth itself was a tribute to the demand for greater professionalism, pumped out a series of do-it-yourself guides whose titles convey the spirit of the times: 'Operational research, models and government'; 'Statistical decision theory'; 'Management by objectives in the civil service'; 'Current issues in cost-benefit analysis'. Bliss it was in that age to be numerate, but to have access to computers was very heaven. Government departments rushed to import the latest American techniques of analysis, notably programme budgeting[28]. Whether in arguing about London's Third Airport[29] or deciding the road building programme, cost-benefit analysis ruled supreme in the brief age of the 'econocrats'[30].

The same spirit that brought new techniques to the corridors of Whitehall also informed the reform of Britain's institutions that characterised this period. For, once again, the drive for rationality demanded that process or technique should be embodied in the structure of institutions. When the Royal Commission on Local Government[31] came to set out the principles shaping its recommendations, it explained that it had settled for the all-purpose authority as its main model because:

A single authority has the great advantage that, through allocation of priorities and co-ordinated use of resources, it can relate its programmes for all services to coherent objectives for the future progress of its area considered as a whole. Being responsible for the total span of local government activity, it can see the full extent of the relationships between different services, what developments in each area are necessary to meet people's needs and what gaps between services ought to be filled . . . This is local government in its simplest most understandable and potentially most efficient form.

In considering the size of the new authorities, the Royal Commission was again influenced by arguments of efficiency. 'An authority', argued the Report, 'must serve a large enough population to employ the wide variety of qualified staff and the financial and material resources necessary'. And from this it concluded that the minimum desirable size was 250 000 since only such an authority would be able to employ the 'range and calibre' of staff – presumably the 'elite of unassuming experts' invoked by Beatrice Webb. Moreover, the Report pointed out, the new structure of local government would mean that 'the full use of new and developing management techniques, computers, and other equipment will be brought within the reach of all authorities', so ensuring that 'the public will be able to obtain increasing value for whatever money they decide to spend'.

The 'value for money' theme was to be taken up, and enlarged upon, by the Baines Report[32] on the management of the new authorities subsequently set up by the government (on a slightly different pattern from that recommended by the Royal Commission). It was this which promulgated the doctrine of a 'corporate approach' to local government policy making, repudiating depart-mentalism and calling for corporate strategies cutting across administrative boundaries:

This corporate approach should be displayed not only within the authority itself but also in its relations with other spheres of local government and with public bodies such as the proposed Area Health Boards and Regional Water Authorities. The allocation of functions to the different local authorities and the freedom given to them to create organisations which are appropriate to local needs only serve to emphasise the need for close co-ordination at all levels for the benefit of the community.

At the same time that local government was being reorganised, so was the National Health Service in an attempt to achieve the aims of its original architects[33]. But the vocabulary and organisational clothes of the reorgani-sation conformed closely to 1970s fashions of reform. Not only were all the different health services brought together under the same organisational umbrella: the Area Health Authority (AHA). But the intention was that the new organisational machinery would make it possible to plan services rationally for the first time. Past shortcomings, explained Sir Keith Joseph in his preface to the 1972 reorganisation White Paper[34], 'were not rational. They did not result from the calculation as to the best way to deploy scarce resources. They just happened.' The reorganised NHS was designed to make sure that things did not 'just happen'. The new AHAs would, for the first time in the history of the NHS, be bodies charged 'to balance needs and priorities rationally and to plan and provide the right combination of services for the benefit of the public'. Furthermore, the White Paper promised in a section entitled 'A sound management structure':

In the reorganised service, there will be a more systematic and comprehensive planning process than now exists. The Department will annually prepare guidance on national policy objectives for AHAs and RHAs who will then draw up their plans for the development of their services to meet these objectives together with their own local priorities. It is intended to seek methods of obtaining improved information and more effective measurements of needs and of performance.

The reorganisation of both local government and of the NHS was carried out by the Conservative government of Edward Heath in the first half of the seventies, although it had been the Labour government of Harold Wilson which had given the impetus to the campaign for institutional reform. But, in any case, the quest for rationality in policy making cut across party political differences. What is significant, indeed, is the extent to which there was a common stock of assumptions and a shared belief in the ideology of national efficiency.

The point can be illustrated by considering the organisational manifesto of the Heath government: its 1970 White Paper on *The Reorganisation of Central Government*[35]. This not only expounded its philosophy of efficiency through rationality but also announced the birth of the Central Policy Review Staff which was subsequently to publish *A Joint Framework*. The aim of the 1970 White Paper was to 'improve the quality of policy formulation and decision-making in Government'. The basis of improved policy formulation and decision taking, it argued, would have to be 'rigorous analysis of existing and suggested government policies, actions and expenditure'. To achieve this, the White Paper announced a number of changes. First, government departments would be joined together, where appropriate, to 'provide a series of fields of unified policy' – a proposal which can claim a direct line of descent from the Haldane Report. Second, to achieve 'a clear and comprehensive government strategy which can be systematically developed to take account of changing circumstances', the government would set up a 'small multi-disciplinary central policy review staff'. Third, there would have to be a 'radical improvement' in the information system available to ministers and in the techniques of analysis available to ministers for taking decisions.

The vocabulary, themes and assumptions of the 1970 White Paper epitomise, as this brief review has sought to suggest, a long tradition of thinking about public policy. It is a tradition which, to pull together the threads of the discussion so far, had a variety of intellectual strands. There is the emphasis on basing decisions on the analysis of information; there is the identification of rationality with adopting a systematic, holistic view of any given problem; there is the reliance on technique and machinery for problem solution, and a strong preoccupation with the organisational structure of policy-making; there is the stress on the key role of coordination as an instrument of rationality – with coordination, in turn, being defined in terms of the coherence, comprehensiveness and consistency of the policies being produced. It is an essentially apolitical tradition, furthermore, which rests on an implicit ideology of neutral, benevolent expertise in the service of consensual, self-evident values such as managerial efficiency; a tradition which, *per contra*, tends to ignore social and economic conflict, and whose underlying assumption is that rationality is possible in the framing of public policy precisely because men are reasonable creatures in pursuit of the common good.

RATIONALITY, COORDINATION AND SOCIAL POLICY

This, then, is the tradition of thinking about public policy which provides the context, vocabulary and terms of reference of *A Joint Framework*. The quest for rationality in social policy, as represented by that document, can only be understood as part of this wider movement. Equally, however, the intellectual dynamics of social policy have themselves largely contributed to the creation of that tradition. For it is no accident that this chapter has throughout drawn on examples from the field of social policy – starting with the New Poor Law – to illustrate its analysis. It is precisely in this field that the benevolent expert – from Chadwick to Beveridge, via the Webbs – has tended to be central in policy making. It is precisely in this field, too, that the dominant academic paradigm – until recently, at any rate – has seen the evolution of social policy as being a consensual, non-conflictual process. In its classic exposition this paradigm saw social policy not only as the product of collective solidarity and altruism but also as the generator of solidarity and collectivism[36].

The reliance on experts and the assumption that the goals of social policy are consensual are, of course, the two sides of the same coin. If the ends of policy are given, then it makes sense to concentrate on the means; if there is agreement about the values to be pursued, then it is only logical to concentrate on improving analysis, organisational structure and the capacity of various agencies to act in a systematic fashion. If needs are defined and measured by professionals, then it is only right to create a machinery for giving full scope to the professional, as in the case of the NHS[37]. If social policy is all about altruism, then it is only reasonable to expect experts and professionals to use their power in the public interest rather than pursuing their own self-interest. It was assumptions such as these, distilled from the then dominant paradigm of social policy, which helped to shape *A Joint Framework*.

But there is another characteristic of social policy which helps to explain, further, the particular distinguishing feature of *A Joint Framework*: the document's insistence that rationality implies *coordination*. This is the defiant, intractable messiness of most social problems. Even to define the nature of a social problem may be contentious. Once defined, there will be uncertainty about causes, and the relationship between causes (of which there may be many) and effects. Depending on the definition of the problem, and the diagnosis of the causes, there will then be a choice of different methods of intervention. Depending on the choice made, the problem will then become the 'property' of a particular service, agency or programme. But the problem will continue to sprawl across administrative boundaries and defy pigeon-holing. Different social agencies may be able to substitute for each other, or their services will complement each other. The action or non-action of one department or agency will often have knock-on, consequential effects on those of others: so that one department's economies may become another department's extra costs. Lastly, the policies of the public sector will inevitably affect, and be affected by, what happens in the private and voluntary sectors.

No wonder, then, that coordination may come to be seen as the master principle, as it were, of social policy. The intellectual history of social policy represents a move from monotheism to polytheism, from a belief in single organising principles ('lesser eligibility' or the 'preventive principle') to a pluralistic approach. In line with this, the actual history of post-war social policy represents a move from single-barrel to multiple-barrel interventions, from seeing better housing or comprehensive schools as *the* solution to deprivation or inequality to experimenting with more complex programmes such as the Community Development Programmes, Education Priority Areas and the Urban Programme which involved the orchestration of a variety of services and inputs[38]. In short, the coordination of different services and inputs may come to be seen as a policy in its own right. It is the rationalist's technique for embracing the complexity and interrelatedness of social problems and for neutralising the craft of policy which we call politics, bargaining, trade-offs and so on. The preoccupation with rationality seen as coordination did not begin or end with JASP. The 1974 reorganization of the NHS which, as already noted, was designed to facilitate coordination across administrative boundaries, was preceded by the setting up of a Working Party on collaboration between the NHS and local government. This took as its theme an argument which was to be repeated in countless documents pumped out by the Department of Health and Social Security over the following decade:

Collaboration between the health and social services will need to be firmly established if the community is to receive comprehensive care. Co-ordination of planning and day to day work will also be important in the fields of education, housing and environmental health[39].

In the event, the legislation creating the new model NHS provided for statutory joint consultative committees, as the forum for health and local authorities to concert their plans and services. This was to be followed, in the mid-seventies, by the introduction of joint finance: i.e. the allocation of funds to health authorities for use in collaborative projects with local social service departments or voluntary agencies. The 1977 document on health and social services priorities, *The Way Forward*[40], stressed that 'the Government are committed to a joint approach to social policy', and exhorted both local authorities and health authorities to engage not only with each other but in wider corporate planning at the local level:

Co-operation at a local level will be particularly important with education authorities on issues concerning the under-fives and the mentally handicapped, on problems such as truancy and on children at risk of injury or personal breakdown; with housing

authorities on matters concerning the care of the elderly, hostels and homes for
mentally ill and mentally handicapped people, and families in need of support; with the
local social security office on all matters of income maintenance; and with the courts
on matters concerning the care of children.

Four years later, with a Conservative administration in power, the same
theme was to be taken up again in *Care in Action*[41]. This once more stressed
that planning and action at the local level was to be cooperative and
coordinated, and from this would flow cost effectiveness and efficiency. It
differed from its predecessors only in emphasising that the scope for
coordination needed to be widened, to include coordination between statutory and non-statutory agencies, between the public, voluntary and private
sectors. For example, it argued that:

The strength of the voluntary sector lies partly in its ability to meet needs as they are
perceived. But if that strength is to be harnessed to best advantage, voluntary and
statutory services must be effectively co-ordinated.

And, in the case of the NHS, *Care in Action* urged health authorities to adopt
'a more imaginative approach to the possibilities of planning and providing
services in partnership with the private sector where it is economical to do
so ...'

So the final irony would seem to be that when governments seek to restrict
the scope of the public sector, they thereby extend the need for coordination:
an irony underlined by the fact that *Care in Action* was published by a
government which largely repudiated the public philosophy that informed *A
Joint Framework*.

THE CHALLENGE OF THE NEW PUBLIC PHILOSOPHY

In July 1983, after the second victory at the polls of the reborn Conservative
Party under the leadership of Mrs Thatcher, the Central Policy Review Staff
was formally dissolved. It was an event significant more for its symbolic
overtones than for any direct implications for the policy making process. The
CPRS had itself lost much of its impetus: the language of JASP had long since
been expunged from the Whitehall vocabulary (chapter 4). But the decision to
dissolve the CPRS reflected the fact that under Mrs Thatcher there was not
only a different ideology of economic management but also a different
ideology of governance. The rationality of politics had, for the time being,
triumphed over the politics of rationality. Analysis was now to be the servant
of politics, instead of being seen as an independent source of ideas and
policies: significantly, the dissolution of the CPRS was followed by the
strengthening of the Prime Minister's personal advisory staff at 10 Downing
Street.

The ideology of governance is, of course, linked to the ideology of economic management. Together they form the new public philosophy which is challenging that of the sixties and seventies. It is a public philosophy which rejects the comprehensive or 'synoptic', in Hayek's phrase, approach to policy making, and is sceptical about the capacity of governments to deal with complex problems. It argues for the disengagement of government. It tends to stress the decentralisation of decision making. It argues for limiting the responsibility of government for the promotion of the economic and social well-being of society. It is, to over-simplify only a little, the public philosophy of an era of economic distress, when governments are anxious to diffuse blame for shortcomings, just as the public philosophy of rational planning was that of an era of economic prosperity, when governments were anxious to claim credit for the fruits of growth. And while the government's own public philosophy is very much linked to its economic ideology, its repudiation of many of the assumptions of the tradition of rational policy making is echoed even by some who strongly oppose that ideology: those who see social policies as the product of conflict not consensus[42] and who are suspicious of expert elites.

In the event, the new public philosophy has imparted a bias to government rhetoric and style but has not, as yet, transformed government actions. There may have been symbolic changes like the dissolution of the CPRS. But the reality is that the process of decentralisation and disengagement has not gone far. Indeed there have been movements in the opposite direction. The 1982 reorganisation of the NHS, in the name of decentralising responsibility, has been followed by increased central control[43]. In the case of local government, the centre has reinforced financial controls and reduced local autonomy in the name of coordinating public spending. And, as noted above, the language of coordination and collaboration remains very much alive in the field of social policy.

So while there may have been disillusionment and disappointment with the vision of the sixties and seventies and the tradition of rational policy making on which it drew, it is clear that neither the vision nor the tradition are dead. Governments still strain after consistency, coherence and comprehensiveness in their policies, and use coordination as the instrument for trying to achieve those aims. The assumption shaping this study is therefore that the quest for rationality in policy making will continue and that it is consequently important to understand the dialectic between the rationality of politics and the politics of rationality. Perhaps it is only by incorporating the rationality of politics into our analysis – by gaining an understanding of power, self-interest and conflict – that we can advance towards a greater measure of rationality in policy making, and illuminate the competing public philosophies of governance.

REFERENCES

1 Central Policy Review Staff (1975) *A Joint Framework for Social Policies*, London: HMSO
2 K. Middlemas (1979) *Politics in Industrial Society*, London: Andre Deutsche
3 N. Harris (1972) *Competition and the Corporate Society*, London: Methuen
4 Jeremy Bentham (1967) *A Fragment on Government*, Oxford: Basil Blackwell, p. 100
5 Michael Oakeshott (1962) *Rationalism in Politics*, London: Methuen
6 Peter Self (1975) *Econocrats and the Policy Process*, London: Macmillan
7 Bhiku Parekh (ed.) (1973) *Bentham's Political Thought*, London: Croom Helm, pp. 222–3
8 Henry Taylor (1958) *The Statesman*, New York: Mentor Books, p. 106. Note that this book was dedicated to James Stephen – one of the great advocates, in the utilitarian tradition, of administrative rationality as against political rationality
9 S. E. Finer (1952) *The Life and Times of Sir Edwin Chadwick*, London: Methuen
10 M. W. Flinn (ed.) (1965) *Report on the Sanitary Condition of the Labouring Population of Great Britain*, Edinburgh: Edinburgh University Press
11 G. R. Searle (1971) *The Quest for National Efficiency*, Oxford: Basil Blackwell. The following pages draw heavily on this study and the quotations come from it when no other source is given
12 Rosamund Thomas (1978) *The British Philosophy of Administration*, London: Longman, p. 48
13 Sidney and Beatrice Webb (1963) *English Poor Law Policy*, London: Frank Cass
14 Ministry of Reconstruction (1918) *Report of the Machinery of Government Committee*, London: HMSO, Cmnd 0230
15 John P. Mackintosh (1968) *The British Cabinet*, London: Stevens
16 Harold Macmillan (1966) *The Middle Way*, London: Macmillan
17 D. N. Chester and F. M. G. Wilson (1957) *The Organisation of British Central Government*, London: Allen and Unwin
18 Ely Devons (1950) *Planning in Practice*, Cambridge: Cambridge University Press
19 F. A. Hayek (1944) *The Road to Serfdom*, London: Routledge
20 K. R. Popper (1957) *The Poverty of Historicism*, London: Routledge
21 Samuel Brittan (1969) *Steering the Economy*, London: Secker and Warburg
22 Lord Plowden (Chairman) (1961) *Control of Public Expenditure*, London: HMSO
23 Hugh Heclo and Aaron Wildavsky (1974) *The Private Government of Public Money*, London: Macmillan
24 Sir Richard Clarke (1978) *Public Expenditure, Management and Control*, London: Macmillan
25 Sir Leo Pliatzky (1982) *Getting and Spending*, Oxford: Basil Blackwell
26 Secretary of State for Economic Affairs (1965) *The National Plan*, London: HMSO, Cmnd 2764
27 Lord Fulton (Chairman) (1968) *Report of the Committee on the Civil Servant*, London: HMSO, Cmnd 3638
28 Rudolf Klein (1972) 'The Politics of PPB', *The Political Quarterly*, vol. 43, no. 3, July/September
29 Mr Justice Roskill (Chairman) *Report of the Commission on the Third London Airport*, *Report*, London: HMSO
30 Peter Self (1975) *op. cit.*
31 Royal Commission on Local Government in England (Chairman: Lord Redcliffe-Maud) (1969) *Report*, London: HMSO, Cmnd 4040

32 *The New Local Authorities: Management and Structure* (1972), London: HMSO
33 Rudolf Klein (1983) *The Politics of the NHS*, London: Longmans
34 Secretary of State for Social Services (1972) *National Health Service Reorganisation: England*, London: HMSO, Cmnd 5055
35 Prime Minister (1970) *The Reorganisation of Central Government*, London: HMSO, Cmnd 4506
36 Richard Titmuss (1970) *The Gift Relationship*, London: Allen and Unwin
37 Rudolf Klein (1983) *op. cit.*
38 Keith G. Banting (1979) *Poverty, Politics and Policy*, London: Macmillan
39 Department of Health and Social Security (1972) *A Report from the Working Party on Collaboration between the NHS and Local Government on its activities to the end of 1972*
40 DHSS (1977) *Priorities for the Health and Personal Social Services: The Way Forward*, London: HMSO
41 DHSS (1981) *Care in Action: Handbook of Policies and Priorities for the Health and Personal Social Services in England*, London: HMSO
42 Ian Gough (1979) *The Political Economy of the Welfare State*, London: Macmillan
43 Patricia Day and Rudolf Klein (1985) 'Central accountability and local decision-making', *British Medical Journal*, vol. 290, 1 June, 1676–78.

2 ~ Investigating policy coordination: issues and hypotheses

Attempts to improve coordination are only one manifestation of the long historical search for greater rationality in public affairs, but they have been central to the history of social policy. From the Charity Organisation Society and the Royal Commission on the Poor Laws to the Central Policy Review Staff and JASP, the leitmotif of coordination has traced a path through a century of concern about social problems. Motivations and objectives have varied greatly, but underlying them has been a constant reality: social issues, needs and problems – and the responses which they invoke – are usually complex and interrelated. As a consequence, a call for greater coordination flows almost ineluctably from any discovery of duplication, inefficiency, ineffectiveness, or of 'holes in the safety net'.

Perhaps surprisingly, given the historical background, coordination in social policy tends to be regarded as neutral and innocuous at worst and as self-evidently good for consumers and clients at best. We do not make this assumption. Coordination can be pressed to the service of many causes and interests; who gains and who loses from coordinative successes and failures must be investigated, not taken for granted. As Pressman and Wildavsky note, in the absence of consensus and common purpose 'coordination becomes another term for coercion'.[1] More specifically, Glennerster has argued that in recent times centrally coordinated social planning has been at least as much about the control and rationing of public expenditure as about the effective meeting of social need.[2] Similarly, social service professionals who ostensibly seek to improve coordination in order to benefit their clients can easily be seduced by that which is personally rewarding or professionally appealing; they can lose sight of how the consumers actually experience services and of what for them amounts to accessible and useful forms of help.[3] These are matters of evaluation which we did not broach systematically in our empirical research. Our sights were firmly set on policy and administrative processes, not on outcomes as such. Nonetheless, there can be no doubt that the search for rationality which characterised the seventies was strongly motivated, at least in part, by a desire to produce policies and outcomes which would be better for the immediate client or consumer. We therefore set off in search of coordination in the belief that it – and the wider demand for rationality in social policy which it represents – could certainly, in principle, be in the interests of the public in contact with the social services.

COORDINATION: ITS MEANING AND POLITICAL RELEVANCE

Precision about the meaning of coordination is rare. We have broadly characterised it as a pursuit of coherence, consistency, comprehensiveness and of harmonious or compatible outcomes. In the sixties and seventies, however, it took on a more specific, dominant form. Within the belief in rational, synoptic planning was to be found a search for *policy* coordination – coordination at the strategic level. Coordination was central, not peripheral, to the style of governance. Indeed, the preoccupation with administrative technique and organisational machinery was at times so strong that it became the major form of substantive policy. The reorganisation of the personal social services, the health service, and local government could all be seen in this light; so, too, could the partnership policies and 'total approach' towards the inner cities.

Coordination is above all the rationalist's technique for embracing the complexity and interrelatedness of social issues and problems, and there can be no doubt that at times rational planning has come to resemble the triumph of administrative technique over the craft of politics. Planning in the sixties and seventies was primarily conceived, by default as much as by design, as a centralised and essentially technical process. As such it threatened to bypass the political masters it was supposedly serving, but it also seemed poised to supplant the more obscure and mundane craft of bureaucratic politics – the bargaining, trade-offs and fancy footwork by which professionals and administrators in the public services defend or promote sectional goals and interests.

It is important to note and hold on to both these notions of politics: what might be called 'high politics' and 'low politics'. The search for rationality in public affairs usually expresses an impatience, even distaste, for the former and always for the latter. It represents an attempt to marshal and discipline the chaos which can arise from a multiplicity of competing, often conflicting, interests. The political craft, on the other hand, is embedded in the recognition of divergent interests – or at least some of them. Our own contrast between the politics of rationality and the rationality of politics must be seen in this light. It is not merely party politicians who threaten to upset the rationalist's carefully arranged apple-cart, it is all actors – high or low – who exhibit a leaning towards *ad hoc* negotiations, deals and opportunistic actions.

To characterise the rational planning of the seventies as essentially a centralist dead-hand on party and bureaucratic politics would be misleading. The tendency was discernible, but the practice was never sufficiently developed to have that outcome. Moreover, the trend towards centralisation was matched by a desire to achieve decentralised forms of coordination. The inner cities provided one notable, not to say notorious, example; the health and personal social services provided another. Both examples added a further piece to the coordination jigsaw: while centrally devised plans could aid coordination by providing a coherent framework, the need at the local level was for collaboration. It was seen to be necessary for local actors and organisations to rise above any minor differences of opinion and interest in order to pursue the common good of the local community in concert. Indeed, it is an abiding feature of the rationality game that people who can see many reasonable – and rational – reasons for differences of opinion and divergences of interest at their own level of operation tend to emphasise the rationality of collaboration at other levels (and fail to see why there should be barriers or obstacles in the path of such a self-evident good).

Centralisation is an inherently relative concept. What was perceived by central government as a valuable or even essential attempt to develop decentralised collaboration was often perceived by local actors and observers as further evidence of centralisation. Corporate planning in local government was a prime example. The attempt, in itself laudable and long overdue,[4] to achieve greater coordination across local government departments became inseparably entwined with the reorganisation of local government into much larger, more remote and more bureaucratically complex units.[5] The same was true of collaboration between the health and personal social services. Moreover, the collaboration in question was between whole departments and organisations and was designed to promote another layer of rational planning. The term 'collaboration' has warmer and more personal overtones than the term 'coordination', but in practice it did not imply too many cosy chats about mutual interests – it merely entailed some attempt to harmonise the actions of large organisations characterised by divergent interests. As we shall illustrate from our own empirical work, it was generally as resolutely technical and technocratic (few local politicians played a decisive role) as the attempt at rational planning initiated within central government.

Nonetheless, these different developments highlighted a single and crucial issue: the large-scale state social services which had been developed in the post-war years could fail to meet – or could even exacerbate – people's needs, as well as resolve them. One central reason for this was that policies, the structure of service systems, and the actual delivery of services all exhibited gaps in coverage, conflicts of aim and failures of communication. Better coordination was the solution and it could take several forms (that there could possibly be other sources of failure and other potential solutions is a point to which we shall return).

The two forms of coordination which we have mentioned – rational planning and collaboration – require a further word of explanation. In one sense they represent the difference between technique and process. *Rational planning* is one technique by which a framework to guide and coordinate action can be achieved. Collaboration is a process of interaction in which two or more parties identify mutual interests and freely agree to work together towards a common goal.[6] *Collaboration* is therefore one way of *developing* a rational plan, and it was seen to be a necessary way at the local level (because many autonomous agencies needed to work together and there was no acceptable means of coercing them to do so). By way of comparison, a second way of engaging in rational planning is for an acknowledged authority to require different groups and interests to submit to a single coherent strategy. *Imperative* (or coercive) and *collaborative* processes may both be involved in the process of rational planning, therefore. Government departments engaged in planning might do so through a combination of these processes. Ministers, Cabinet and trans-departmental bodies (such as the CPRS) might exercise authority or persuasion, but much might also hinge upon unforced collaboration across sections, divisions and departments. These central government processes are explored in detail in chapters 4 and 5.

However, we later use the term '*collaboration arena*' in a quite specific sense which should be distinguished now. It is used to refer to the field of local interaction between the health authorities, local authorities and voluntary agencies. Its use reflects the fact that central government policies have characterised coordination and joint planning at this level as *essentially* collaborative precisely because the organisations involved are autonomous of one another and, to varying degrees, of central government.[7] Any plan of action agreed by such agencies would immediately take on a different role within those separate agencies – it would be authoritative – but it would itself be the product of purely collaborative interaction. In reality, joint planning has never been innocent of authoritative action by central departments. The Department of Health and Social Security (DHSS) has long favoured joint planning and, since 1970, it has had responsibility for both the health services and one of the relevant bits of local government – the personal social services. The DHSS has established machinery to facilitate joint planning at the local level, imposed collaborative working as a legislative duty, and developed financial inducements to lubricate the collaborative wheels.[8] Moreover, the ten-year development plans initiated by DHSS in the early sixties and again in the seventies were designed to guide local agency planning in compatible directions and thereby to ease fruitful interaction.[9] Joint planning has been heavily mandated from above. Nonetheless, central government writ runs but imperfectly at such local levels and collaboration has remained the essential ingredient. Hence we use the term '*collaborative arena*' to specify joint planning between health and local authorities and voluntary bodies.

Even before 1979, no actuary would have taken a risk on the life expectancy of rational planning; the more grandoise hopes and ambitions had already begun to crumble and decay. Once the first Thatcher administration had come to power, it was only a matter of time before the life support machine was switched off altogether. What had finally disappeared, after a long period of false alarms, was the entire post-war tradition of consensus politics. Most fundamentally, the competence and role of the state had been re-evaluated and re-defined. State paternalism – and 'dirigiste' central planning – were an anathema. Yet, as we have argued in the first chapter, the need for policy coordination has survived this dramatic change in political ideology. It has everywhere undergone a change of style or of name, it has on occasions gone underground, but in only a few cases has it gone out of the window. A considerable degree of continuity of practice has accompanied sharp changes in principle. What, then, is to be learned about coordination and the politics of rationality from the experiences of the early eighties?

The first lesson is that a market oriented philosophy throws a different light on the whole issue of rationality and coordination in the social policy field. It re-defines the problems and highlights different potential solutions. Ideally, rational decision making and coordination is left primarily to the individual consumer at the point of consumption. The emphasis, in principle, is on consumer choice between outputs rather than on political or bureaucratic decision making and the coordination of inputs and policy processes. Consumers are expected to be able to put together their own package of social provisions. Coordination is still necessary if government is to create the right framework within which a mixed economy of statutory, voluntary or private producers can operate. It is also still necessary within and between statutory producers. But the weight of coordinative responsibility is decentralised somewhat and the parties covered by the coordinative imperative are different – coordination between public and private producers grows in importance.

The second lesson is that the 'rationality of politics' has been reasserted in a major way at the strategic level. The tendency to de-politicise policy issues has been swept aside. What was always clear to many has become perfectly clear to all: rationality resides in the choice of means to ends, but the choice between ends is inherently political. Faith in consensus has been at a minimum; divergent and conflicting interests have come out of the closet. Yet this reassertion of the rationality of politics has been highly selective. It has been confined to the national tier of government and to 'high politics'. Neither differences of interest and viewpoint between centre and locality, nor bureaucratic politics have been countenanced as legitimate barriers to the implementation of key policies. Coordinated action has remained very much in demand once political decisions have been made: *instrumental* rationality has lost none of its appeal. It is any lingering belief in *substantive* rationality – a uniquely appropriate understanding of the public good which can be discerned through sophisticated policy analysis – which has disappeared from view.

A third, obvious but often overlooked, lesson has also been forcibly restated. The more grandiose formulations of the rational synoptic planning approach contained a deep-rooted paradox. They were an attempt to contain and discipline the ad-hoc and short-term nature of purely political decision making and yet they were fundamentally dependent on the support and commitment of politicians. This is especially so in the British context, as we shall detail in chapters 4 and 5. The British civil service is deeply conservative in its ways and resistant to implanted foreign bodies such as policy units and think-tanks; only civil service loyalty to committed ministers could offset the deleterious consequences of departmental and sectional loyalties for the vital organs of the rational approach. Ministerial support for synoptic planning was patchy and uncertain at best before 1979, but it ceased altogether thereafter.

COORDINATION: COMPONENTS AND DIMENSIONS

Coordination remained a key aspect of the style of governance which characterised the early eighties, but it was shorn of most of the trappings of rational planning. The issues to which it was seen to be most pertinent also changed. Public expenditure control moved sharply up the agenda, as did law and order and, more gradually, the link between education/training and 'manpower planning'.[10] But what does coordination entail? What kind of phenomenon or process are we discussing? Now that the rhetoric and organisational machinery of the rational planning era have been jettisoned, it is somewhat easier to perceive the essential elements. Coordination in social planning may refer to one or more of the following:

(a) ensuring consistency and coherence between the *various objectives and elements of a single policy or project*;

(b) ensuring consistency and coherence within a *set of interacting policies or projects* 'owned' by one or more departments or organisations;

(c) ensuring that policy is translated into a consistent and coherent set of *appropriate actions* within one or more departments or organisations;

(d) ensuring that *service delivery practices* at the field level are such that a consistent, coherent and comprehensive package of help is available to people with specified needs;

(e) ensuring that the *services actually consumed* by the public in contact comprise a consistent, coherent and comprehensive package appropriate to expressed wants.

To begin with the last, we have noted that the market philosophy places considerable emphasis on coordination at this stage as a function of consumer choice. In a more traditional public service frame of analysis, this view of implementation implies the evaluation of outputs and outcomes from the consumer's perspective. The first four forms of coordination fit readily within the public service perspective: the first two emphasise coordination in policy making, and the second two underline the importance of policy implementation. Both these 'levels' of coordination were covered in our empirical research and the interrelationship between them is underlined in later chapters.

Coordination can also be specified in terms of the kinds of activities involved. Three distinctions are especially pertinent:

(a) coordination as a *cerebral or analytical activity* (e.g. establishing an appropriate mix of objectives and methods in a policy or project at the planning stage);

(b) coordination as the *interaction of formal organisations* (agencies or departments of a large organisation) *or groupings* (e.g. professions) and the possibly competing or conflicting interests which they contain or represent;

(c) coordination as the *interaction of individuals* – usually as representatives or members of organisations or groupings (e.g. politicians, chief officers, middle managers, professionals and other field workers).

Each of these facets of coordination present different issues. The first was the jewel in the rational planning crown, though some account had necessarily to be taken of the second. However, the rational planning era did tend to obscure the importance of the second and third; they were less glamorous and also less amenable to centralised control through paper planning exercises. But for our own purposes they are central: the interactive elements of the coordination process were the key object of our empirical research.

Coordination can finally be characterised in terms of a series of dichotomies. Two of the most significant – *centralised/decentralised* and *authoritative/collaborative* – have already been mentioned. They are broadly indicative of important variables rather than precise specifications. The third – *formal/informal* – is similar in this respect. By formal we mean coordination attempted through official channels or special machinery (e.g. Joint Consultative Committees); by informal we mean the interaction of individuals or small groups as representatives and as people. The latter introduces the human element: the importance of personalities and interpersonal interaction. As such it is pervasive. Interpersonal interaction may tip the balance in favour of a particular outcome within a highly formal committee meeting just as much as over a drink at the bar afterwards. We do not intend these dichotomies to be seen as mutually exclusive polarities, therefore. They are important dimensions of our analysis which are best summarised briefly in this manner for the time being.

The analytical component of coordination was explored at considerable length in a large body of academic writing before and during the rational planning era. Changes in the process of governance were strongly underpinned by theory. But they were also strongly criticised by alternative bodies of theory. Moreover, once the emphasis shifts from coordination as policy analysis to coordination as organisational interaction it is quite apparent that the body of academic writing which could be drawn upon as a guide to understanding is immense. Consequently, in developing guiding hypotheses for our research we had to be severely selective. We drew upon a wide range of literature, but concentrated on key ideas relating to the interactions which we most wanted to study and understand. It is to this academic framework that we must now turn.

THEORIES AND HYPOTHESES

To begin to understand the approach taken towards rationality in the seventies one has only to look at the one comparatively coherent and manageable body of literature advocating rational synoptic planning,[11] or – in later revisionist versions – mixed scanning.[12] But there is also a need to understand the likely limits of and impediments to these routes to coordination, and the literatures in this case are altogether more diverse and intimidating. It is true that the rational planning literature was counterbalanced by the 'incrementalist school'[13] which trenchantly criticised both the feasibility and desirability of the rational synoptic approach, but simply to draw on this would not be wholly appropriate. The image of a sharp antithesis between the 'rational planning' and 'incrementalist' schools was always overdrawn and resulted in fundamentally distinct issues being conflated. For example, the idea of incremental policy processes seemed to convey a single, coherent phenomenon, but incrementalism could, in fact, convey any or all of the following:

the avoidance of grand strategies in favour of single issue decision taking;

the avoidance of elaborate policy analysis in favour of political judgement and the 'intelligence of democracy';

the avoidance of centralised policy making in favour of more decentralised decision taking;

the avoidance of dramatic change in policy objectives in favour of more conservative patterns of change; and the acceptance of undramatic or conservative shifts in policy outputs at the expense of radical change.

Neither sophisticated analysis nor radical policies necessarily mean radical changes in outputs (or vice versa), but these small matters of causality were often lost sight of in the partisan heat of a great academic debate. However, given the qualifications and intellectual disentangling which are now possible, the incrementalist literature obviously proved to be a valuable source of ideas and guiding hypotheses when first we began our research. Nonetheless, we faced a further problem. Both the rational synoptic planning literature and – to a lesser extent – the incrementalist rejoinder, concentrated on 'high politics': on the nature of policy making rather than on the whole politico-administrative process. We therefore needed to draw additional perspectives, especially on organisational interaction, into our theoretical net. We had also to identify a simple framework within which ideas from these various literatures could be marshalled.

Notwithstanding the dangers of over-generalising and of drawing unduly hard distinctions between literatures characterised by diversity and subtlety, two broad traditions of thought can certainly be discerned. We will label them, for convenience, the 'optimistic' and 'pessimistic' traditions. However, it is important to emphasise that we only present them as optimistic and pessimistic in relation to our chosen issue: the possibility and likelihood of achieving coordination as an expression and outcome of a wider commitment to rationality in public affairs.

THE 'OPTIMISTIC' TRADITION

The 'optimistic' tradition is characterised by persistence in the face of recurring disappointments; it follows a cyclical pattern of enthusiasm, disillusionment and resurrection. Its rhetoric is enduring because it evokes commitment to a particular way of viewing the world:

The first of the shared commitments is to rationality. Coordination strategies carry an authoritative ring of technical competence and planning ... The most obvious point is that integration of human services makes sense ... A reform strategy that claims to bring order out of chaos becomes very appealing. There is a deep and pervasive vein of current conventional wisdom, namely that all things should be unified, quantified, ordered, consolidated and computerised ... Unification is good, duplication is bad ... official order is safe, pluralistic order is less than safe. Coordination appeals to this proposition.[14]

In short, the 'optimistic' tradition survives because it reflects and embodies the ideology of public bureaucracies concerned to bring about predictability and regularity in a turbulent world. Without coordination there will be conflict or wasteful competition.

The primary focus of this tradition in recent times, apart from the process of rational synoptic planning itself, has been the organisational framework necessary for the survival of that process. Organisational dysfunction, as we have noted, was widely diagnosed as the major barrier to effective coordination throughout the sixties and seventies: organisational structures, formal machinery and planning processes were highlighted as the crucial prerequisites of progress. Examples of what this meant in social policy practice will be outlined in the next chapter in relation to the two client groups – the elderly and children under five – on which we focused during our empirical work.

The prerequisites and assumptions entailed in the 'optimistic' tradition underline the organisational and behavioural demands and expectations which it involves. At minimum, the idea of rational planning implies:

(a) a broad, system wide perspective rather than a narrow or sectional view of problems, needs and issues;
(b) the existence, or achievement, of broad areas of consensus on goals, the nature of the problems to be tackled, the most acceptable and efficacious methods of intervention, and on priorities;
(c) a significant capacity for rational analysis, combined with authoritative backing;
(d) organisational arrangements appropriate to the analysis of problems and the implementation of solutions.

The assumption is that rational planning springing from such a conducive environment will provide the authoritative framework within which coordination will occur at all levels. As we have noted, the exception – a very major exception – arises from the frequent absence of imperative coordination: collaboration is necessary if policy and action is to be coordinated across the boundaries of autonomous organisations and groupings. However, collaboration, as Webb and Wistow have indicated,[15] implies further and no less demanding requirements:

(a) that a system-wide perspective will pervade all organisations and groups which do, or which ought to, interact;
(b) that 'system-gain' (e.g. the greater good of the client or community) will be readily identified by all and will act as a sufficient reward for the achievement of consensus;
(c) that where pursuing system-gain conflicts with short-term and sectional interests, the latter will triumph – 'organisational altruism' will be the order of the day.

The matter of organisational altruism is crucial precisely because the rational tradition under-plays the power of divergent interests. It assumes that consensus is readily achievable and it has no solution to offer – other than authoritative action by a higher body – if it is not forthcoming. Given the reality of divergent sectional interests, collaborative rational action must therefore depend to some extent, possibly a major extent, on the altruistic willingness of organisations or groupings to forego some of these sectional interests. It is one of the issues which we clearly had to build into the hypotheses and propositions which guided our empirical research.

THE 'PESSIMISTIC' TRADITION

While the rational tradition optimistically posits an underlying social harmony, the many alternative viewpoints are united precisely in their pessimism – or realism – on this point. The assumption is that 'harmony of needs is not only undiscoverable but non-existent'.[16] In the tradition of Hayek and Popper, true rationality resides in process – the interplay of individual preferences and decisions – not in the imposition of a collective strategy. 'Pluralistic disorder' is positively embraced, or at the very least acknowledged. The notion of an overarching rationality is seen as a snare and delusion leading to the 'preceptorial society'.[17]

Beyond the prescriptive and tendentious elements of this perspective there is a central observation with which observers from all points of the ideological compass have been able to concur: individual and group interests are multiple and divergent, and the net result is competition, bargaining and conflict. As with the tradition of optimism about rationality, routes back to some form of relatively harmonious social order are typically sought and prescribed – whether in the classical liberal advocacy of the market or the classical Marxist advocacy of a wholly novel socio-economic order. Nonetheless, theorists in the 'pessimistic' tradition begin by recognising divergent and conflicting interests and it is this preliminary observation which throws much light on the deficiencies, and indeed the potential dangers, of the search for a rational consensus in public affairs. Without a class or conflict perspective, for example, it would be much more difficult to highlight the enormous potential of 'coordination' as an instrument of neglect (benign or otherwise), of official evasion, or of repressive social control. But for the purposes of guiding our empirical research, a potentially vast literature which was explicitly or implicitly critical of the rational optimistic tradition had to be translated into a manageable number of insightful propositions and guiding hypotheses on three topics central to the coordination issue:
  information;
  the nature of policy; and
  the nature of interaction between organisations.

INFORMATION: COPING WITH OVERLOAD

Failures of communication and pleas for better information exchange are perennial. They are the smoke-screen for incompetence and bad faith, but also the time-honoured fig-leaf with which to disguise the unpalatable fact of divergent interests where harmony and rational collaboration are presumed to reign. However, even assuming that communication is the problem and not the scapegoat, the 'optimistic' tradition tends towards naivety. Information is treated as costless, as self-evidently good and as a force for unity rather than division. The alternative is to stress the costs of both generating and processing information, and the problems of coping with it.

The most familiar result of viewing information as problematic is to conclude, with Simon, that individuals and organisations will tend to 'satisfice' rather than 'optimise'.[18] The rational model assumes that maximising information and analysis will maximise the quality of decision making. That, in practice, the costs of pursuing perfect information are great is indisputable, but the argument can be taken further. For the individual actor learning to cope with a particular kind of information is an 'irreversible investment'; the 'code' has to be learned. For the organisation this process represents a significant accumulation of 'capital': once created, therefore, organisations have distinct identities which are comparatively inflexible due to the costs involved in changing codes.[19] The process of coping with information consequently erects barriers to coordination, especially to collaboration.

The more efficient an organisation (or profession) is in developing its own code – i.e. its way of handling and interpreting information – the more difficult it may be to communicate with other organisations. A similar conclusion is suggested by cognitive theory. Organisational actors develop analytical paradigms which allow them to cope with uncertainty and ambiguity in dealing with information. In Steinbruner's words:[20] 'Pertinent information may enter the decision process or it may be screened out, depending on how it relates to the existing pattern of belief'; information 'which is threatening to established belief patterns' may be rejected. This, in turn, may lead to 'grooved thinking': the organisational actor's decisions 'are programmed so that once he determines which category obtains, the decision follows without further question'. This is first cousin to the notion of Standard Operating Procedures (SOPs), described as follows by Allison:[21]

Rules of thumb permit concerted action by large numbers of individuals, each responding to basic cues. The rules are usually simple enough to facilitate easy learning and unambiguous application. Since procedures are 'standard' they do not change quickly or easily. Without such standard procedures, it would not be possible to perform certain concerted tasks ... Some SOPs are simply conventions that make possible regular or coordinated activity. But most SOPs are grounded in the incentive structure of the organisation or even in the norms of the organisation or the basic attitudes and operating style of its members. The stronger the grounding, the more resistant SOPs are to change.

Once again, the more efficient organisations are in developing their own analytic paradigms and SOPs – i.e. in coordinating their internal activities – the more difficult they may find it to enter into a dialogue with other organisations, since they will be using different organisational languages.

The problems of organisational information-handling raise some further questions about the assumptions made – if only implicitly – in the 'optimistic' rational model. If coordination is about information exchange (among other things), what actually is being exchanged, and by whom? One way of organising the collection of information within the organisation is through hierarchy: the information flows up the official lines of authority. But this, as Downs[22] argues, introduces bias since 'all types of officials tend to exaggerate data that reflect favourably on themselves and to minimize those that reveal their own shortcomings'. Such bias introduces information distortion. Thus Tullock[23] calculated that if, in an organisation with seven levels, the average official screens out only half the data given him by his subordinates, the winnowing process would eliminate 94.8% of the data originally gathered by the time the information reached the top of the office. Yet a central feature of coordination, as we discovered, is precisely that it depends both upon detailed understanding of the key issues at the level at which coordination is to occur and upon decision making authority. The choice of personnel to discuss and negotiate new arrangements is therefore a perennial problem and a crucial determinant of outcomes.

POLICY: A MISLEADING CONCEPT

The very idea of policy implies a degree of orderliness, even consensus; a way forward has been agreed and delineated. In the social policy field, moreover, the term policy is typically taken to refer to the specification of the needs which are to be met and the means by which this is to be achieved. The implication – widely reflected in official policy on the inner cities and on the care of the elderly and other 'priority client groups' – is that what is required is coordination between different policies, each of which is designed to meet one of an interlocking set of needs. The real problem of coordination is seen to lie at the interface between the major strands of social policy and the major service departments and agencies which enact them.

This is a wholly misleading picture and it is one which arises from the conceptualisation of policy as a coherent, relatively self-contained, complete and authoritative guide to future action. However, this misleading picture also arises from the tendency in the post-war decades to split social policy off from the rest of the body-politic and to treat it as a hermetically sealed arena of state intervention co-terminous with the departments and agencies of social policy. In reality, policy processes are altogether more complex and messy. The conflicts and power struggles which determine the *outcomes* of social policy (as opposed to the content of statements of objectives which are merely *inputs*) are to be located throughout the government system and not only in the 'social policy departments'.[24]

One way of expressing some of this complex reality is by thinking, as Webb and Wistow suggest,[25] in terms of *streams of policies* which interact, compete and conflict, rather than in terms of policies as discrete and authoritative blueprints. They argue that social policy outcomes are best seen as the end-product of at least three streams of interacting policies:

(i)   *service, or output, policies* – which specify the social needs to be met and the choice of appropriate means and methods of intervention;

(ii) *resource policies* – which specify broad patterns of expenditure, detailed allocations between competing uses, and the dominant approaches taken to resource management (e.g. to maximise long-term cost effectiveness or to minimise total expenditure in the short term);

(iii) *governance policies* – which specify the general view taken of the role of the state as well as the philosophy of management and control to be adopted within public authorities (e.g. centralisation or decentralisation, detailed intervention or *laissez-faire*).

To these can be added a fourth:

(iv) *fiscal policies* – which specify the general view taken on the level and structure of taxation to be aimed at as well as the specific tax 'subsidies', benefits or breaks which are to be permitted.

What this formulation immediately reveals is the importance of seeing policies as a means of *expressing* conflicting interests rather than as the product of conflict resolution. A policy to ease the lot of institutionalised mentally ill people which founders for lack of resources can only be seen in the rational 'optimistic' tradition as a failure of communication and coordination. But it may more accurately be understood as the triumph of one interest (expressed through resource allocation policies) over the interests of mentally ill people (expressed through a service policy). It is therefore essential to look for competition and conflict between policies and also to recognise the divergent value systems, goals, dominant interests, and informational codes which may underpin differences between various policy streams.

To turn this perception of conflicting interests on its head is to reveal another dimension of coordination: to achieve a particular outcome for a vulnerable and weak interest group such as the mentally ill will not only depend on coordinating different social service organisations and objectives. It will depend on the degree of coordination achieved across the service, resource and fiscal policy streams, which in turn will depend upon the adoption of a governance strategy designed to effect congruence between service goals and resource commitments. In short, coordination is not merely a neutral technique. It can be a crucial element of any strategy to overcome – or to enhance – the bias in favour of dominant interests and ideologies which is inherent in our – and every – system of government. Coordination is itself about power and the purposeful use of power.

POWER-DEPENDENCE AND ORGANISATIONAL INTERACTION

The rational tradition tends to assume that the guiding ideology of public service organisations is the pursuit of the common good. One of the popular alternative viewpoints is that organisational actors are self-interested 'utility maximisers':

Bureaucratic officials in general have a complex set of goals including power, income, prestige, security, convenience, loyalty (to an idea, an institution, or the nation), pride in excellent work, and desire to serve the public interest ... But regardless of the particular goals involved, every official is significantly motivated by his own self-interest.[26]

This view of organisational actors as economic men who will weigh up the costs and benefits to themselves of any given course of action, sensitises us to incentives and disincentives to coordination (or any other desired objective).

Following on from this model, public sector organisations can be seen as bodies dedicated to securing their resource base. In an extreme version, this viewpoint prompts the conclusion that bureaucratic organisations will invariably seek to maximise their budgets.[27] But this does not necessarily follow from the basic premise. If organisations collectively are (like the individual actors within them) utility maximisers, they may seek to maximise their autonomy or their security and it is possible to imagine a budget-maximising strategy which imperils all these goals (such as taking on new responsibilities for a heterogeneous, difficult to deal with client group). In short, organisational self-interest may point in the direction of refusing to take on extra responsibilities, even if these bring in extra money. The crucial factor may be precisely the *ratio* between resources and responsibilities: i.e. the amount of 'organisational slack'.

Viewing public service organisations as bodies dedicated to protecting their resource base (as distinct from necessarily seeking to maximise their budgets) has some further implications. It suggests that such organisations will seek to mobilise political support for their activities – and budgets – just as private sector business firms will seek to attract customers for their products. After all, in a period of resource stress even support for baseline activities cannot be taken for granted. Such support mobilisation strategies may take a variety of forms, but one self-evident strategy consists of proclaiming the organisation's special and unique role in protecting the interests or well-being of a popular or politically strong client group. To establish a monopoly of care or provision for such a group is to assert the claim that any attack on the organisation – such as budget retrenchment – is also an attack on those clients. In a sense, popular clients are valuable property, to be defended against other, competing organisations. Conversely, of course, one might expect public sector organisations to be less interested in the care of less popular client groups. Willingness to collaborate would, therefore, be most unlikely where one organisation sees itself as having established a desirable monopoly and most likely where a client group is seen as marginal to the agency's main role or as imposing burdens which do not bring in any compensatory inputs of support. In this respect, the rational strategy for public sector organisations would be similar to that for professions, in so far as the process of professionalisation can be seen as the assertion of monopoly control over certain social functions or skills (a conclusion which would, in turn, suggest that a public sector organisation containing a strong professional element would have a double incentive to warn possible competitors off its policy patch).

The notion of seeking a monopoly of service provision by colonising a particular policy area also links up with the idea of territoriality. As Downs puts it:[28]

The *interior* of the bureau's territory is where it exercises the dominant role over social policy. It consists of two sub-zones: the *heartland*, in which the bureau is the sole determinant of social policy; and the *interior fringe*, where it is dominant, but other social agencies exercise some influence. No single bureau is dominant in *no-man's land*, but many have some influence ... The *exterior* of the bureau's territory is where other bureaux dominate social policy. This consists of two sub-zones: the *periphery*, where it has some influence but another bureau is dominant, and *alien territory* where it has no influence whatever. The heartland of any bureau is alien territory to all other bureaux.

The rational perspective draws heavily on Weber and a host of modern interpreters united by the basic tenets of the classic theory of bureaucracy, but alternative viewpoints spring from a variety of disciplinary perspectives and often lack even a common vocabulary. Nonetheless, a central theme is the insistence on viewing organisations as 'bargaining and influence systems'. If individual actors seek to maximise utilities, groups and even whole organisations can be understood in the same terms. Organisations compete for resources with the result that the normal mode of co-existence is not harmonious collaboration but bargaining, power play and conflict.

Lindblom's[29] early contribution to the debate rested on the assumption that organisations would coordinate their activities only if it was in their own self-interest; attempts at exhortation or at establishing formal coordinative machinery would not be likely to have much effect. Lindblom's approach was consistent with a heterogeneity of literature sailing under the flag of exchange theory. One of its great merits is that it identifies many of the barriers and opportunities which shape bargaining processes.[30] The starting point is that bargaining, or exchange, is a function of interdependence: interdependent organisations 'must take each other into account if they are to accomplish their goals'.[31] Interdependence consists of interlocking patterns of demand and supply for resources: material resources such as capital, income flows, labour and clients, but also less tangible resources such as information, expertise, authority and the capacity to authorise. Bargaining depends upon complementary patterns of demand and supply for such resources and also upon the likelihood of substituting readily available alternatives for needed resources possessed exclusively by a rival organisation.

Organisational bargaining may be expected to have many of the characteristics of any other 'market place', but how important is the buoyancy of the entire inter-organisational economy for the level of bargaining? Does interaction peak in good times or bad? One answer is that organisations will interact strongly through bargaining both in times of abundance and in times of great scarcity.[32] When organisational budgets are growing rapidly, the costs of trading (and of any poor deals) are easily borne; when budgets are very tight, the benefits of avoiding duplication and of pooling resources are great. This latter possibility has had particular and obvious relevance in the social policy field in the last decade. But the evidence for these propositions is less than clear-cut.

Aiken and Hague have argued that for bargaining and exchange to take place 'there must be some slack in the resource base'.[33] Subsequent empirical findings suggested that scarcity may provide the motive but that 'those agencies most willing to act upon this motive are those relatively rich in clients and non-human resources'.[34] The obvious proposition – which informed our own choice of empirical research sites – is that a finely balanced experience of pressure and comparative security (or room for manoeuvre) provides the strongest spur to exchange through bargaining.

However, the picture is further complicated by the transaction costs involved in inter-organisational exchange. Negotiation ties down staff and involves uncertainty and risks. These costs may in turn depend upon the networks, if any, which link organisations. As Thrasher has argued, 'networks which persist over time are likely to exhibit different exchange patterns than those which are newly created'.[35] The need to create networks and engender trust can be a major transaction cost. What this suggests is that formal machinery may have no relevance where the preconditions for bargaining are absent, but it may play a real role in giving permanence to networks and lowering transaction costs.

The importance of networks underlines the fact that the rewards sought on behalf of organisations and those sought by their representatives as individuals differ. Individual actors may aspire to many non-material rewards: status, social approval and friendship.[36] Nonetheless, the individual actor, just as much as the organisation, is viewed essentially as self-interested rather than altruistic.

To recognise networks and diverse non-material rewards is to accept that exchange and bargaining constitute a complex social game which is likely to be played according to rules – rules which define socially acceptable behaviour and transactions.[37] Relationships between organisations, groupings and policy streams may be based on competition and conflict rather than on consensus, but competition and conflict are constrained by 'basic rules of conduct'.[38] Moreover, interlocking transactions may take place in more than one arena: 'some resources gained in one arena may be used to win prizes in another arena'.[39]

The complexity of the bargaining relationships through which policies and actions may become more (or less) coordinated point to two crucial issues for empirical research: the structuring of arenas by government and the role of 'middlemen'. The first of these is summarised in Webb and Wistow's phrase, 'the structuring of local policy environments'.[40] Health and local authorities, for example, do not relate one to another in a vacuum. Central government systematically, though not necessarily intentionally, influences the resources needed by and available to these organisations. It structures the formal organisational arrangements which impinge on the development of networks of relationships, and it determines many of the costs and benefits of interaction. It may also affect the availability of 'middlemen'.

Reticulists[41] – which, as a term, is preferable to 'middlepersons' – are specialists in inter-organisational politics who cultivate networks of relationships and provide access to information. Enthusiastic reticulists seem to discount the costs and frustrations of negotiation and information gathering against the rewards of manipulation – the manipulation of inter-organisational relationships. The fact that they may have to discover rewards where other actors only perceive costs underlines the need to take a sophisticated view of the model of self-interested behaviour at the heart of the bargaining/ exchange perspective. It underlines the array of costs and benefits, for multiple actors, which must be predominantly positive on balance if exchange is to lead to coordinated action. It also underlines the challenge to government of harnessing organisational self-interest as a route to coordination; to depend on altruistic, rational patterns of coordination may be to court disappointment, but it is certainly the easy option.

The superficial attractions of the rational 'optimistic' tradition are even clearer when it is remembered that stable patterns of exchange and bargaining rest upon a broad symmetry between organisations and a recognition that opportunities exist for rewarding exchange. The first is crucial, not least because it raises the ghost at this feast: power. Bargaining and exchange arise from dependence: a wholly independent organisation with no pressing unmet resource needs can afford to go its own way without reference to others. But dependence bestows power on the resource-rich party; undue dependence implies dominance by another. Reasonably symmetrical patterns of dependence are therefore the stimulus to exchange. Moreover, a symmetrical pattern of dependence has to be *perceived*. Opportunities for exchange which go unnoticed, and exchange possibilities which are seen to include unduly high costs, or risks of dominance, will simply result in non-interaction – even the active avoidance of interaction.

Highly asymmetrical patterns of dependence can themselves lead to coordination: imperative coordination. Powerful organisations can and do impose their will on others and enforce interactions on their own terms, just as they can and do pursue their own courses of action with scant regard for weaker organisations which are greatly influenced by them. As Schmidt and Kochan[42] have persuasively argued, the power and the bargaining/exchange views of inter-organisational behaviour are complementary. If power is interpreted in terms of inter-organisational demands for and supplies of resources, interaction can arise from exchange in the context of symmetrical relationships and the exercise of power can arise from asymmetrical relationships. The ability of central government to enforce coordination on subordinate organisations is precisely to be understood in these terms.

The obvious caveat which must be appended to this power-dependence/bargaining-exchange model of organisational interaction is that power may be too narrowly conceived. Wrong suggested the narrowness of the approach taken by arguing: 'I do not see how we can avoid restricting the term "power" to intentional and effective control by particular agents'.[43] Emerson, even more specifically, asserted: 'The power of A over B is equal to, and based upon the dependence of B upon A'.[44] These views of power could be stretched to include all that we would wish to include, but it is better by far to follow Lukes and adopt a more catholic formulation.[45] The kind of power most readily incorporated within the approach suggested by Wrong and Emerson and many others, is essentially overt – it is a behavioural approach to power. It comprises what Bachrach and Baratz called the first face of power.[46]

In their terms, the second face of power added another ingredient: non-decisions. This concept has been much ill-used, but Bachrach and Baratz applied it in situations in which possible lines of action or behaviour were intentionally excluded from discussion, or were kept off the agenda, by power holders. To take an example, a highly self-sufficient organisation may perennially disregard calls to coordinate its actions with those of a less powerful organisation; an arrogant insularity may keep the coordination issue off the agenda altogether.

Lukes developed these two views of power and added a third which he called the radical view of power: both overt power play and non-decisions may prove unnecessary if power takes the form of influencing the very way in which a problem is defined or perceived, or the way in which phenomena come to be regarded as problematic. Deeply entrenched views of the world, which are unremarkable precisely because they are deeply entrenched, are a most valuable bulwark for those interests which they favour. This third, or radical, view of power also points to the likelihood of failures of coordination, therefore. For example, the curative model of medical practice enjoys a reputation for hegemony which must alert us to its likely consequences for coordination between health and other local services. Medical doctors have, until recently at least, successfully shaped the way in which other professions, and policy makers, think about issues involving health and sickness.

From the point of view of central government departments seeking to encourage coordination in social policy, the 'pessimistic' tradition of academic analysis makes dismal reading. The central government tendency has always been to rely on the rational model. Organisations and professions are exhorted to look beyond their sectional interests and to work together for the greater good of clients and the community. Such altruism is expected to be its own reward. The 'pessimistic' academic tradition underlines all the barriers not only of self-interest *per se*, but of exceedingly complicated patterns of self-interest. Interaction may occur through bargaining and exchange and it may possibly lead to desired patterns of coordination. But it may, even more plausibly, lead to no such thing. Organisational relationships, where they occur, may fall far short of such well-developed exchanges. Partisan mutual adjustment, to use Lindblom's old expression, may merely involve organisations in changes of practice which are designed to avoid or minimise conflict. It may facilitate unilateral development, which Glennerster identifies as the dominant contemporary mode of action in the social policy field,[47] rather than presaging close collaboration. Unilateral change by one organisation to accommodate the policies of another may produce desired coordination, or it may merely represent two ships of state passing in the night.

While non-interaction and failures of coordination may be the most readily explained phenomena, the 'pessimistic' tradition does hold out hope of more concerted action. It points to the possibility of systematically structuring arenas so that they facilitate and promote collaborative exchange. The conditions may be demanding and government action may need to be finely tuned if it is to succeed, but the message – in essence – is simply that 'policy implementation' ought to be as central and as well informed a feature of government as 'policy making'. That opportunities for concerted influence do exist is the optimistic part of the 'pessimistic' tradition from a governmental point of view.

What is also apparent is that these academic perspectives are substantially complementary, rather than in conflict. The great rational synoptic planning versus incrementalism debate obscured this complementarity. An emphasis on power-dependence and bargaining needs to be balanced by reference to the possibility – however slight – that social service organisations and professions may at times take a broad, altruistic view and elevate system (or client) gain above sectional interests. However, to speak of altruism in this context could be misleading, for it is the value base and service ethos of the social services which may produce such a 'rational' outcome. If government neglects to build and mobilise such a value base, it is indeed relying upon pure altruism to generate collaboration.

Similarly, the 'pessimistic' emphasis on processes of interaction, bargaining and conflict is needed to balance frequent references to structures. The elegant mansion of rational synoptic planning was constructed without sufficient regard to the need for adequate foundations or to the problems of managing a large and disputatious household. Nonetheless, it did at least recognise that walls and roof are more likely to join, and skilled workers are more likely to be brought together, when everyone has a blueprint in their hands. Neither the emphasis on structure nor that on planning is irrelevant; together they may, as we have argued, provide the context in which networks develop and flourish – networks which are vital to processes of interaction. The real purpose of our empirical research, therefore, is not to test the ideas and hypotheses which flow from rival academic traditions, but to explore the extent to which they – alone or in concert – can explain the barriers and opportunities, costs and benefits, failures and successes, of the perennial search in public affairs for better coordination.

To this end we note below some of the key propositions which we extracted from the literature. They are related to the two broad traditions of 'optimism' and 'pessimism' about the likelihood of securing coordination through a rational and disinterested pursuit of public good, but we ourselves see them as largely complementary emphases on different facets of political and bureaucratic life.

PROPOSITIONS AND RESEARCH METHODS

Propositions generated by the 'optimistic' rational perspective
1 Coordination can be pursued imperatively: through *authoritative* forms of planning, or through *collaborative-altruistic* forms of planning.
2 Both forms of planning are essentially synoptic and rational.
3 Both forms of planning will require a substantial capacity for policy analysis and a large measure of consensus on the nature of problems and acceptable solutions.
4 Collaborative planning will require a degree – possibly a high degree – of organisational altruism: short-term and sectional interests will need to be subordinated to considerations of 'system gain'.
5 Planning will be sustained by and substantially conducted through formal structures and processes developed for the purpose.
6 Formal machinery will be much in evidence and its use will be associated with a high level of output.
7 Interaction between organisations and actors will be intensive: it will occur frequently and freely through formal, and also through informal, processes.
8 Coordination and interaction leading to jointly agreed policies and projects will be particularly strong when need is high but resources are scarce.

Propositions generated by the 'pessimistic', power-dependence/bargaining perspective
1 Coordination is problematic both in terms of process and output.
2 Organisations and other actors may not perceive a need for interaction or may consciously avoid interaction.
3 Coordination may result from unilateral, non-interactive adjustments or from mutual adjustment designed to minimise interaction and conflict, but the kinds of coordination desired in social policy are most likely to result from interactive processes.
4 Interactive processes leading to greater coordination may include bargaining/exchange and power/dominance relationships, but the former are most likely to lead to desired forms of coordination.
5 Interaction is based on the exchange or appropriation of valued resources and proceeds by estimation of the costs and benefits of the interaction process itself and of its outcome.
6 Interaction through exchange is most likely when organisations perceive mutual benefits and lowest when neither perceive a benefit (e.g. symmetrical relations of interest and disinterest, respectively).

7 Interaction through dominance is most likely when one organisation perceives the possibility of securing benefits without incurring exchange costs (e.g. asymmetrical relations of power-dependence).

8 Interaction and its scope (e.g. uni-, or bi- or multi-lateral) are determined wholly by perceived costs and benefits and not by system-wide thinking or altruism.

9 The influence of formal machinery and of structure (e.g. the impact of structural complexity on interaction) is mediated through, not independent of, the costs and benefits associated with different patterns of action.

10 Interaction is therefore conditional and likely to be sporadic rather than consistent.

11 Interaction is locally determined and negotiated rather than externally imposed or mandated, but the structuring of local environments by superordinate bodies is a crucial influence on both the likelihood and nature of interactions.

12 The domains over which organisations seek control include the supply of their inputs, the speed and characteristics of throughput and the timing and flow of outputs; interaction may be directed at protecting or modifying any or all of these. Professional domain considerations may be offset when the other benefits of interaction are distinctly positive, but they are a crucial limiting factor when the benefits of interaction are marginal or uncertain.

13 A scarcity of resources is likely to affect interaction in one of several ways:

   (a) Severe and unrelieved scarcity experienced by organisations which are substantially independent and broadly equal in terms of power is likely greatly to inhibit interaction.

   (b) A disproportionately powerful organisation faced by scarcity may appropriate resources by exercising its dominance over other organisations.

   (c) However, weaker organisations, faced by this possibility, may accordingly avoid all opportunities for interaction.

   (d) Where no one organisation is able or likely to exploit a position of dominance, and thereby impose costs without benefits on other organisations, mutual scarcity may foster coordination designed to increase the efficiency with which existing resources are used.

   (e) An overall position of scarcity combined with the availability of some flexible or additional resources is most likely to facilitate such coordination.

   (f) Additional resources can act as a major incentive for interaction if they are made conditional on the achievement of coordination.

These propositions were used to inform all our empirical research, which began with an exploration of the history and fate of the proposal, emanating from the Central Policy Review Staff (CPRS), that a Joint Approach to Social Policy be attempted. It seemed appropriate to use this proposal as the initial focal point for our research and to identify as fully as possible the extent of its impact during its brief period of direct influence on central government policy making. This exploration of the JASP initiative was undertaken by William Plowden and drew on his contacts and detailed knowledge as one of the members of CPRS at the time. The empirical research took the form of in-depth interviews and the analysis of papers.

Two policy 'tracers', which will be introduced fully in the next chapter, were selected as focal points for the remainder of the empirical research: children under five and the elderly. In contrasting ways they highlighted problems of policy coordination within and across organisational and professional boundaries; attempts at active policy coordination had been made within central government in both cases. Our strategy was to examine the structures, processes and attitudes surrounding these policy fields within central government and then to use the same tracers in studying relationships between professions, departments and organisations in a selection of local areas.

Although the ambitions outlined in the original JASP proposal were soon thwarted, our empirical research was designed to identify any and all examples of effective coordination, and failure to coordinate, with respect to our two tracers. The 'optimistic' tradition, as it affected governance in Britain in the seventies, placed great store on coordinative structures such as joint committees or policy units; it also emphasised formal policy making at the strategic level (Cabinet committee and top of the office in central government, and members and chief officers at the sub-national level). One of the clear messages highlighted by the 'pessimistic' tradition of writing and analysis, however, was that interaction may be expected to result from self-interested bargaining and power play at all levels. It therefore seemed essential to cast our net so as to include informal as well as formal processes at all levels of decision making. Hence, we cut a vertical slice through the system of public administration from Cabinet level down to the highly local level of individual projects and fieldwork arrangements within health and local authorities and between these statutory bodies and voluntary organisations.

Informal processes are far more difficult to study than formal decision making structures. Our interest in them dictated a research method which relied heavily upon a qualitative fieldwork approach: in-depth interviews, observation and the analysis of papers were our stock in trade at the local level. The same was true within central government departments – with the exception that observation of meetings was not possible. However, several members of the team had participated in central government decision making in other capacities and the lack of opportunity to observe was not too keenly felt. The access obtained within local and health authorities was excellent; very few doors were closed to us. Access within central government was less straightforward, but by no means impossible. Many officials at all levels gave generously of their time and were keen to explore issues with us that many of them recognised to be of importance to the good conduct of public administration. The conclusions which we have reached are firmly our own, but they are founded on a degree of access to central departments which is often considered to be impossible to obtain in the face of the British obsession with official secrecy.

The emphasis on qualitative research methods was counter-balanced by a systematic attempt to quantify the amount and level of use made of formal coordinative machinery. This attempt at quantification was extended to cover the amount and range of coordinated outputs of all kinds, no matter what their origin or provenance. This limited indulgence in 'bureaumetrics' seemed an essential complement to our qualitative methods for two reasons. The quantification of formal machinery was obviously appropriate because the 'optimistic' tradition had prompted an investment in such coordinative machinery. It seemed wise to see whether machinery had in fact been developed and whether it was actively used. To discover whether it was at all effective, however, we had to have some quantification of coordinative outputs: jointly developed policies, programmes, projects and practices. Measures of machinery and output could be compared and causal links could be traced, however tentatively. Even more importantly, the quantification of coordinative outputs provided a 'back-stop' for our examination of informal processes. If we did not identify informal processes sufficiently well, but did identify outputs, we could gain some assessment of the importance of informal processes by tracing outputs back to see if they originated from formal machinery or had emerged in other ways.

Our overall research strategy therefore involved three interlocking empirical studies and an account of our findings is structured in the same way. Our approach, and the structure of the major part of the book, can be summarised as follows.

(a) A restrospective study of the origins and fate of the JASP proposal initiated by the Central Policy Review Staff during the mid seventies. The main research methods were in-depth interviews and the analysis of papers, though William Plowden's experience as an 'insider' was also vital to the research. Chapter 4 is devoted to this topic.

(b) An in-depth study of policy coordination at central government level in the late seventies and early eighties, using policies towards children under five and the elderly as 'tracers'. The research methods were as noted above. The work was shared between the research teams at Bath and Loughborough Universities. The findings are discussed in chapter 5.

(c) In-depth studies of six localities in which relationships between health authorities, local authorities and voluntary organisations were studied through the same two tracers employed at the central level. The main research methods were in-depth interviews, the analysis of papers, non-participant observation, and the approximate quantification of coordinative machinery and outputs. The approach was similar to, though less intensive than, that which Glennerster has labelled 'organisational anthropology'[48] – with a touch of 'bureaumetrics'. The work was again shared between the Bath and Loughborough teams. The detailed research methods, selection of sites and the findings are discussed in chapters 6 to 9.

One task remains before the exploration of our empirical findings can begin; the two policy tracers at the heart of our research need to be introduced. It was not part of our intention to produce a detailed history or analysis of policies towards children under five and elderly people as studies in their own right. They were employed merely as a manageable means of tracing the complexity surrounding major issues of social policy. Nonetheless, the policy backgrounds do need to be outlined. The next chapter is devoted to this task and also, *inter alia*, to an exploration of the various attempts made during the seventies to establish coordinative machinery and processes in these policy fields.

REFERENCES

1 J. L. Pressman and A. Wildavsky (1979) *Implementation*, Berkeley: University of California Press
2 H. Glennerster, *et al.* (1983) *Planning for Priority Groups*, Oxford: Martin Robertson
3 A. Webb and M. Hobdell (1980) 'Coordination and teamwork' in S. Lonsdale, A. L. Webb and T. L. Briggs, *Teamwork in the Personal Social Services and Health Care*, London: Croom Helm
4 See J. D. Stewart (1974) *The Responsive Local Authority*, London: Charles Knight; R. Greenwood and J. D. Stewart (1974) *Corporate Planning in English Local Government*, London: Charles Knight
5 J. Bennington (1975) *Local Government Becomes Big Business*, London: CDP Information and Intelligence Unit; C. Cockburn (1977) *The Local State*, London: Pluto Press; R. J. Haynes (1980) *Organisation Theory and Local Government*, London: Allen and Unwin

6 A. L. Webb (1986) 'Collaboration in planning: a prerequisite of community care', reprinted in A. L. Webb and G. Wistow, *Planning, Need and Scarcity: Essays on the Personal Social Services*, London: Allen and Unwin, p. 155

7 G. Wistow (1982) 'Collaboration between health and local authorities: why is it necessary?', *Social Policy and Administration*, 16, 1, 1982, pp. 43–62, reprinted in Webb and Wistow (1986) *op. cit.*

8 *Ibid.*; see also T. A. Booth (1979) *Planning for Welfare: Social Policy and the Expenditure Process*, Oxford: Blackwell

9 Webb and Wistow (1986) *op. cit.*

10 P. M. Jackson (ed.) (1985) *Implementing Government Policy Initiatives: The Thatcher Administration 1979–1983*, RIPA

11 C. E. Lindblom (1959) 'The science of muddling through', *Public Administration Review*, 19, 2, 1959, pp. 79–88; Y. Dror (1964) 'Muddling through – "science" or "inertia" ', *Public Administration Review*, 24, 3, 1964, pp. 154–7; A. Faludi (1973) *A Reader in Planning Theory*, Oxford: Pergamon; M. Carley (1980) *Rational Techniques in Policy Analysis*, London: Heinemann

12 A. Etzioni (1967) 'Mixed scanning: a "third" approach to decision-making', *Public Administration Review*, 28, 5, 1967, pp. 385–92; J. I. Gershuny (1978) 'Policy-making rationality: a reformulation', *Policy Sciences*, 9, 1978, pp. 295–316

13 Lindblom (1959) *art. cit.*; C. E. Lindblom (1965) *The Intelligence of Democracy*, New York: The Free Press

14 J. A. Weiss (1981), 'Substance and Symbol in Administrative Reform: The case of Human Service Coordination, *Policy Analysis* 7(1) pp. 21–47

15 A. L. Webb and G. Wistow, 'Collaboration: a case study in social planning', *Journal of Social Policy*, forthcoming

16 C. E. Lindblom (1977) *Politics and Markets*, New York: Basic Books, p. 251

17 *Ibid.*

18 H. Simon (1965) *Administrative Behaviour*, New York: The Free Press

19 K. J. Arrow (1974) *The Limits of Organisation*, New York: W. W. Norton & Co.

20 J. D. Steinbruner (1974) *The Cybernetic Theory of Decision*, Princeton: Princeton University Press

21 G. T. Allison (1971) *Essence of Decision*, Boston: Little Brown & Co.

22 A. Downs (1967) *Inside Bureaucracy*, Boston: Little Brown & Co.

23 G. Tullock (1975) *The Politics of Bureaucracy*, Washington DC: Public Affairs Press

24 R. M. Titmuss (1968) *Commitment to Welfare*, London: Allen and Unwin; H. Heclo and A. Wildavsky (1981) *The Private Government of Public Money*, London: Macmillan (2nd edition)

25 A. L. Webb and G. Wisto (1982) *Whither State Welfare?*, London: Royal Institute of Public Administration; Webb and Wistow (1986) *op. cit.*

26 Downs (1967), *op. cit.*, pp. 212–13

27 W. A. Niskansen (1971) *Bureaucracy and Representative Government*, Chicago: Aldine Atherton

28 Downs (1967), *op. cit.*, pp. 212–13

29 Lindblom (1965), *op. cit.*

30 Peter Abell (ed.) (1975) *Organisations as Bargaining and Influence Systems*, London: Heinemann; S. B. Bacharach and E. J. Lawler (1981) *Bargaining*, New York: Jossey Bass. For a comprehensive summary of power-dependence/bargaining-exchange literatures as they apply in this field, see R. Rhodes (1981) *Control as Power in Central–Local Relationships*, London: Gower; see also Glennerster *et al.* (1983), *op. cit.*

31 E. Litwak and L. P. Hylton (1961) 'Interorganisational analysis: a hypothesis on coordinating agencies', *Administrative Science Quarterly*, 1961, pp. 395–420

32 *Ibid.*; R. J. Adamek and B. F. Lavin, 'Interorganisational exchange: a note on the scarcity hypothesis' in A. R. Negandi (ed.) (1971) *Organisational Theory in an Interorganisational Perspective*, Kent, Ohio: Kent State University Press

33 M. Aiken and J. Hage (1968) 'Organisational interdependence and Intra-organisational structure', *American Sociological Review*, vol. 33, pp. 912–30

34 Litwak and Hylton (1961), *art. cit.*

35 Michael Thrasher (1983) 'Exchange, networks and implementation', *Policy and Politics*, vol. 11, no. 4, October 1983, pp. 375–93

36 Michael Thrasher and David Dunkerley (1981) 'The contribution of social exchange theory to the study of public policy implementation', mimeo. Paper presented to the ECPR Planning Session on Implementation, University of Lancaster, March/April 1981

37 Rhodes (1981) *op. cit.*

38 F. G. Bailey (1980) *Strategems and Spoils*, Oxford: Basil Blackwell

39 *Ibid.*

40 A. L. Webb and G. Wistow (1985) 'Structuring local policy environments' in S. Ranson, *Studies in Central-Local Relations*, London: Allen and Unwin

41 J. K. Friend, J. M. Power and C. J. L. Yewlett (1974) *Public Planning: The Intercorporate Dimension*, London: Tavistock

42 S. M. Schmidt and T. A. Kochan (1977) 'Interorganisational relationships: patterns and motivations', *Administrative Science Quarterly*, 22, June 1977

43 D. H. Wrong (1967) 'Some problems in defining social power', *American Journal of Sociology*, vol. 73, pp. 673–81

44 R. M. Emerson (1962) 'Power dependence relations', *American Sociological Review*, vol. 27, pp. 31–41

45 S. Lukes (1974) *Power*, London: Macmillan

46 P. Bachrach and M. S. Baratz (1970) *Power and Poverty: Theory and Practice*, London: Oxford University Press

47 Glennerster *et al.* (1983), *op. cit.*

48 *Ibid.*

3 ∼ Policy coordination for children under five and for elderly people

COORDINATION AND POLICY FOR THE HEALTH AND
PERSONAL SOCIAL SERVICES, 1971–1981

Collaboration and coordination were explored in the research by detailed investigation of two policy areas at both central and local government levels. The areas were day care for children under five and policy for elderly people. These two 'tracers' were chosen from several possible candidates. As chapter 1 made clear, policy statements about the health and personal social services have, for many years, stressed the importance of collaboration. Particular examples have included statements about specific client groups like mentally handicapped[1] and mentally ill people[2], but the drive towards coordination has been evident in documents with a wider remit like the Consultative Document in 1976[3], *Care in Action* in 1981[4] and before that, the circular in 1972[5] which launched the 'Ten Year Plan' initiative. This circular provides a convenient point at which to begin a more detailed account of the development of the idea of coordination in relation to the health and personal social services than was given in chapter 1, an account which will also make clearer the reasons for choosing children under five and elderly people as the two tracer groups.

The Ten Year Plan circular was perhaps one of the clearest statements of the belief in rational planning and it is worth quoting at some length to give the flavour of much of what was to come for client specific policies and for policy in the health and personal social services more generally:

The Secretary of State is concerned to secure that, in the future, following the reorganisation of the National Health Service and local government into matching areas of administration, the needs of each area for health and social care should be assessed and provision made through coordinated planning of services by the new area health authorities and local authorities ... The Department proposes to develop both for the new health authorities and for local authority services, arrangements for forward planning which will provide for annual reviews by both types of authority, will enable them to draw their plans into relationship with one another, and enable local government and central government jointly to review at regular intervals the development of the services and to determine the best use of resources[6].

Ten year plans were introduced at a time when expenditure on services was expected to increase by 10% in real terms each year, for ten years. In other words, there was to be a growth increment which authorities could use to change the balance of services in line with guidelines issued by the government. These guidelines were intended to:

provide a basis for projecting the direction and the balance of development of the services, and will make possible an orderly and regular review of them[7].

There seems little doubt, as Booth has pointed out, that the government's motives in introducing ten year plans were mixed, with the desire for a degree of control over local social service authorities being part of the admixture[8]. But it is also clear, and consistent with the other major reforms of the period (Seebohm, local authority and NHS reorganisation), that the Heath government believed in the value of rational comprehensive planning. The suggestion that central and local government should review the plans together also indicated that the government wished to see closer collaboration between the centre and the local authorities, a theme that also appeared in the 'partnership' initiatives on the inner cities[9]. There were commentators at the time, however, who felt that the system was far from comprehensive. A leader in the *Municipal Journal* commented:

in the same week that local authorities received the Bains Report advocating a corporate approach, they also received circular 35/72 from the Department of Health seeking to encourage local authorities to establish ten year plans for their social services departments.
  It is a perfect example of how the expressed good intentions of Whitehall – to give local government greater independence and freedom from unnecessary interference – are constantly being contradicted by day to day practice. And it is clearly time the Whitehall departments put their heads together to eliminate this contradiction[10].

The circular was at pains to point out that coordination should include non-statutory as well as statutory bodies[11]. Furthermore the Secretary of State wished the views of clients 'to be brought into consideration' wherever possible. A few social service departments did attempt this; Mr Potter, Director of Surrey SSD, said that Surrey was holding informal discussions with voluntary organisations but 'it is also hoping that some of its one million residents will put forward their individual suggestions'[12]. In general however consultation, let alone cooperation and coordination, with the voluntary and informal sectors was very thin and patchy[13]. This was not too surprising since SSDs had been given only six months in which to prepare, approve and submit their plans, but coordination with the non-statutory sectors is a theme which has reappeared in every major policy document since.

Ten year plans did not survive infancy. Only one set of plans was completed. The rational planning system was defeated by the 'irrationality' of industrial disputes in 1974 and the 'irrationality' of economic crisis. The DHSS was swamped by material from the local authorities, some of which has never been analysed, and the preoccupation with NHS and local government reform sealed the system's fate. Nevertheless the Consultative Document, *Priorities in the Health and Personal Social Services*[14], promised a new era of rational planning in this area of social policy. The Secretary of State for Social Services, Barbara Castle, promised guidelines for planning which would 'reflect' the views of health authorities, local authorities, voluntary bodies and 'others with a close interest in these services'. The significance of the document was made very clear on its opening page:

This Consultative Document is a new departure. It is the first time an attempt has been made to establish rational and systematic priorities throughout the health and personal social services. Such an attempt is long overdue but it is given even greater urgency by the economic limitations outlined in the White Paper on Public Expenditure up to 1979/80 – the period on which this document concentrates. The level of resources which will be available over the next few years means that difficult choices will have to be made. It is essential that they should be made in full knowledge of the facts facing the services as a whole: the likely changes in demand by different client groups; the areas where past neglect had led to serious 'deficiencies'; the ways in which the available resources can be used to get the best return; the vital importance of joint planning. It is essential too, that central government and those who administer the services locally should work out together what the broad priorities should be.

There was no suggestion in the body of the document that there might be differing views about what the priorities should be, that full information is unobtainable and that partial information is always more partial than it at first appears, that the social and medical problems of human beings may not be amenable to solution, or that professional rivalries affect the ways in which concerned individuals see problems. It was left to an Annexe of the document to spell out some of the harsher realities:

In health and personal social services a complete breakdown of expenditure by objectives (e.g. treatment of specific medical conditions) would be extremely detailed and complex, and far too cumbersome for an across-the-board review; the necessary data is not in any case available. The programme budget does not therefore contain the kind of information needed for evaluating options in detail[15].

The next document, *The Way Forward*, spelled out the planning arrangements of the DHSS, the personal social services and the NHS, and talked of the benefits to be gained from close collaboration. Major structural problems were glossed over, as in the case of the divide between the health service and the provision of personal social services by local government, and instead virtue was found in the arrangement:

For the personal social services, planning procedures will need to fit in with the wider planning arrangements and decision-making processes of local authorities concerned. Whereas in central government the health and personal social services are combined in a single department, the local authorities are separated in the field from the health authorities but combined with, or closer to, the authorities responsible for education, planning, housing and other matters of local concern. Their work with children also puts them into a close relationship with the courts and the probation service. The central responsibilities in relation to these functions are distributed among a number of government departments. Corporate planning at local level has therefore concentrated on those activities for which local authorities hold direct responsibility[16].

The Conservative government's *Handbook of Policies and Priorities for the Health and Personal Social Services in England: Care in Action*[17] upheld the importance of good, rational planning. A great deal more emphasis was placed upon the involvement of the non-statutory sectors in service provision while the role of central government was played down, but the spirit of the documents of the seventies was clearly discernible. Planning and action at the local level was to be cooperative and coordinated and from this was to flow cost effectiveness and efficiency. The document contained sections specifically devoted to planning at the local level; the one on the voluntary sector started:

The strength of the voluntary sector lies partly in its ability to meet needs as they are perceived. But if that strength is to be harnessed to best advantage, voluntary and statutory services must be effectively coordinated[18].

The equivalent section in this chapter on the statutory services stated quite clearly the place of collaboration:

Health and local authorities have a statutory duty to cooperate to 'secure and advance the health and welfare' of the population. This collaboration will continue to be important when the new district health authorities are established. Joint consultative committees remain a legal requirement and informal machinery involving voluntary bodies will continue to be needed as well[19].

The chapter on the private sector, entitled 'Partnership with the private sector', spelled out the government's view:

The present constraints on the resources available to the NHS should encourage a more imaginative approach to the possibilities of planning and providing services in partnership with the private sector where it is economical to do so ... In certain circumstances either party could benefit from the use of facilities at full capacity, whereas facilities provided separately might be underused[20].

This brief review of policy statements underlines the importance and the persuasiveness of the ideas of coordination and collaboration; they have survived changes in government and changes in economic fortunes. With this as a backdrop, choosing areas in which to explore the practicalities of coordination was difficult precisely because there were so many candidates from which to choose.

THE TRACERS: CHILDREN UNDER FIVE AND ELDERLY PEOPLE

The reason for choosing these two particular client groups as tracers was that taken together they included a wide range of local and central agencies. Policy towards young children had put particular emphasis on the relationship between social services, education and the voluntary sector; policy towards elderly people had stressed the need for collaboration between social services, health, housing, social security and the private sector. In both cases there had been an exceptional amount of attention given to coordination and collaboration in a series of letters, reports, consultative documents and a White Paper from central government urging a partnership approach. It is the detail of these papers, discussed in the short tracer profiles which follow, which made them such good candidates.

Children under five

Day care for children under five has been an area of social policy in which the belief in the benefits of collaboration and coordination has been particularly apparent. The importance of day services for children was stressed by the Plowden Committee and this view was endorsed in a number of government papers throughout the 1970s. The provision of social and educational care for the very young has been seen as being one of the ways in which the breakdown of families can be prevented and a child's capacity to cope with the social, emotional and educational aspects of life can be enhanced. Responsibility for provision has always been fragmented, with the local education authorities (LEAs) providing nursery education and the local social service authorities (LSSAs) providing day nurseries for social priority children. There has also been a lot of private and voluntary provision in the forms of childminding and playgroups. Health authorities, especially through health visiting services, have also had a major stake in care for this client group.

This rather general account of the organisational arrangements for providing for children under five does not convey, however, the severity of fragmentation in this policy area. Challis[21] has noted that in one London borough alone, not one of the study areas reported on in this book, over 20 different organisations, not counting the private and voluntary sectors, were involved in the planning, running and delivering of day care. At a central government level this included the Department of Health and Social Security (DHSS), the Department of Education and Science (DES), and the Department of the Environment (DOE); at the local level the list included the Inner London Education Authority (ILEA), the Directorate of Social Services, the Directorate of Amenity Services, two Health Districts, the Directorate of Development, the Directorate of Finance and Management Services, the Greater London Council, the Council for Community Relations, the National Association of Local Government Officers (NALGO) and the National Union of Public Employees (NUPE). Furthermore some of these

Table 1 *Organisations involved in formulating policy and planning, running and delivering day care services for under-fives (examples of one Inner London borough)*

Organisation	Relevant responsibilities[a]
Central government[b]	
*Dept of Education and Science	All aspects of nursery education service.
*Dept of Health and Social Security	All aspects of personal social service responsibilities. Regional officers, specialist officers, administration and information services, building and cost advice (until recently – loan sanctions).
Dept of the Environment	Urban programme, inner city partnerships, local government rate support grant (RSG), planning and land matters.
Health Service	
Regional Health Authority	
Area Health Authority	
*Health Districts (2)	Health visitors, child health clinics, creches, district nurses, visiting medical officers.
*General Practitioners	
Community Health Councils	
Local government	
*Inner London Education Authority	All aspects of nursery education. *County Hall* – advice, professional support, policy, resources, administration. *Division* – local planning and administration etc.
Greater London Council	
*Directorate of Social Services	Day nurseries, playgroups and registration, registration of childminders, field social work, private and voluntary schemes, grants to organisations, training, personnel, etc.
*Directorate of Amenity Services	Libraries, books and toys, storytelling, one o'clock clubs, mother and toddler clubs, play space.
*Directorate of Development	Physical planning, design.
Directorate of Housing & Property Service	
Directorate of Construction Services	
*Directorate of Finance	Budgets, audit, etc.
*Directorate of Management Services	Establishment, organisation.
Corporate Planning Unit	
Other agencies	
*Council for Community Relations	Special projects.

58   *Policy coordination*

Table 1 (*cont.*)

Organisation	Relevant responsibilities[a]
*NALGO and NUPE	Trade union matters for professional and non-professional staff.
*Voluntary organisations	Enormous range: advisory and major service providers.
*Private organisations	Day nurseries, etc.
*Childminders	Between 400–500.
Additional bodies with interests in under fives provision[c]	
Inner City Partnership	ILEA/Social Services Local Standing Committee
-Partnership Committee	
-Officer Steering Group	Standing Committee for Coordination.
-Under-fives Sub-group	
	ILEA/LA Members standing Committee.
-Inner City Consultative Group	
-Sub-group on Under-fives	Coordinating Group on Under-fives.

Notes: * indicates those agencies most closely concerned with direct service provision
[a] Responsibilities outlined for agencies marked * only
[b] Omits Treasury and Employment etc.
[c] Large, complex committees with membership of officers and/or members and/or consumers.
From Challis, 1980.

organisations had different sections within them dealing with different aspects of the service; the Directorate of Social Services, for example, had staff in different sections dealing with playgroups, childminders, field social work, training, personnel matters and so on. More detail is given in table 1.

Alongside this organisational fragmentation has gone a shortage of places. Both in terms of demand for day care and in terms of officially stated guidelines for provision, the last 15 years have been marked by a substantial shortfall. In 1981 there were 2 779 000 children in England aged under five[22]. In 1982 the number of places in local authority day nurseries was 29 143; there were 98 000 places with childminders. There were also 15 362 playgroups[23]. Fewer than half a million children in England were attending nursery education on a full or a part-time, mostly part-time, basis[24]. It is difficult to estimate the coverage of services because some children may attend more than one type of provision, but several things are clear. Firstly it is clear that the number of children receiving full day care in local authority day nurseries fell below demand for such places and secondly, that children receiving nursery education (39% of population aged three and four years) fell below the Plowden estimates. These two factors, fragmentation and shortage, have rendered this policy area ripe for the application of a coordinated approach.

The Seebohm Report had stated that day care services for pre-school children should attract more resources and that there should be a national policy. The Report noted:

The lack of such a policy arises in part from the fragmentation of responsibility at both national and local level, but it also reflects society's ambivalent attitude towards working mothers[25].

There was some hint in this that organisational and professional rivalries might stand in the way of a rational approach but also apparent was the belief that if all parties were to behave sensibly and put the needs of the customers first, the problems would disappear:

All of us join in stressing how important it is that more nursery schools and classes should be provided and specially that the division of responsibility between local education departments and social service departments for somewhat similar services for young children should not be used by either as a pretext for evading responsibility[26].

The implementation of the Local Authority Social Services Act 1970 and the creation of social services departments in 1971 did not eliminate these divisions; indeed it is difficult to see how organisational reform on its own could have hoped to 'tidy up' the confused area of responsibility for provision. Policy on day care became largely a governance policy; suggestions as to ways in which the authorities could coordinate their activities so as to produce more provision with greater efficiency.

The Consultative Document stated that coordination at the local level was a high priority and a joint letter by the DHSS and DES to local authorities in 1976 urged the setting up of coordinating machinery. Such machinery it was argued would increase the effectiveness of services already provided and would:

create a situation in which the various departments and agencies (statutory and voluntary) concerned with under fives can exchange information, discuss common problems and improve coordination[27].

The letter included an annexe of examples of consultative arrangements, cooperation and liaison. The specific examples given were combined centres where education and social service provision was made under the same roof, joint training of education and social service staff, and joint appointments.

The Way Forward and a DHSS/DES report on combined nursery centres, both published in 1977, stressed the importance of collaboration[28]. Another

DHSS/DES letter in early 1978 continued the theme and gave examples of the benefits to be gained from having close working relationships between authorities. More extensive examples of good practice were included; once again the list had combined centres on it but, in addition, day nursery links and home visiting, playgroup advisors, fostering links between childminders and nursery schools and classes and peripatetic teachers were recommended. Whilst the letter stated that:

The Departments hope that these approaches and the examples of local practice ... will be of assistance to authorities generally in considering what further action they can take, within the limit of available resources, to achieve closer liaison between the various organisations concerned with the under fives, including volunteers and voluntary organisations active in this field,

the central departments were not willing to see joint committees with executive powers set up. Instead, ministers were to meet regularly to review progress on coordination at central government level[29].

In its paper, *A Joint Framework for Social Policies*, the CPRS had argued that one area of policy which should be examined was that of the employment of women and the care of children. The report of this examination was published in 1978 and contained the following recommendation to ministers:

At the local authority level there should be joint committees for children under 10, with equal representation from social service departments, from education departments, and advisors from the Area Health Authorities. These policy committees would cover the provision of advice, support, development and care, and the provision of pre and post statutory school age extended day services ... Centrally, there should be a joint unit (staffed by the DES and the DHSS) responsible for overseeing policies and expenditure for young children. The allocation of responsibility for this joint unit to the Minister of State from both DES and DHSS would help mark its importance. The policy of the unit would be to encourage local flexibility on the kind of response made but to ensure that basic standards were met and general guidelines followed[30].

Neither these proposals nor the CPRS proposal that a capital fund for development be established was accepted by the government.

The Conservative government continued to stress the importance of coordination and cooperation in this area and added greater emphasis to the role to be played by the private and voluntary sectors in making provision. It was clear that education and social service responsibilities were to be kept distinct, it was also clear that any government money directed towards the under-fives was to go to the non-statutory sectors. Day care was not a high priority for the government; *Care in Action* noted:

A prime objective of both statutory and voluntary services should be to encourage the development of self help and community activities involving children, and through these to help parents look after their children better. The development of play groups, family centres and home visiting schemes can all make a significant contribution[31].

The report of a study, sponsored by the DES and the DHSS, by Martin Bradley quoted many examples of coordination and joint initiatives[32]. The report had the express purpose of publishing instances of good practice, some of which were found in only a few localities, others were found in many places. By and large they followed the same patterns of good practice highlighted in other publications like the joint letters and reports by the ACC/AMA[33] and the TUC[34]. The list included the by now very familiar examples of the publication of comprehensive directories of service for the under-fives; home link projects; advisory home visiting; family centres; links between service providers; multi-disciplinary training; information exchange.

A survey of the use of joint finance money conducted by the National Association of Health Authorities found that the total number of schemes specifically designed for the under-fives was relatively few. Those that did exist fell into four main groups: services for mentally handicapped children; prevention of non-accidental injury; day care; and services for the physically handicapped pre-school child.

The Secretary of State, Norman Fowler, announced at the end of 1982 that £2 million would be made available from Health Service money for work with pre-school children. He stated:

The emphasis will be on helping voluntary bodies which work with the under fives and which support families with very young children[35].

Although extra resources on any substantial scale were not to be committed to this policy area the emphasis on coordination has continued. A conference organised by the DHSS and DES in October 1981 concentrated on local cooperation and the benefits which could accrue from this. A small change was introduced into the Education Act 1980 (Section 26) to allow LEAs to provide nursery teachers to day nurseries but apart from this no major revision of organisational responsibilities has been introduced. Policy has remained primarily one of governance; coordination and cooperation at the local level will bring better use of existing resources.

Elderly people

Policy for elderly people has remained the same for at least twenty years. The 1976 Consultative Document stated it quite succinctly:

The main objective of service for elderly people is to help them remain in the community for as long as possible.

The realisation of this policy objective has however been thwarted by two major factors.

The first of these is the demographic profile of Great Britain's population.

The numbers of elderly people have increased from 5 332 000 in 1951 to 7 985 000 in 1981[36]. As a proportion of the total population the elderly have risen from 10.9% to 15.0% in the same period and by the year 2001 are projected to account for 15.3% of the total population of Great Britain. Perhaps even more serious is the increase in the numbers of very old people, those people aged 75 and above; in 1981 there were 3 052 000 as compared with 1 731 000 in 1951 and further increases are expected before the turn of the century. It is this group, because the need for services seems to grow with increasing age, which is causing the greatest concern. There are simply more very old people in a severe condition who need help if the objective of keeping elderly people in the community is to be realised.

The second factor which has undermined the desire of policy makers to see community care become the dominant mode of care for the elderly is that it is a very difficult policy to implement. Study after study has shown that the elderly are a socially needy group and that their homes fall below the standards achieved by other age groups. The elderly are amongst the poorest groups in society in terms of income. Nearly three-quarters of elderly people are at or below the poverty line compared with one-fifth of the non-elderly[37]. Many elderly people living at home are disabled in some way. Hunt found that 26% of her sample were unable to bath themselves without difficulty or help and that 12.4% were unable to get out of the house unaided[38]. They live in conditions which can only be described as vulnerable with 29.7% living alone and 52.6% living with one other person, usually an elderly spouse. In general the housing of the elderly is in poor condition; 5% of all households with elderly people in them had access to an outside WC only, nearly half a million households did not have exclusive use of an inside WC and bath. Not only that but elderly people live in houses which are larger than average; in 1981 the numbers of people per room amongst the elderly living alone was 0.2, of the 1 094 000 elderly people living alone in owner occupied property nearly 60% had five or more rooms[39]. A policy which seeks to maintain the elderly in the community has somehow to deal with the fact that sizeable numbers of elderly people have little money at their disposal, are in a poor state of health and living alone in substandard accommodation or with someone else who is old[40].

But the enormity of the difficulties which arise from these conditions are exacerbated by the complexity of the organisation of services intended to implement policy. A 'map' of these services, given in table 2, helps to convey the magnitude of the task and it should be borne in mind that different services offered by the same organisation nevertheless have separate admission criteria and procedures. The picture is in reality even more complicated than a simple chart can indicate.

Table 2 *Outline of main organisations involved in formulating policy, planning and delivering services for elderly people*

Organisation	Relevant responsibilities
Central government	
Dept. of Health and Social Security	*Personal Social Services*
	All aspects of personal social services. Regional officers, specialist officers, administration and information services, building and cost advice. Policy advice.
	Social Security
	Pensions, Supplementary Benefit, Extra Needs Payments (ENPs), Heating, etc.
	Health
	All aspects of health services. Policy guidance for Regions, Areas and Districts. Information and cost advice.
Dept. of the Environment	Housing and sheltered housing. Housing investment plans (HIPs). Local government and finance. Land use.
Health service	
Regional Health Authority	Community nursing (district nurses,
Area Health Authority	health visitors and psychiatric nurses),
Health Districts	day hospitals, psychogeriatric units, acute care, orthopaedics, aids (wheelchairs, hoists etc.), voluntary service organisers, ambulances, hypothermia equipment, registration and inspection of private nursing homes.
General Practitioners	
Community Health Councils	
Local government	
Social Services Department	Home helps, meals on wheels, social workers, luncheon clubs, day centres, aids and adaptations, transport, Part III, elderly mentally infirm units, fostering, laundry service, night attendants, bath attendants, volunteer organisation, hypothermia prevention, registration and inspection of private and voluntary residential care homes.
Recreation and libraries	Recreation centres, social clubs, domiciliary library, large print books, tapes.

Table 2 (*cont.*)

Organisation	Relevant responsibilities
Housing	Rent and rate rebates and allowances, sheltered housing, wardens, alarm systems, improvement grants.
Planning	Physical planning and design.
Finance	Budgets, audit etc.
Personnel	Establishment, organisation, staffing.
Other sectors	
Voluntary	Volunteer bureaux, good neighbour schemes, meals on wheels, supporting the carers groups, residential homes, hospices, information centres.
Private	Residential care, nursing, domestic services.

For example, the Department of the Environment has key responsibilities for local government finance which of course affects the amount which can be funded at the local level. It also has responsibility for housing and more specifically for sheltered housing and alarm systems etc. The Housing Corporation also has a role in its relationship with housing associations which have a key part in the provision of sheltered housing. The DHSS has many interests in care of the elderly and those interests fall within different parts of its internal organisation. Pensions and supplementary benefits are separate, so too is hospital provision and Part III, local authority residential provision, so too are community nurses and home helps, and so on.

Central government's response to the challenge of community care policies has, not surprisingly, laid heavy emphasis on coordination and collaboration. The 1976 Consultative Document made this quite clear:

it should be emphasised that for the elderly coordinated planning is required across administrative boundaries. Joint Consultative Committees and Joint Care Planning Teams should be fully used to coordinate planning between the health and personal social services, but coordination of the latter with other local authority services is equally important. As stated, housing is of special importance to the elderly and every effort should be made to increase the amount of sheltered housing[41].

This view was reaffirmed in *The Way Forward* in 1977.

The Labour government issued a Consultative Document on policy for elderly people, *A Happier Old Age*, in 1978[42]. The document raised an impressive list of questions about care for the elderly ranging from preparation for retirement to psychiatric provision, and invited people to give their views on these topics so that a White Paper could be prepared. A substantial part of the chapter of this document dealt with the issue of coordination and collaboration. As the authors put it:

the promotion of a satisfactory quality of life for elderly people, and adequate provision for their care involves many different organisations and individuals. But the effectiveness of all the various efforts depends a great deal on the extent to which people work together and play their part in changing attitudes where these bar progress. It is also important that we get the right balance between various forms of provision[43].

The importance of formal structures, committees etc. and of good inter-personal relationships was recognised and so too were some of the barriers to good cooperation. The different boundaries of health, social service and housing authorities were seen as an example of the structural obstacles and different professional attitudes as an example of factors which might inhibit good working relationships between individuals. The document also noted that the local authorities might not be fully aware of the part that voluntary organisations could play in care of the elderly and summed up the question which it would like answered as:

How can collaboration between all the various organisations and individuals involved in providing help for elderly people be improved in order to make the best use of all available resources and increase the effectiveness of the contribution of each agency or individual?

The White Paper, *Growing Older*, was eventually published in 1981[44] by the Conservative government and had, not surprisingly, a similar flavour to *Care in Action*. The constraints on public expenditure were emphasised and so too was the role of the informal, voluntary and private sectors. Once again the paper was littered with references to 'partnerships', 'collaboration' and 'mutual support' and it was clear that, whatever might be meant by these terms, the government expected it to be happening at the inter-personal and inter-agency levels. What was also clear was that the government expected greater effectiveness and efficiency to flow from such endeavours.

Unlike central government's advice to local authorities on coordination of services for children under five which gave considerable detail on the mechanics of coordination, guidance on the machinery for service planning and delivery to the elderly concentrated on the importance of using joint planning and finance provision which was already in place.

Joint planning and finance are the natural successors of the philosophy expounded in the Ten Year Planning initiative and before that, in the Seebohm Report. The hopes of its architects were apparent in the Consultative Circular in 1976 and in the subsequent circular issued in May 1977[45].

Services provided by local authorities (LAs) (specially those which are the responsibility of their social services committees) have a considerable impact on health services, and vice versa. This interdependence makes it essential to have effective arrangements for joint planning to secure the best balance of services and to make the most effective use of the resources available for the elderly, the disabled, the mentally handicapped, the mentally ill, children and families, and for socially handicapped groups such as alcoholics and drug addicts. Effective joint planning is vital to the government's overall strategy of developing community based services so that wherever possible people are kept out of hospitals and other institutions and supported within the community. The Secretary of State's aim is to encourage joint planning by health and local authorities in which each authority contributes to all stages of the other's planning, from the first steps in developing common policies and strategies to the production of operational plans to carry them out. Only by full collaborative planning in partnership can health and local authorities devise and implement effective complementary patterns of services.

The machinery for collaboration was based upon the recommendation made by the Working Party on Collaboration between the NHS and local government. There is a statutory obligation on health authorities and the relevant local authorities to set up Joint Consultative Committees (JCCs) composed of members of the two sets of authorities. The responsibilities of the JCCs were set out in the 1977 Circular:

When agreement has been reached between authorities on the key areas for joint planning, JCCs should prepare, for endorsement by their constituent authorities, advice on the broad strategy for future development of the relevant services, taking account of national policies, the existing pattern of local development and the level of resources expected to be available to the AHA and LA.

The authorities were also to set up a Joint Care Planning Team (JCPT) of officers to advise them. Links between health and social services were to be forged and maintained by, among others, a specialist in community medicine and some LSSAs appointed health coordinators to act as a channel for communication between the two services.

Joint finance was first referred to by Mrs Castle in November 1975 in a speech at the Local Authority Association's Social Services Conference. The amount of money allocated each year was to increase and was intended to pay for the fruits of joint planning. The different systems of funding the NHS (central exchequer from taxation) and the personal social services (rates and central government grant) were seen as a barrier to effective collaboration: it was not easy to move money around and consequently not easy to move people around in fulfilment of a policy of reducing institutional/ hospital care. The Health Services Act of 1980 gave health authorities powers to give funds to local authorities for personal social service functions.

As with joint planning, so with joint finance; details of the scheme were given in considerable detail. The types of projects to be funded were specified:

the health authority accepts that the recommended spending justifies the use of NHS resources in the terms prescribed and can be expected to make a better contribution in terms of total care than would deployment of equivalent resources directly on health services[46].

And so too was the balance between capital and revenue projects, the tapering arrangements and even the procedures for processing recommendations for the use of joint finance:

Proposals may be initiated by either authority. Recommendations for joint financing should be submitted by the JCPT to the JCC and simultaneously to both authorities. Proposals should relate to services which stand referred to local authorities' social services committees only, save that in non-metropolitan counties, joint finance support can be given, if agreed with the County Council through the joint consultative machinery, to spending by a district council under section 31 of the National Assistance Act 1948 as amended by the National Assistance Act 1948 (Amendment) Act 1962 (i.e. provision of meals and recreation for old people in their homes or elsewhere). Some under the exceptional arrangements mentioned in paragraph 11 below or as an interim measure as described in paragraph 10, joint finance is to be used in support of LA spending, and not, for example, as a contribution to the AHA's share of joint NHS/LA activities[47].

Evidence from the National Association of Health Authorities (NAHA) index of joint finance schemes confirms that it has been used to develop projects for elderly people as well as for other client groups. In addition, the joint care awards sponsored by the *Health and Social Services Journal* gave some idea of the range of innovation occurring across service boundaries. Examples included links between sheltered housing, social service old people's homes (Part III) and the health services; nursing care in Part III; joint care assessment panels; intensive domiciliary support for frail elderly people; very sheltered housing; hospital discharge schemes; home visiting and community care centres.

Although evidence from various sources has suggested that the joint planning machine has not been a great success in planning for elderly people[48] there does not seem to have been a shortage of good ideas about developments in care. The health and social service press has been full of such ideas. There have been articles about good neighbour schemes, the Kent community care project, Part III homes as community service resource centres[49], psychogeriatric assessment panels[50], advice on rehousing/rehabilitation projects[51], fostering, nursing homes[52] and many more. Nearly all of these have laid great stress on collaboration and coordination.

It has taken longer for the realisation to dawn that the non-statutory sectors of care are very important in care of elderly people. All the policy handbooks have mentioned the role of the voluntary sector but not until *Care in Action* in 1981 was recognition afforded to the private sector and greater emphasis put on the informal sector. The orthodoxy of community care has been challenged by an increasing body of writers as being a way of putting more stress and strain on female carers. The Equal Opportunities Commission[53] and the Policy Studies Institute[54] have both published reports which contain this as a central theme. Similarly the importance of the private sector has been given some credence as shown by the report *At Home in a Boarding House*[55] and the Consultative Document *A Good Home*[56]. A systems-wide perspective would clearly have to be developing some means for collaboration with both the private and informal sectors as well as with the voluntary sector and with other statutory bodies.

This then was the background against which the study sought to explore the realities of coordination. This exploration was carried out in a variety of ways. First, coordinative machinery was identified and its outputs established. Secondly, schemes which had been identified in the literature as examples of coordinative activity were logged and their origins examined to see if they arose from coordination or by some other process. This approach was adopted at both central and local levels.

REFERENCES

1 DHSS (1971) *Better Services for the Mentally Handicapped*, Cmnd 4683, London: HMSO
2 DHSS (1975) *Better Services for the Mentally Ill*, Cmnd 6233, London: HMSO
3 DHSS (1976) *Priorities for the Health and Personal Social Services: A Consultative Document*, London: HMSO
4 DHSS (1981) *Care in Action: Handbook of Policies and Priorities for the Health and Personal Social Services in England*, London: HMSO
5 DHSS (1972) *Local Authority Social Services Ten Year Development Plans 1973–1983*, Circular 35/72, 31 August
6 *Ibid.*, para. 5
7 *Ibid.*, para. 18
8 T. A. Booth (1979) 'Forward planning of local authority services', chapter in Booth, T. A. *Planning for Welfare*, Oxford: Blackwell and Robertson
9 DOE (1977) *Policy for the Inner Cities*, Cmnd 6845, London: HMSO
10 *Municipal Journal*, 13 October 1972, p. 1365
11 DHSS (1972) *op. cit.*, para. 10
12 *Municipal Journal*, 29 December 1972, p. 1810
13 A. Webb and N. Falk (1974) 'Planning and social services', *Policy and Politics*, vol. 3, no. 2, pp. 33–54
14 DHSS (1976) *op. cit.*
15 *Ibid.*, Annexe 2, para. 2
16 DHSS (1977) *Priorities for the Health and Personal Social Services: The Way Forward*, London: HMSO, para. 3.13
17 DHSS (1981) *op. cit.*
18 *Ibid.*, para. 3.19
19 *Ibid.*, para. 4.15

20 *Ibid.*, para. 6.5
21 L. Challis (1980) *The Great Under Fives Muddle: Options for Day Care Policy*, University of Bath
22 OPCS (1983) *Census 1981: National Report: Great Britain Part I*, CEN 81 NR (1), London: HMSO
23 DHSS (1983) *Children's Day Care Facilities, 31/3/82, England*, AF 826, London: DHSS
24 DES (1983) *Statistical Bulletin*, London: DES
25 Cmnd 3703 (1968) *Committee on Local Authority and Allied Personal Social Services* (Seebohm Report), London: HMSO
26 *Ibid.*, p. 61.
27 DHSS/DES (1976) *Coordination of Local Authority Services for Children Under Five*, DHSS/DES Letter LASSL (76) 5
28 DHSS/DES (1977) *Combined Nursery Centres*, Report by HM Inspectors of Schools and by the Social Work Service, Medical and Nursing Officers of the DHSS, London: DHSS.
29 DHSS/DES (1978) *Coordination of Services for Children Under Five*, DHSS/DES LASSL (78) 1
30 CPRS (Central Policy Review Staff) (1978) *Services for Young Children with Working Mothers*, London: HMSO
31 DHSS (1981) *op. cit.*, para. 5.2
32 M. Bradley (1981) *Coordination of Services for Children Under Five: Final Report*, Liverpool: St Katherine's College, Liverpool Institute of Higher Education
33 ACC/AMA (1977) *The Under Fives*, London: Association of County Councils and the Association of Metropolitan Authorities
34 TUC (1978) *The Under Fives*, Report of a TUC Working Party, London
35 *Hansard*, November 1982
36 OPCS (1983) *op. cit.*
37 C. Rossiter and M. Wicks (1982) *Crisis or Challenge: family care, elderly people and social policy*, Study Commission on the Family
38 A. Hunt (1978) *The Elderly at Home*, OPCS, London: HMSO
39 OPCS (1983) *Persons of Pensionable Age*, CEN 81 PEN, London: HMSO
40 L. Challis (1984) 'A profile of the elderly: some implications for policy', *Political Quarterly*, January
41 DHSS (1976) *op. cit.*, para. 5.14
42 DHSS (1978) *A Happier Old Age: A Consultative Document*, London: DHSS
43 *Ibid.*, para. 8.1
44 DHSS (1981b) *Growing Older*, London: HMSO
45 DHSS (1977) *Joint Care Planning: Health and Local Authorities*, DHSS HC (77) 17, LAC (77) 10, London, May
46 *Ibid.*, para. 6(a)
47 *Ibid.*, para. 4
48 H. Glennerster with N. Korman and F. Marslen-Wilson (1983) *Planning for Priority Groups*, Oxford: Martin Robertson & Co.
49 D. Wilkin, B. Hughes and D. Jolley (1982) 'Better care for the elderly', *Community Care*, 6 May
50 B. Warwick (1982) *Health and Social Service Journal*, 19 August
51 A. Larkin (1982) *Roof*, July/August 1982
52 P. Roe (1982) *Health and Social Service Journal*, 7 October
53 EOC (1982) *Caring for the Elderly and Handicapped: Community Care Policies and Women's Lives*, Manchester: Equal Opportunities Commission

54 M. Nissel and L. Bonnerjea (1982) *Family Care for the Handicapped Elderly: Who Pays?*, London: Policy Studies Institute
55 *At Home in a Boarding House* (1981) Report of an Independent Working Group. National Institute for Social Work
56 DHSS (1982) *A Good Home*

4 ~ Whatever happened to JASP?

The attempts made within central government between 1971 and 1978 to improve the coordination of social policies can legitimately be regarded as probably the most sustained single attempt to apply the 'optimistic' model. In fact, the attempt comprised several different episodes, with an almost cyclical fluctuation in the balance between the 'optimistic' and what might be called the 'pragmatic' elements in the approach – culminating in an acceptance so total of the 'pessimistic' approach that the role of the centre diminished to complete inaction.

Although the notion of a centrally-steered 'joint approach' is inseparable from the existence and purposes of the CPRS, JASP had two immediate predecessors. The first disappeared without progeny; the second could be regarded, if not as a parent, at least as a godparent of JASP.

The first sustained attempts at coordination in the 'social' or welfare field began in 1967 when Michael Stewart took over from Douglas Houghton both the chairmanship of the Cabinet's Social Services Committee and an extremely ill-defined task as social services coordinator. He acquired as an official 'adviser' a civil servant from the Ministry of Education, Paul Odgers. Stewart and Odgers, working through the Social Services Committee (and its supporting committee of civil servants), started to explore the problems and possibilities. They took their brief to cover social security, health, probation, rent rebates and sheltered housing, and aspects of education such as school meals. With support from the Prime Minister, the Treasury and the Cabinet Office, they started to develop the notion of a 'social services budget'; the distribution of this among the several social services would be determined by the Social Services Committee chaired by the coordinating minister. At the level of principle some progress was made, but as one participant later observed, 'when it came to really large issues Ministers and their departments fought their corner like tigers', and the conflicts had to be resolved in Cabinet.[1]

In April 1968 Stewart was replaced by Richard Crossman, who, it was agreed but not announced, was due to take over in the autumn as Secretary of State at the newly merged Department of Health and Social Security. Odgers began to expand his small staff; it grew to a total of 20, seconded for about two years from the main welfare departments and grouped into three divisions for social security, health and welfare, and research. (The basic task of this last was to develop some kind of relationship between the research activities of the several departments concerned with 'social' problems. For example, there was no central record of relevant research commissioned by Whitehall.) The staff was based in the Cabinet Office (and stayed there even when Crossman moved to the DHSS headquarters at the Elephant & Castle).

Crossman had in fact been urged by the Cabinet Secretary, Sir Burke Trend, to stay at the centre rather than moving either to the Ministry of Health or to the Ministry of Social Security. ('You can only coordinate from the central point of power where people come to be coordinated, the Cabinet Office ... Why not keep the title of Lord President and your coordinating staff under Paul Odgers? ... You're doing an even more important job [than that of a departmental minister] when you're getting the basis of block budgeting for the social services worked out.')[2]

In November the departments were formally merged and Crossman himself moved his office to the headquarters of the new DHSS south of the river.

The unit continued to work for Crossman in his coordinating capacity, which in principle was distinct from his role of Secretary of State at DHSS. The unit tackled major topics such as pensions policy, the reorganisation of local government, the health service and the personal social services, and the Community Development Programme. At a level of finer detail it briefed Crossman for his role as chairman; it chaired and serviced interdepartmental committees on topics such as poverty, social service training and advisory machinery, and the youth service.

The unit continued in being after the arrival of the Conservative government in June 1970. The new Secretary of State, Sir Keith Joseph, acquired the children's services previously at the Home Office. This move marked the end of a long and bitter struggle within Whitehall; it would, in the words of the October 1970 White Paper on the reorganisation of central government, enable 'the effective development of a new, broadly-based service to deal with family needs in accordance with the objectives of the Seebohm Committee'. It was consistent with the philosophy, set out in the same document, of grouping 'functions together in departments with a wide span, so as to provide a series of fields of unified policy'.[3]

However, while gaining the children's services Joseph had lost Crossman's broader coordinating role. The Social Services Committee was abolished. The unit went on working but it now had no client and no forum. It rapidly lost impetus. The possibilities were discussed of merging the unit with the new Central Policy Review Staff, but the functions of the CPRS were felt to be too different. In August 1971 Odgers returned to his department and shortly afterwards the unit was wound up. Only the division concerned with research survived in the Cabinet Office until 1977 its files and one remaining member were transferred to the DES.

It was all too typical of Whitehall that the experience of the coordinating staff died with it. Odgers himself never returned to work in this area and neither he nor his staff were encouraged to pause and reflect on what might be learned from the experiment. The page was turned and when the CPRS, as described below, launched itself into exactly the same turbulent waters it started with a completely blank map. The CPRS was to venture into some of the very same rapids, to miss some of the channels discovered by the coordinating unit, and to bump painfully into some of the identical rocks.

The next attempt to develop joint approaches followed the logic of Crossman's move from the Cabinet Office, and was led not from the centre but from the periphery – from the Department of Health and Social Security which Crossman had headed until the general election of 1970. Behind its reassuring title, the DHSS had continued to operate as two separate departments linked only at the very top. Its permanent secretary from 1970 to 1975 was Sir Philip Rogers, whose most recent previous posts had been in the Civil Service Department, Treasury and Cabinet Office. To Rogers, with this experience at the centre of Whitehall, it was all too clear that if the rhetoric of the White Paper was to be made a reality something had to be done both to improve working relationships between the separate parts of his own department, and to reduce the frequent divergence of objectives not only between DHSS and other departments, but also between Whitehall and local authorities. Rogers tried to develop a leading role for DHSS in coordinating the policies of several 'social' departments in tackling shared problems – for example, those of particular groups such as children under five. The first two other departments involved were the Department of Education and Science (DES) and the Department of the Environment (DOE); later, other departments such as, inevitably, the Treasury as well as Employment, Home Office, Welsh and Scottish Offices were drawn in.

These attempts continued through 1971 and 1972, steered by a committee of permanent secretaries chaired by Rogers himself. The concern of the DHSS was to develop a very broad consensus on the need for 'joint planning', and within this to identify particular policy areas in which this approach might be useful. The department mainly concerned – often, inevitably, the DHSS – was to take the lead in each case.

Other departments were willing broadly to support the principle – the main exception being the Department of Education and Science, reluctant to concede that the objectives of educational policy could be defined widely enough to overlap with those of 'social' or 'welfare' policies. But most departments were wary lest this DHSS-led initiative should infringe their own autonomy or threaten their own budgets, and there was much suspicion of DHSS 'empire building', linked with sceptical comments about the inflexible application of theory to the untidy variety of the 'real world'. By the middle of 1972, it was becoming clear to Rogers that his initiative was generating for DHSS not only a great deal of work but also – as one cause of this – a growing amount of friction with other departments. Rogers tried to interest Sir Burke Trend, the Secretary to the Cabinet, in the possibility that the Cabinet Secretariat should take over the management of the project from the DHSS. Trend's view of the job of the Secretariat did not include this kind of policy making function, and he was not very responsive. It was at this point that the CPRS came on to the scene.

To explain the interest and the role of the CPRS it is helpful to look back at the main purposes for which it had been set up. These in turn need explanation in terms of the ways in which government policies are normally made.

Collective nouns such as 'Whitehall' or 'the government' are obviously necessary and desirable shorthand terms for referring to complex organisations made up of many individuals and sub-units. The term 'government policy' can be helpful, too, in indicating a broad set of attitudes (or, negatively, their absence: 'the government seems to have no policy on this'). But all these terms are distinctly unhelpful in their implications that the civil service, or ministers collectively in their departments, both think like a single person and have a single will fixed on agreed ends. 'Policy' or, still more, 'strategy' are just as misleading if they are taken to imply that explicit decisions have been taken about the different priority to be given to particular objectives, that the means subsequently chosen will reflect those priorities, and that those means will always be compatible with each other.

In other words, coordination is imperfect. There are many reasons for this. But the most important are, first, that government is fragmented; its resources and ambitions are divided, in particular, among a dozen major departments, each with its own minister, clienteles, policies and objectives. As the CPRS put it, in a report mentioned later in this chapter, 'The concept "central government" is ... an abstraction which conceals reality'.[4] A minister's reputation is enhanced by actions which take effect in the specific policy area for which he is responsible – opening a new hospital one week, calling for cuts in NHS administrative staff the next – and his officials make their reputation by effectively advancing their minister's and their department's objectives. Secondly, at the strategic level most coordination consists not of a unilateral planning process but of a series of bilateral bargains and adjustments struck at the margin between the competing policies of two or more spending departments and/or the Treasury.

This last point applies just as much to the budgetary (or public expenditure control) process as to any other. The annual (often more frequent) process of reconciling departmental spending plans with the Treasury's overall proposals for total public expenditure may appear to be a genuinely collective business, and one in which the Treasury as the arbiter between competing departmental programmes allocates more resources to (or takes fewer resources away from) those of higher priority in the government's overall strategy. In practice, however, although some broad sense of priorities obviously does influence the decisions taken, the main determinant is often the relative political weight and forensic skill of the individual ministers struggling to defend their departmental budgets against the Chancellor.

Finally, the Cabinet is often presented as the embodiment of genuinely collective policy making. Here all the leading ministers, including the Chancellor of the Exchequer, meet to make decisions – and, in theory, to set these in the fullest possible context of objectives, resources and other constraints. In practice, however, the Cabinet, like other bodies of its kind, inevitably tends to deal piecemeal with issues as they arise, week by week. The terms of debate about any specific issue will be largely established by the protagonists, i.e. the two or three ministers principally involved; pressures of time and of mental stamina, plus the convention that 'dog don't eat dog', will greatly limit the willingness of their colleagues to broaden the discussion by trying to put the issue in context. Moreover, the Cabinet does not act as a true coordinating body in the sense either of planning policy – it reacts to events – or of overseeing its implementation; this is left to departments to work out among themselves, striking such bargains and making such compromises as are needed for the continued support of the several departments that may be concerned.

These issues are discussed in more detail in the following chapter. They constitute a large part of the background against which the CPRS was created in 1971, and against which in turn the CPRS was to embark upon the task of trying to improve the coordination of government-wide policies in the 'social' (or welfare) field.

The main purposes for which the CPRS had originally been created might be summarised as being to apply analysis (and, implicitly, 'reason') to the process of working out a government's priorities, to try to ensure that individual decisions reflected those priorities, to offset the fragmentation of governmental policy among different departments and agencies, and to ensure a more deliberate relationship between different decisions – probably taken at different times – about different policies. The so-called 'Joint

Approach to Social Policies', or JASP, grew directly out of these purposes. The aim of JASP was to apply the general principles just mentioned in the field of 'social', or welfare, policies – which, it might be assumed, had in common at least the objective of modifying the effects of inequitable distribution of resources and opportunities in the community.

The JASP episode lasted about six years. It fell into three distinct parts: the first comprised the initial 'selling' to ministers of the general principle that resource constraints now made it necessary to give more thought to questions of priorities in the social field; the second phase perhaps came closest to an attempt to apply the ideal model of rational and coordinated policy making to the untidy processes prevalent within Whitehall; it saw an ambitious, schematic and completely unsuccessful attempt to devise a comprehensive system for doing this; thirdly, a much more modest attempt, based on an implicit acceptance of at least some elements of the 'pessimistic' model, to encourage 'joint' thinking and action in a limited number of specific contexts. In the middle of this last phase, the CPRS, against its own better judgement, found itself once again involved in a second unsuccessful attempt to produce a comprehensive plan.

The germ of the JASP idea was on the agenda of the CPRS from its earliest days. Very soon after the CPRS had formally begun work, in the early spring of 1971, and before all its staff were in place, it organised a 'trawl' around Whitehall soliciting suggestions for items for its future work programme. One topic suggested was 'interdepartmental aspects of social policy'. The suggestion was recorded and filed and became part of the CPRS's steadily evolving ideas bank.

Meanwhile the CPRS was steadily developing a broad line of analysis which was to be one of the central themes in its activities for the next ten years. It concerned the relationship between patterns of resource distribution and the priorities of the government. A long series of CPRS papers and presentations were to confront successive generations of ministers with pictures of the ways in which resources were currently, and might on current trends be in the future, distributed among different programmes and – at least implicitly – allocated to identifiable objectives: and then to enquire of ministers whether the ordering of programmes and objectives was in fact that which they were willing to approve. For one of the first of these presentations, in the summer of 1972, the CPRS produced an enormous chart showing the national distribution of all productive resources between activities of every kind (industry, defence, public administration). It also produced a separate paper on 'social affairs'. This analysed and discussed the distribution of resources between social programmes and tentatively argued the need for greater coordination within central government and between it and other agencies.

A little later, the CPRS suggested that a ministerial 'strategy group' for social affairs should be set up to discuss these larger questions of priorities. It was to be briefed by the CPRS. This proposal was not resisted by the DHSS or by other departments. The Cabinet Secretary, Sir Burke Trend, was acquiescent if not particularly enthusiastic.

The ministerial group met for the first time early in 1973. With the help of the management consultants McKinseys, the CPRS submitted to the group not a conventional civil service memorandum, but an oral presentation supported with slides. (In a further departure from custom, the meeting was held not during normal daytime hours in an official committee room, but over and after dinner in the Whitehall flat of one of the ministers concerned.)

The aim of the CPRS presentation was to persuade ministers that total public spending on social programmes could not continue to increase at current rates – or, in other words, that the resources available for social programmes would inevitably be quite inadequate to meet all future demands. Some difficult choices would therefore have to be made. These would need to derive from some set of priorities agreed by ministers collectively. Agreement on priorities would require a new and more analytical (as opposed to adversarial) approach to policy making. The CPRS proposed that it should develop such an analytical approach.

Faced with these very general propositions (which as presented did not explicitly challenge the priorities of any individual minister present), and perhaps relaxed by the informal circumstances, the ministerial group agreed that the CPRS should do some further work on the subject.

This was the starting-point of what might be called 'JASP Mark I' – an application of the 'ideal model' of collaboration in an extreme form. Great reliance was placed on the ability of analysts, or planners, to develop a reliable synoptic view of the whole field of social policy, of the relative severity of the various problems perceived there and of the relative quantities of resources currently devoted to each problem. Moreover, it was also assumed that policy makers, i.e. ministers, once faced with this battery of facts would be able to read off the appropriate decisions and would be prepared to act accordingly.

During the next year the CPRS (still assisted by McKinseys who seconded a consultant to work virtually full-time with the CPRS) worked on the production of what was intended to be a comprehensive analytical framework for developing and imposing coherent priorities in the 'social' field. The aim was to ensure that patterns of resource allocation corresponded more closely to ministers' priorities, which should in turn reflect a better understanding of where the most urgent problems lay. This understanding was to come largely from an analysis by the CPRS of the needs of different client groups and of the impact of government programmes on each of these.

During this period the Home Secretary, Robert Carr, was given the task of leading a coordinated interdepartmental work programme directed at urban problems. There was an echo here of the Houghton/Stewart/Crossman post of coordinating minister, with the major difference that Carr was given no special non-departmental staff to help him in his task. The CPRS, which was invited to join a small group to oversee this programme, took the chance to 'adopt' the Home Secretary as honorary sponsor of its own programme. (How this arrangement would have worked it is hard to say; the Home Secretary had not been able to play much part in developing urban policies, let alone take a close interest in the activities of the CPRS, before the economic and political crisis of the winter of 1973/74 and the fall of the Conservative government in February 1974.)

In the autumn of 1973, 'JASP Mark I' reached its climax. The results of the CPRS work were circulated as a paper to ministers. Though it appeared over the signature of the Home Secretary in his capacity as 'coordinator', it was, in fact, largely drafted by the head of the CPRS, Lord Rothschild. The paper proposed that the CPRS should help ministers think comprehensively about priorities by analysing needs and programmes in terms of 'client groups', and by setting up a continuous monitoring process to be known as the 'Social Audit'. These two approaches together would help ministers to identify which programmes were under- or over-resourced in relation to ministerial priorities, and so to decide where to increase or to cut expenditure. The whole proposal was couched in the assertive, 'scientific' prose, admitting of little uncertainty or possibility of compromise, which was characteristic of Lord Rothschild.

It was probably the style of the paper, as much as its extremely ambitious content, which made its proposals unacceptable. Ministers, presumably briefed by their departments, declined to endorse these in any way. The CPRS was instructed to go away and talk to departmental officials, and to come back with something much more modest. These talks revealed widespread scepticism within Whitehall about the value of the approach, combined with the fear that it would lead to a great deal of additional work for departments. DHSS officials, in particular, resented the swamping or possible frustration of their own earlier more modest activities in this 'comprehensive' exercise, as well as what they saw as a CPRS attempt to take over some of their responsibilities by insisting that these be discussed collectively. The CPRS, faced with the prospect that the whole initiative would founder, went back to the drawing board.

This was the start of 'JASP Mark II', an enterprise far more successful, at least in the short term. The approach reflected elements both of the 'optimistic' and of the 'pessimistic' models. Optimistic was the continuing firm assumption by the CPRS that a 'joint approach' was necessary and practicable, and that ministers in particular would see the case for this. Pessimistic was the recognition that departments, now highly suspicious of the CPRS's attempts to collectivise decision making in 'their' policy areas, would not accept the case for a joint approach across the board; the approach would have to be developed 'with the grain', in specific contexts where departments saw some benefit to themselves. Pessimistic, too, was the assumption that laggards would need to be chivvied by external forces, notably ministers themselves and public opinion. The whole style was to be far more incremental and consensual, and much less grandiose in its absence of pretension to a comprehensive approach to problems and policies. The CPRS team determined to pick a series of specific issues to which a joint approach seemed likely to be relevant, to study them in some detail and to draw up proposals for action in each case.

JASP Mark II was also much more political in the CPRS's acceptance of the need for allies and for stratagems. Thus, in particular, from now on the CPRS sought to work very closely with the Cabinet Secretariat under its new head, Sir John Hunt. Hunt was as sceptical as any other permanent secretary about the value or practicability of the comprehensive approach of JASP Mark I. But he was conscious of what he later called 'the hole at the centre' of government, which 'in the absence of a Chief Executive with his own staff . . . an over-worked Cabinet seemed incapable of filling'.[5] Hunt was sensitive to Prime Ministerial demands on the Cabinet Secretariat for advice on the substance of policy (as opposed to its traditional products of neutral briefs and minutes of meetings), and was eager for the Secretariat to be capable of providing this. He saw the CPRS, in JASP as in other contexts, as a valuable resource for this purpose. His own previous experience as the senior Treasury official responsible for managing the public expenditure process had left him dissatisfied with its mechanistic bilateral nature. He was also a friend, as well as a colleague, of Sir Philip Rogers and approved of his efforts to encourage interdepartmental working. All this led Hunt to welcome the CPRS's attempt to develop 'strategic' thinking in the social welfare field. He agreed to convene and to chair a new committee of permanent secretaries, to oversee developments and encourage progress in JASP, and to underpin the group of ministers already set up by the CPRS. (This was, in effect, the successor to the Rogers group, but without the stigma, in the eyes of other departments, of being chaired by one of themselves.) This deliberate alliance with the Cabinet Secretary, normally the most influential single official in Whitehall, could again be said to reflect the 'pessimistic' model. Hunt's support was invaluable and probably essential.

The nature and pace of the programme was not greatly affected by the general election of February 1974 and the replacement of the Conservatives by a Labour government under Harold Wilson. The CPRS as a whole found itself temporarily in the doldrums; the new administration had no experience of the CPRS and regarded it initially as a Conservative inheritance which might have to be abolished. It therefore had little work to do. CPRS members working on JASP were thus fortunate in having a continuous activity. Probably the most important aspect of the change of administration was the arrival at the DHSS of Mrs Barbara Castle, an implacable promoter of her departmental interests with a strong commitment to truly 'socialist' policies in the welfare as in other fields. An almost equally important arrival at the DHSS with Mrs Castle was her distinguished policy adviser, Professor Brian Abel Smith of the London School of Economics. Neither a career bureaucrat nor a politician, but a genuine expert with his own well-developed views about what should – and could – be done, he was an ideal intermediary for the CPRS team in its attempts to develop policies which would take account of political and bureaucratic realities yet which would not be unduly constrained by either.

A similar change connected with the arrival of the Labour government was the creation in 10 Downing Street of a new 'Prime Minister's Policy Unit' under Dr Bernard Donoughue. One member of the unit was David Piachaud, seconded from the London School of Economics, a leading academic expert on social security. He, too, was a valuable link between the JASP team and the politicians.

Another change of some importance for JASP was the departure of Lord Rothschild in the middle of 1974 and his replacement by Sir Kenneth Berrill, formerly head of the Government Economic Service at the Treasury. Berrill had no close personal interest in or knowledge of the social welfare field. More important, he obviously did not share Rothschild's commitment to the ambitious yet simplistic approach which had been so badly received in Whitehall the previous year. The JASP team were thus left free to develop their programme in the way that they thought best. The ministerial group set up by the Conservatives had been dissolved and not replaced, and there was thus no political pressure from above for results.

This way included a great deal of outside consultation. One of the best features of the Rothschild regime had been the free and, by conventional Whitehall standards, indiscreet use made by the CPRS of outside experts of all kinds. Following this tradition the JASP team virtually co-opted Professor David Donnison, then director of the Centre for Environmental Studies. It also tried to develop a link with the Centre for Studies in Social Policy, a small research institute newly set up and founded by Rowntree. But the attempt to plug the CSSP into JASP as a permanent consultant on a retainer basis failed largely owing to the Centre's lack of any spare capacity which could be used in this role.

Throughout the lifetime of JASP, the task for the CPRS was to preserve the legitimacy of a programme of activities which involved departments in a great deal of work which, left to themselves, they would not have done. The CPRS also had to overcome the suspicions, on the part of officials and of ministers, of possible takeover bids for 'their' areas of responsibility and the perennial unease of the Treasury – which grew steadily stronger over time – at enquiries which threatened to excite demands for additional expenditure. If anything, the Treasury regarded outside interests and pressure groups as less worrying in this context than were ministers.

The first main item in the new work programme was one of some interest to all departments but which threatened none in particular. In effect, its aim was to apply to decisions involving resources of all kinds in the social affairs field the principle which for some years had guided public expenditure decisions – that demands on resources ought to be looked at in relation to resources as a whole and to other likely demands, over a period of time. The 'early warning system' for social affairs, devised by the CPRS in association with departments, was a modified version of a technique which the CPRS had tried – unsuccessfully – to apply right across the field of policy a couple of years before. Its aim was simple: to look forward six months and to identify issues coming up which would call for decisions, or at least discussion, by ministers. The hope was that if ministers could see each issue in even this limited context, this would help them to think slightly more systematically about the relative significance of each and about the appropriate action.

Each department produced its own list of issues and events – expected report of a Royal Commission, second reading of major Bill, decision on a pay claim. These were grouped by the CPRS under various broad headings and the whole thing was circulated around all departments.

Meanwhile, the CPRS was trying to put together the programme of discrete studies already mentioned. Choosing the subject for study was a long and painful progress: service departments were extremely reluctant to see an interdepartmental initiative led by the CPRS intruding on to their territory, or to agree to studies which might threaten cherished policies. The list of justifications offered for not choosing particular subjects was long: that the subject had already been so exhaustively studied that nothing more remained to be said or done (under fives), that it could be better approached in other ways (the 'social' impact of housing policies), that it was unsuitable for collective discussion (this was the Treasury on the matter of the interaction of taxation and social security policies), that it was not worth doing (school-leavers). The Department of Education and Science was particularly sceptical about the likely value of any activities of the kind suggested; the Treasury were particularly uneasy at the idea that discussion of needs, and of how to meet them more effectively, might excite spending ministers into a collective demand for higher public expenditure which the Chancellor would be unable to contain.

However, throughout the long series of bilateral talks between the CPRS and departments during 1974 a small group of topics emerged for which special studies seemed not only potentially useful but politically feasible. To help the process of consultation each department was asked to nominate one person to act as permanent link with the CPRS. To help develop consensus about the value and objectives to the exercise, these departmental representatives were also brought together from time to time in an informal interdepartment group chaired by the CPRS. This was specifically a 'group', not a conventional interdepartmental 'committee'; it met, not in the customary surroundings of one of the committee rooms in the Cabinet Office, but in the Civil Service College, Belgrave Road – in easy chairs arranged in a horseshoe shape. These physical arrangements were intended to emphasise that the group consisted of individuals engaged in a joint activity, of almost an intellectual kind, with common objectives, rather than representatives defending sectional interests. Indeed, departments were specifically asked by the CPRS to treat the group as, in effect, advisory to the CPRS; their advice and information was essential but the CPRS would take full responsibility for the papers which it produced on the basis of the group's discussions. The departments involved, and thus represented on the group, included the Central Statistical Office, Welsh and Scottish Offices, Lord Chancellor's Office, Home Office, Departments of Employment, Environment, Health and Social Security.

This approach worked remarkably well; it ensured that the CPRS was fully aware of departments' views on proposals discussed in the group but avoided the sterile wrangling over detailed issues and points of drafting which are so typical of interdepartmental activities in Whitehall. In any case, departments had an effective long-stop in the form of their representatives on Sir John Hunt's committee of permanent secretaries.

The proposals discussed and broadly agreed by the group included the setting up of a 'strategic' group of ministers to discuss social policies and problems; continuing the 'forward look' exercise already mentioned; some interdepartmental work on 'financial poverty' and in particular on the interaction of long-term cash benefits and shorter-term means-tested benefits; the working relationship between Whitehall departments and local authorities with particular reference to the ways in which these relationships affected the possibility of developing coherent 'packages' of services adequately related to the needs of prospective 'clients'; the 'social' aspects of housing policy; a study of a specific client group – preferably the disabled, which would make it possible to build on work already being done by an interdepartmental committee chaired by Mr Alfred Morris, a junior minister at the DHSS; a longer-term study, perhaps future policy towards women at work or the family.

The single main transdepartmental activity, and probably the most resource-intensive element in the whole package, was the better preparation, dissemination and use of 'social' statistics. This was in effect all that remained, though greatly modified, of the data-based approach of JASP Mark I. With the enthusiastic support of the Central Statistical Office it was agreed that a new 'Social Group' should be set up in the CSO, to oversee a Whitehall-wide campaign to produce better statistical information about social policies and problems, and to present this to ministers in forms which they could understand and, hopefully, use. A valuable ally here was Anthony Crosland, then Secretary of State for the Environment; he had proposed that ministers faced with decisions about changes in social policies ought to have some idea of their distributional consequences – which groups in the population would gain, or lose. The CPRS and CSO adopted this suggestion, and suggested that departments putting forward new expenditure proposals in the social field should attach to them a summary of their likely distributional effect, particularly on different income groups. The whole package of work was to be supported by an effort to improve the dissemination and presentation and use of statistical material.

These proposals, in the form of a draft report for ministers, were discussed by the Hunt Committee in the spring of 1975. Some permanent secretaries were still expressing disquiet at the whole project, fearing – as ever – that in identifying unmet needs and proposing new approaches to deal with these JASP might provoke discontent among spending ministers and, if the document became public, pressures from outside interests. These feelings were reinforced when, in April, a long article appeared in the *Times Educational Supplement.* This gave a comprehensive and fairly accurate account of the draft report, but went on to argue that the main aim of the whole project was to find new ways of cutting social expenditure, especially on education, that an 'inner Cabinet' or senior ministers would be 'ganging up' and forcing upopular decisions on individual spending ministers; and that the whole activity (in ways undefined) would diminish the authority of parliament. Even Sir John Hunt was affected by his colleagues' reservations. He insisted that the working title be changed from 'A Joint Approach to Social Policy' to 'A Joint Framework for Social Policies' to make it clear that the main purpose was to provide a better framework for ministerial decision taking in relation to client groups rather than to promote CPRS policies as such. However, he urged the CPRS not to pay too much heed to the doubts of departments nor to their suggestions for further dilution of the wording of the report.

In fact, the momentum of the programme carried it forward. In May the report was discussed in the new Cabinet Committee chaired by the Prime Minister. The simplest way of describing the meeting is to quote the account given by Barbara Castle, who through an oversight sent her Minister of State, David Owen, in her stead:

I was annoyed to find this morning had been pre-empted by a meeting of a Cabinet Committee on Joint Approach to Social Policies. Glancing at my papers, I couldn't even remember what it was all about, so I sent David in my place. He told me afterwards that I clearly should have gone: the PM was in the chair, all the top Ministers were there and they discussed the CPRS paper on a 'joint framework for social policies'. I had forgotten all about it. The pressure of hand-to-mouth work is so great these days that anything more profound one has read some weeks ago gets totally submerged. Since this new committee is part of Tony Crosland's bid for better 'social monitoring' (which is all right in itself, except that it is part of his continuing attacks on my expenditure) I would have liked to be there. There has certainly been no more 'wasteful expenditure' than in the housing field, and I am glad to learn that one of the short-term studies which CPRS proposes is on the social aspects of housing policy – as long as 'social aspects' does not rule out a study of cost-effectiveness. I learn that the CPRS paper is to be published, that the PM is to preside over a ministerial group on strategy, that social monitoring is to be carried out by a 'social group' of senior statisticians in the Central Statistical Office, that the group of Permanent Secretaries is to process all this, and that the first strategic ministerial meeting is to be held at Chequers soon. I certainly must not miss any more of these meetings. Harold must have felt aggrieved that I was not there.[6]

The report was duly published, with only marginal amendments, in July.[7] At one point it was firmly intended that it should be launched at a press conference by the Prime Minister; this was at the height of the government's attempt to sell to the trade unions the concept of the 'social wage', that is to persuade them to acknowledge the money value of the many welfare benefits received by their members and to accept these in lieu of increased cash through pay increases. The JASP report, with its emphasis on trying to increase the real value of services to those who needed them most, looked like a useful instrument in this campaign. However, in the event discussions of the social wage became bogged down and the press conference was postponed; rather than allow the JASP report to miss the tide of interest which, it was hoped, had been generated by the earlier press stories it was thought best to launch it on its own without further delay.

Thus published, the report constituted quite a forthright statement of the incoherence of social policies, and of the need to relate patterns of resource allocation to some explicit views about priorities in the social welfare field. Though published under a Labour government, its origins in the 'resource allocation' paper put to Conservative ministers three years earlier were clearly reflected in its emphasis on the need to reduce the growth in welfare expenditure and to 'cut back on some plans in the social field, as elsewhere'. But in going on to argue that this called for clear thinking about priorities, it added that this would be necessary whatever the public expenditure situation. Drawing on painful experience, and accurately anticipating the major obstacle to any inter-organisational venture of this kind, the report stated as its 'key assumption' the need for departments and ministers to be 'prepared to make some adjustments, whether in priorities, policies, administrative practices, or public expenditure allocations'. It went on to propose the several separate pieces of work already mentioned.

It is worth noting that the publication of the basic 'JASP report' set a precedent for the rest of the JASP programme, which contrasted markedly with the rest of the CPRS programme, still more so with the practices of the rest of Whitehall, then or later. The only major piece of JASP work not duly published was the report of the Treasury-led group on financial poverty. The same was true of some of the earlier Social Briefs. The result was an interaction between the JASP teams and the outside world that was as valuable as it was undamaging. The CPRS allowed itself some quite blunt language in its reports; ministers came to accept that these were public property, and did not object. Meanwhile the JASP received a steady stream of comments – not always complimentary – from academics, the media, pressure groups and politicians.

The work programme thus launched ran for about two years. At a purely administrative level, the interdepartmental group chaired by the CPRS met every few months to review progress on the various elements in the work programme, to agree on future development and to consider what might be said to the rather rarer meetings of Sir John Hunt's group of permanent secretaries and the 'strategic' group of ministers. This last, initially chaired by the Prime Minister, was later taken over by Mrs Shirley Williams (Secretary of State for Prices and Consumer Protection). The group on financial poverty, chaired by the Treasury, met regularly. Its main contribution was to draw together in reasonably concise and readable form a great deal of information about the various groups who comprised 'the poor', the nature of their situations, the impact of them on the current 'anti-poverty' programmes and the scope for helping them by selective improvements in social security benefits. The originality of the group lay in the fact that it was set up not to deal with an urgent specific problem, nor even to process a specific measure (such as a draft Bill), but to survey the whole of a wide field, to analyse the nature and interrelationships of the various problems discovered there, and to think about the most effective combinations of solutions to deal with these. By the restrictive standards of interdepartmental committees it was an untrammelled and creative body.

A group was set up to look at relations between central government and local authorities, despite the objections of the Department of the Environment that this would cut across the work being done by the Layfield Committee on local government finance. Most untypically for Whitehall, this group consisted of civil servants plus four local authority officials (a director of education, two chief executives and a director of social services). It also included a Treasury official who, again untypically, accompanied members of the group on some of their visits to local authorities. (In one midlands county, the introduction of the Treasury man provoked a spontaneous round of applause from the local authority representatives who rightly recognised the unique nature of this visitation.)

A great deal of work was done by the Central Statistical Office, with the help of departmental statisticians, both in assembling the data needed in the several studies and also in two activities which were, in effect, statistical ends in themselves: planning and producing periodic statistical digests related to social affairs, and devising ways of implementing the Crosland proposal about the distributional effects of new policies. The digests took specific topics, such as the geographical distribution of the poor, or population change; the current situation and recent trends were shown in diagram form, supported by a fairly neutral commentary. Originally these 'Social Briefs' were classified and were circulated only within Whitehall. By the end they were publicly available. All these activities drew on the experience and interest acquired by the CSO in recent years in the production of its annual volume *Social Trends*. For the CPRS – which had briefly considered recruiting its own statisticians – the value of the resources of the CSO was obvious; for the CSO, direct and almost daily contact with the CPRS stimulated thought about the relevance of its material to senior decision makers and about ways of improving its presentation and thus its value.

All this work continued, at different speeds, throughout 1975 and 1976. The interdepartmental group met every two or three months to review progress and to discuss the conclusions of the different studies as they emerged. Sir John Hunt's groups and the ministerial 'strategy' group met more rarely.

The first of the working groups to produce a full-scale report was the poverty group; its report went to ministers but, unusually in JASP, was not published. The next, which was later published, was produced by the group on central/local government relations. The report was completed, submitted to ministers and in 1977 published, on *Relations between Central Government and Local Authorities*.[8]

The motivation and conclusions of this report were so closely related to the themes of this project that a brief description is justified. The report began with the assumption that joint approaches at local authority level could be greatly helped or hindered by the actions and attitudes of central government. It concluded that there were 'real defects' in the central/local relationship. Whitehall departments – the contrast was made with the Scottish Office – acted 'for most purposes in isolation from each other, and conduct their relationships with local authorities accordingly'. The relationship was also greatly confused by uncertainty about the respective responsibilities of central and local government. The report recommended that central departments should act more corporately, should desist from heavy-handed intervention in the detail of local authority services, and should get to know local authorities, and their problems, better.

A major product of the statistical side of JASP was another report, also published in 1977, on *Population and the Social Services*.[9] This simple but elegant piece of analysis was based on projections till the end of the century of the size of the various main age-groups in the population. It spelled out the implications of these projections for demand for the main social services and thus for the cost of these services.

The even and moderate tenor of this programme was abruptly disturbed when, in late 1975, the CPRS found itself unexpectedly commissioned by ministers to carry out what it had long since concluded was impossible – a comprehensive review of spending on social programmes leading to some better-informed decisions about priorities across the board. This commission originated with a Cabinet discussion of the need for a review of the social services akin to the annual defence review – with the implicit hope that such a review would give 'social' professionals, especially the doctors, the chance to articulate their demands for resources as cogently as the military seemed to do. It seems fairly clear that this was, in effect, a counter-attack mounted by Barbara Castle on what she saw as the threat to her own programmes represented by the Department of Education and Science and by Anthony Crosland at the DOE.

For the CPRS the commission was doubly unwelcome – first because it would create a great deal of work on top of the JASP activities, and second because it was in effect a throw-back to an approach which all concerned had now explicitly rejected. It was uncomfortably reminiscent of the earlier Rothschild paper with its assertion that clear decisions on spending priorities could be read off from a picture of the amount of resources already allocated to each of a list of 'client groups'.

However, it was agreed that the review of social spending or 'ROSS', as it half-jokingly became known, should at least be handled by the institutions already concerned with JASP. This ensured that the creature would not develop an independent life of its own since everybody concerned would be personally aware of the continuing demands of JASP. The CPRS concluded that ROSS should aim to be comprehensive only in taking a sweeping glance at the public expenditure figures and that it should then, with as much of a contribution as possible from ministers themselves, try to focus on some limited topics for more detailed work – the approach already underway in JASP.

With a great deal of help from the Treasury and the CSO, the CPRS assembled some statistical time series showing expenditure on the main social programmes, at constant prices, backwards to 1952 and forwards to 1980 (the end of the public expenditure survey period). Using figures for other countries derived from the Organisation for Economic Cooperation and Development and elsewhere, and with the advice of an academic expert, the CPRS then produced some international comparisons showing levels of expenditure on selected major programmes, correcting for the 'purchasing power' of each country; in discussions with ministers and their officials the CPRS then tried to tempt the former to indicate their own views of high and low priorities among needs or programmes.

The responses included, from Anthony Crosland, a reply as thoughtful as it is rare in ministerial thinking about expenditure priorities – an attempt, starting with the assertion that current priorities were not right, to look right across the board of government spending and to indicate which programmes (including some of his own) were receiving too much and which too little.[10]

The outcome of this work took the form of a CPRS 'presentation' to ministers – a device by now very well established in the private sector but almost unknown in Whitehall, where the preferred mode of putting complex options to ministers is to summarise the situation in two pages of typescript supported by bulky factual annexes, the whole thing being introduced to his colleagues by the minister responsible who may, or may not, be personally familiar with the subject matter. As Barbara Castle recalled:

The 'Think Tank' was due to give a presentation of its 'synoptic' view of social policy as the first stage of its 'fundamental review' . . . Harold was in the chair . . . It turned out to be quite illuminating. Ken Berrill introduced a succession of his younger experts, who proceeded to show slides which effectively illustrated some of the things I have been arguing in PESC, e.g. the relative advantage education had enjoyed over the years in public expenditure, despite the move of demographic factors in favour of the health and personal social services . . . The international comparisons . . . showed our expenditure on the social services to be below the European average . . .[11]

The CPRS went on to argue that these aggregate figures did no more than indicate where further investigation might be worthwhile. It might be helpful to look also at the relationship between supply of services and the need for them, the fit between services provided and consumers' preferences, the important role of local authorities in all this and the sharply rising cost of manpower.

The presentation itself was well received. But it proved very hard to translate ministers' approval of this broad-brush approach into departmental agreement to do anything in particular. The senior ministers concerned were so reluctant to discuss the CPRS proposals for the next stage that the task was given to a group of junior ministers. In the face of endless departmental prevarication and haggling over the details and terms of reference of individual follow-up studies, the CPRS finally secured agreement that the (independent) National Consumer Council should be commissioned to do some work on housing provision and clients' preferences, and that it might itself initiate some work on regional variations in service standards and needs. It proved impossible to launch some work, to be led by the Department of Employment, on trends in social service manpower.

Part of the problem here was the by now extreme sensitivity of the Treasury to any activity which might increase, not so much pressure for higher expenditure, as resistance to the cuts which the desperate economic situation was thought to require. Barbara Castle commented on ROSS that 'for some incomprehensible reason the CPRS review was labelled "Confidential" and not published by the Government'.[12] In fact, nothing could be easier to understand than reluctance to publish semi-official, and all too well-authenticated, comparisons showing Britain near the bottom of the international spending league on social services.

But little work had been done on the ROSS studies when a series of decisions were taken which effectively brought an end to the work of the CPRS not only on ROSS but also on JASP, and their involvement in the interdraft aspects of social policy. These decisions were in fact initiated by the CPRS itself.

Very early in 1977, the CPRS had a collective two-day meeting at the Civil Service College, Sunningdale. This was the third such annual meeting, organised at the insistence of some of the middle-ranking members of the CPRS and acquiesced in rather reluctantly by Kenneth Berrill. The aim was for the CPRS itself to have a 'strategic' discussion of its objectives and priorities, as the basis for planning its own work programme. The JASP team put to the meeting the proposition that the time might now have come to run down JASP and to turn the CPRS manpower to other uses. (Some six people were now spending 5% to 75% of their time on JASP activities.) The arguments for pulling out were that JASP had now, over time, absorbed more CPRS man-hours than probably any other CPRS study, that it no longer seemed to arouse a proportionate degree of ministerial interest (which suggested that for the CPRS the opportunity costs were fairly high, given its constant need for the approval of its clients), and that the CPRS was in any case an analytical and not an executive body.

The CPRS, led by Kenneth Berrill himself, saw no reasons to question this judgement.

In February the JASP team put the same proposition, rather more emphatically, to the interdepartmental group, and met much the same response.

The result was that from the spring of 1977 JASP, as a linked group of activities overseen by the CPRS, ceased to exist. Work continued on one or two major studies, notably those which were later published as *Housing and Social Policies* and *Services for Children with Working Mothers*.[13] The Social Group in the Central Statistical Office continued to produce Social Briefs, which were not formally abandoned until the coming of the Thatcher government. The special ministerial committee and Sir John Hunt's group continued to exist on paper but ceased to meet. The CPRS continued to take a general interest in social problems and policies (as witness its subsequent report, unpublished in Britain but available in pirated copies on the Continent, on alcoholism), but did not claim that this related to any kind of wider vision or more comprehensive scheme of things.

Commentators on the JASP episode have used it to make several points in particular. JASP has been taken, by many people concerned at the apparent ineffectiveness of the state's response to social problems, as an example of the kind of approach which is essential if new issues are to be identified, old bureaucratic shibboleths and organisational rigidities ignored and resources used so as to have the maximum impact. For others, it has exemplified the high-water mark of a naive faith, born in the 1960s, in the practicability and value of central coordination; even many supporters of the principle have seen JASP as very much 'of its time', unrepeatable a decade later. Others have suggested that there was a failure to relate an ambitious central design to the realities of actually implementing the necessary policies.

The main question to ask in the context of this study is whether and how far the JASP experience supports the case for the 'optimistic' or 'pessimistic' model. There is no doubt that for the CPRS, many guiding assumptions even of JASP Mark II were firmly rooted in the 'pessimistic' model. JASP Mark I had tested this model to destruction. Rothschild, whose hand was extremely apparent in the paper that went to ministers in autumn 1973, drew from his scientific background the belief that for any problem there was probably a 'best' technique and a 'correct' solution; in this case the technique was to analyse the world in terms of client groups, and so precisely to define their situations that ministers could almost automatically infer the most effective course of action. This approach played straight into the hands of departmental officials; adopting the 'practical man' pose which is a favourite blanket response to threatening proposals from outside, they had little difficulty in showing that the client group/social audit approach would ignore as many problems as it promised to solve. The consequent confrontation greatly damaged the credibility of the CPRS, and its legitimacy as an actor in the social policy field. It took the CPRS over a year to recover the ground thus lost. (The process was made easier for the CPRS JASP team by Rothschild's loss of interest in the subject and by his subsequent replacement by Kenneth Berrill, whose main interests anyway lay elsewhere.)

But even CPRS members who thought Rothschild's approach mis-conceived, and who were much less certain that the techniques of social science could discover objective or generally acceptable truths in the field of social policy, were optimistic in their belief that ministers would appreciate an exercise which consisted of applying analysis to the identification of problems, and defining solutions which would be more effective than current policies by virtue of being transdepartmental. It was also hoped that ministers would be willing to choose the more effective solutions even when these required some loss of departmental sovereignty, whether by themselves or by their colleagues. The whole emphasis in JASP Mark II placed on better information, and the key role given to the Central Statistical Office, underline the point. The aim of the interdepartmental JASP group was to develop consensus as a basis for CPRS recommendations and for interdepartmental action.

On the other hand, the 'pessimistic' model was not denied. Even the procedures of the interdepartmental group conceded the impossibility of guaranteeing a consensus in every case; the CPRS explicitly reserved the right to produce its own reports without necessarily securing the agreement of all members of the group. Moreover, for the CPRS the significance of Sir John Hunt's chairmanship of his committee of permanent secretaries was that he was thus institutionalised as an outside authority to whom appeal might be made in the event of obstruction. Hunt's efforts to involve the Prime Minister in JASP enhanced this authority and were naturally welcomed by the CPRS. The CPRS did not hesitate to exploit contacts with politicians through intermediaries such as Brian Abel-Smith and the Downing Street Policy Unit. The 'assumption' stated in the original JASP report, that departments and ministers 'must be prepared to make some adjustments, whether in priorities, policies, administrative practices, or public expenditure allocations' reflected precisely the recognition that departments and ministers would be extremely reluctant to do this. Finally, the eagerness of the CPRS to publish the reports produced by JASP groups reflected their wish to enlist outside opinion in the struggle to persuade departments and ministers to 'make adjustments'.

Taking all these factors together it might be said that the CPRS was, implicitly, operating on the basis of a 'mixed' model, containing both 'optimistic' and 'pessimistic' elements. The same might be said, at another level altogether, about the involvement of the CPRS in JASP at all. In one sense the CPRS could be said to have been led to JASP by the process of applying pure reason to an area of government policy: analysis of the scale of the problems and of the inadequacy of current responses to them then justified a relatively large resource investment by the CPRS.

On the other hand, for the CPRS JASP was equally consistent with the assumptions underlying the 'pessimistic' model. CPRS influence, and thus both its future resource security and budget, could only be enhanced by CPRS involvement in the massive field of social policies and expenditure. One departmental official discussing JASP subsequently commented that it seemed to be a case of the CPRS 'making a role for itself', and this could be said to be a perfectly fair comment.[14] For the CPRS, a successful JASP was its own justification – provided always that it was seen as successful by ministers, and that it did not divert CPRS resources from other activities which would appeal to ministers more. This logic, which justified CPRS's original entry into this field, correspondingly underlay its withdrawal when, in 1977, first the JASP team and then the CPRS as a whole concluded that the exercise was starting to pay diminishing returns in terms of the costs of CPRS time weighed against the benefits of ministerial satisfaction. If all this is taken as indicating simply the simultaneous presence of elements of institutional self-interest and of institutional altruism, that would be acceptable shorthand.

For the DHSS, too, institutional self-interest justified a joint approach. The background to the rise and fall of the 'Rogers initiative' has already been outlined. For Rogers, the main aims were to improve internal coordination in the DHSS, and to develop effective working relationships with local authorities. As a joint exercise, the weakness of this initiative was that it was seen by other departments as being of primary interest to one department in particular – the DHSS. For the Department of Education and Science, with its increased share of resources apparently secure, participation in the Rogers' activity could be seen as little more than a damage-limitation exercise, and much the same was true of the DOE. For the Treasury, the prospect of a united front among this group of spending departments was always a threat. Hence, by mid 1972 the loss of the initial impetus generated by Rogers' group of permanent secretaries, as departments started to drag their feet in response to DHSS leads. This was the point at which, for the DHSS itself, the slowly growing administrative cost of keeping the project going started to outstrip the prospective benefits.

But at least for the DHSS the value of the benefits did not diminish. Hence the active support given to JASP by Rogers and some senior colleagues. One of their main targets was, and remained, the Department of Education and Science. It was strongly felt in the DHSS (as in other departments) that some way must be found of bringing the DES into the realm of social policy; its senior officials ought to recognise that their department had obligations, and its activities effects, beyond the narrow world of education. A senior DHSS official commented on the 'appalling problems' caused for the social work service by the unilateral way in which the DES had handled the major policy change of raising the school leaving age in 1973. 'Educational perfectionists who would accept no policy that fell in any degree short of their own ideal', as one ex-minister at DHSS put it. 'The most outward looking of all Whitehall departments – in its concern with its own clients and its lack of corporate sense' was the judgement of a very senior non-DHSS official. Rogers and some of his colleagues felt that their own initiative had helped DHSS to make real, if limited, progress in developing dialogues with the DES and other departments. It was their belief that the holistic approach of JASP Mark I was going to lose all the ground thus painfully gained that led to their feelings of frustration which, in part, were responsible for the confrontation with the CPRS in November 1973.

But there were other views within the DHSS about the value and purpose of joint approaches. In the first place, there were 'target' departments other than the DES. For some, the main target was the Treasury: JASP was felt to be a means of increasing the influence of the DHSS and so to enable it to deal on more nearly equal terms with the Treasury in discussing the interactions between cash benefits, administered by the DHSS, and the Treasury's fiscal activities. Others in the DHSS had their eye on the housing divisions of the Department of the Environment, others again on the residual welfare responsibilities – focused on the inner cities through the Urban Programme – of the Home Office.

But there were also divisions of opinion between those at the top of the DHSS and their colleagues lower down. Rogers and, later, Nairne had well-developed views about the value of interdepartmental working and put a good deal of time and effort into encouraging it. Some of their juniors felt that they had had their perspectives altered by their experiences in the Cabinet Office, to the detriment of their willingness simply to fight the DHSS corner against all comers. (Nairne had in fact come to the DHSS only as his last posting in a career otherwise spent wholly in the Cabinet Office and the defence departments.) Some people in DHSS middle management saw JASP in particular as abstract, idealistic and unlikely to contribute to achieving the central purposes of the DHSS. JASP studies, which threatened to reveal how far existing levels of service provision fell short of needs, would be likely only to excite demands for additional resources which would not be available, and damagingly to expose the gap between the rhetoric of ministers and officials on the one hand and actual performance on the other.

In any case, it was argued within the DHSS, as far as JASP focused on the personal social services, provided by local authorities, it cut across the main political interests of DHSS ministers, which were to protect those budgets for the spending of which they were directly responsible, viz. health and social security. If cuts were to be made under Treasury pressure, it was politically much easier to see these made in services for which local authorities were answerable. One respondent said that this attitude led to deliberate attempts to 'foil the DHSS: I had no doubt that there was a "network" at assistant secretary level who conspired to foil, for example, the demographic work launched by JASP'. And although some DHSS officials conceded that JASP had encouraged them both to think more interdepartmentally and to develop closer working relationships with their opposite numbers in other departments, others argued that perfectly adequate relationships had been and could be developed without JASP.

Finally, even though JASP in principle offered the DHSS a vehicle for use in competing for resources with other departments, officials did not always want to take advantage of this, for fear of disturbing the balance of power to their own detriment. For example, using JASP as a means of prying resources out of the DOE housing budget might have alienated the support of DOE in helping to keep the CPRS out of DHSS territory.

Later discussions with DOE officials suggest that this caution on the part of the DHSS was probably justified. Within the DOE JASP seems to have been seen mainly as an exercise imposed upon the department from outside and offering it little of value, and whose main purpose was to provide the DHSS with a means of solving problems which it could not solve within its own departmental boundaries. In the early days of JASP there seem to have been within the DOE several different attitudes towards it – all more or less sceptical. First, that it was not the task of departmental officials to try to think transdepartmentally: this should be left to others. Secondly, that on the other hand something should be done to reduce the inconsistencies between the main cash payment systems, in particular supplementary benefit and rent/rate rebates – but that little effective could be done here without the active commitment of the Treasury. Thirdly, that there were some programmes, notably housing, where better coordination would in principle allow the more effective use of resources and so was, in principle, welcome: but that in practice the CPRS showed no signs of being better able to achieve coordination between departments than was the DOE, struggling with the problems of coordinating its own activities.

One DOE official said that in the circumstances his own attitude towards JASP had modified over time – from his initial general belief that the exercise was worth the effort, to scepticism. However, he conceded that he had at least acquired one important insight from taking part in the central/local relations study, namely that central government's attempted interventions in local programmes were often quite inappropriate to local needs. The questions whose asking had prompted these insights were not ones which the DOE would have been likely to ask spontaneously.

None of the other participants, individual or institutional, in JASP had quite the same interest as the CPRS or the DHSS in coordination as such. The closest was probably the Cabinet Secretariat; Sir John Hunt's attempts to develop the Secretariat's policy coordinating role were well served by the CPRS's interventions in social as in other policy areas. His sympathy with Sir Philip Rogers' objectives led him to put the weight of the Secretariat behind the CPRS when it took over the lead from the DHSS.

Two other departments whose general interests were served, in rather different ways, by more coherent approaches to policy making were the Treasury and the Scottish Office. For the Treasury, a 'strategic' approach to social policy was entirely consistent with its own insistence that increased resources for some programmes must be balanced by savings elsewhere; JASP seemed to offer more chance than did the established PESC process of looking at programmes and policies in the multilateral way needed to achieve this. It was a pity, commented a Treasury official later, that JASP did so little to identify the relatively low priority areas from which resources might be transferred – thus unconsciously harking back to the embryonic 'social services budget' of the Crossman era. However, for the Scottish Office, JASP offered some prospect of developing among Whitehall departments the closer working relationships that were relatively easily achieved in Edinburgh where their single Secretary of State was, in effect, equivalent to a Cabinet committee in London. Though the Scottish Office had no specific programme interests in JASP, it had a general interest in more effective working relationships in Whitehall: 'If the DES and the Home Office were at loggerheads over, say policy towards children, it didn't help us in trying to develop a common policy on the subject in Edinburgh'. Otherwise, commented a Scottish Office official, the department's interest in JASP was probably 'genuinely altruistic, in thinking that we had something to offer Whitehall ... We were perhaps the department whose perspective was closest to that of the CPRS.'

Most others involved saw the chance of using the momentum generated by JASP to promote specific objectives of their own. For the Central Statistical Office, JASP offered a role which promised lasting benefits. The immediate attractions of JASP to the CSO was the potentially important part in it for statistics and statisticians; its longer-term value was as a 'lever' for establishing and enhancing the role of statistics in the 'social' field equivalent to their by then well-established role in economic policy. JASP gave the CSO the chance of building up an effective network, with itself at the centre, of the statisticians in the social departments and, at the same time, of strengthening the links between them and policy makers. JASP in general, and the preparation of Social Briefs in particular, brought the two groups into much closer contact than normal; it also obliged the statisticians to think positively about the policies which they were ultimately serving.

If the attitudes of the Treasury, Scottish Office, DHSS and DOE were fairly consistent over time, those of some other departments derived much more particularly from specific experiences or objectives, sometimes quite personal in nature. Perhaps the most interesting was the change of view ascribed to the DES by one of its senior officials. The educational budget, and the determination of the DES that the allocation of this should be guided exclusively by educational criteria, were for many people the main targets of JASP. This was indeed how the DES itself saw JASP. In the early stages of JASP the DES saw no prospective benefit in 'joint' policies. 'We had defined "educational policy", and had a government commitment to it in the form of Mrs Thatcher's 1972 white paper (Education: a Framework for Expansion) ... So we plowed our own furrow, with only lip service to the DHSS and its "day-care" interests ... Although we were willing to go to Sir Philip Rogers' meetings we did not want to do much of substance ...'

These attitudes underlay the DES's reluctance to contribute constructively in the first stages of JASP. By the later stages, however, things were changing. 'The resources that we had thought "tied up" were now being eroded through inflation or act of government. So we had more to gain, and less to lose, from interdepartmental activities.' It was indeed a DES proposal which led to one of the more successful JASP studies, that on *Social Policies and Demographic Change.* The arguments offered at the time for this study were entirely consistent with the change of attitude outlined above: just as falling numbers of school children had been used to justify cuts in the educational budget, would it not be appropriate to consider the possible implications of these and other demographic changes for the budgets and medium-term strategies of other spending departments?

But it would be misleading to suggest that every department had a well-developed 'institutional' view about JASP and its likely costs and benefits to the department. As one official commented, all the main social departments had to play at least a formal part in JASP as long as it was seen to have the backing of the Prime Minister. But the depth and detail of departmental commitment was inevitably greatly influenced by the views of individuals about the relevance of JASP to their own personal interests. An economist who acted as his department's 'link-man' in JASP recalled there being no departmental view about JASP, partly because of the absence of a coherent management structure which would have made possible the development of such general departmental policies. But in this vacuum he could himself exercise considerable discretion in deciding the kind of part the department should play. In practice his own interests were served by playing an active part, since this helped to strengthen his own role as an economist without specific line-management functions. 'So long as JASP did not make major demands on departmental resources our finance people were happy to let it go on ... My unit did the coordinating and did the rest of the department no harm.' In that JASP in this way helped to develop a role for a central planning unit it had the support of the department's permanent secretary, who himself had a personal interest in more effective central management control.

At the margins departmental participation in JASP was, in effect, optional. In the right circumstances JASP could serve as a vehicle for advancing particular current policy interests. This was the case with the Lord Chancellor's Office – not normally known for its broad concerns with welfare objectives or for its transdepartmental perspective. But in the mid 1970s one of the department's concerns was the promotion of 'law centres' (voluntary organisations, mainly financed by central or local government, providing free legal services in deprived areas). JASP provided a framework within which to develop the Lord Chancellor's bid for putting more resources into legal services in general and law centres in particular, for arguing the case for expanding legal services in ways which would help to serve the interests and maintain the confidence of the more deprived groups in society, and for obtaining cash for these from the Urban Programme – then run by the Home Office. In particular, 'JASP provided a degree of network and a context within which these causes could be advanced'. Another career official from the department commented on the value of JASP as an activity involving the department in urban problems, in which they were concerned to take an interest.

Finally, ministers. The difficulty faced by the CPRS throughout JASP, and in many other similar contexts, was two-fold. On the one hand there was the all-too familiar problem of developing a sense of collective purpose strong enough to overcome the inevitable pressures towards departmentalism. This was reflected in the passage in the original report, already quoted, about the need for adjustments in departmental policies and priorities. On the other there was the danger that in thus persuading ministers to take sufficient interest in the principle of JASP one would be risking their greater disappointment when they saw how slow was the process of producing real changes and improvements at a practical level.

As it happened, the Labour Cabinet of 1974–75 found it fairly easy to applaud the principle of JASP, given its relevance to the concept of the 'Social Wage' and its apparent promise to enhance the real value of that wage. Harold Wilson's agreement, abandoned only at the last minute, personally to launch the published report at a press conference is the best evidence of this. Even the highly departmental Barbara Castle sensed that something potentially important was happening and regretted her failure to attend the ministerial meeting at which the original report was discussed. Her Minister of State David Owen, concerned with the needs of the under fives and irritated by lack of cooperation on the part of the 'perfectionists' at the DES, later commented that 'JASP was useful in getting something interdepartmental going'.

But once the initial initiative had been taken and announced, ministers found it hard to keep their interest in the details of the inevitable long grind that followed. Few ministers see the point of JASP-type approaches, reflected one senior DHSS official: Sir Keith Joseph did; Mrs Castle did not; David Owen might have but was distracted by other issues. Despite the Scottish Office's interest in JASP at official level, an official recalled his disappointment at the lack of attention paid to it by his ministers. JASP lacked political appeal, was the view of a DOE official: 'It was more a permanent secretaries' thing than a Ministers' thing'. Another suggested that individual Labour ministers were more attracted by the detail of social policy expenditure – which 'tends to strengthen departmental rather than corporate thinking'. He, too, felt that JASP was, in a sense, 'too rational, too a-political'. It might have had more impact, was the view of one senior Cabinet Office official, if more effort had been put into involving ministers directly and in identifying a small number of problems in which they were interested. But, as Lord Hunt later remarked, 'Few Ministers whole-heartedly supported JASP; most of them saw it more as an intrusion into their own bailiwicks'.[15]

It is clear that for all concerned the degree of their interest in and commitment to JASP depended on a fairly shrewd calculation of the value to themselves and/or their department of taking part in this attempt to improve the coordination of social policies. This value was seen differently by individuals in different parts of the same department, and differently at different times. Few of those concerned thought in terms of the value of coordination as such – probably only the CPRS and the Cabinet Secretariat, and the DHSS to the extent that successive permanent secretaries were interested in better coordination of the several activities of the DHSS and also wanted to influence the policies of other departments in ways which would serve DHSS ends. The cause of coordination, as preached by the CPRS, thus had little intrinsic appeal to most of the others concerned. Their attitudes were probably best summarised in the two summary conclusions expressed by one official who had been actively involved throughout JASP. Objectively, he suggested, there were few policy areas in which coordination promised major improvements in outcomes; causes of policy failures were official inertia, the pressures of outside interests and the size and complexity of public sector bureaucracies. Secondly, and related to this, line managers' inevitable response to central attempts to improve coordination was 'How will this help me?' – a reasonable question to which the answer was all too often 'Nothing'. Attempts to coordinate usually simply created more work, and rarely generated any feedback from the centre to the periphery.

These and similar views doubtless influenced respondents' assessments both of the decision by the CPRS to pull out of JASP and of the validity and impact of the exercise as a whole.

Very few people expressed surprise or regret at the termination of JASP. Several people felt that JASP had suffered from inherent weaknesses in conception and in execution. It had started with a 'grand vision' but had lost this in 'a welter of detail', said one basically sympathetic official. It had had too many projects on the go at once. The CPRS had not been tough enough in enforcing its own line of thinking. The most important defect of JASP, said a senior official in a long and reasoned critique, was that it was inadequately related to the fundamental resource allocation process, institutionalised as PESC. Simply setting up little working groups could serve no purpose if these were not geared into some central machinery. As it was, JASP could be regarded as a threat to Treasury influence as exercised through the customary public expenditure control procedures – but without itself having adequate political backing. This weakness was exacerbated by JASP's inherent need for a period of economic stability as background for the kind of shifts envisaged between spending programmes. Even where such shifts could be agreed in principle, the CPRS probably underestimated the difficulties of implementing them; in concentrating overmuch on strategic thinking it took too little account of the inertia in the system and of the power of large vested interests such as local authority trade unions. It was also at odds with ministers' inevitable preoccupation with issues of detail and with the short term.

Like many other points made about JASP, this last one – which might be said to express the 'pessimistic' approach – can be matched by its 'optimistic' counterpart. Thus an official from another department argued that ministerial shortsightedness was precisely the kind of propensity that JASP should have aimed to change. JASP had wrongly tried to influence the detailed aims and methods of departments whereas it should have concentrated on getting ministers to identify broad priorities in the social field. This should have been the main purpose of the special ministerial and other committees.

Views differed about the value of these committees. Lord Hunt felt that although his permanent secretaries group had some symbolic value, it was of little practical use. Meeting at long intervals for perhaps two hours at a time, it was not a suitable forum for considering complex transdepartmental issues; these really called for sustained discussions among full-time members of 'project teams'. An ex-minister felt that the special ministerial committee on long-term social policies was itself of little use. His view was that the political overview should be taken in the regular 'home affairs' committee, chaired by a 'determined Home Secretary'. The chairman would need non-departmental support, possibly from the CPRS. This should help him to play an active and positive part in developing social policies, across departmental boundaries where necessary. 'How often at present does the Home Secretary (as chairman of the committee) actually ask for the papers to be brought forward to HA Committee?' The role envisaged here is close to that briefly played by Richard Crossman as coordinating minister, chairing the Social Services Committee and supported by the coordinating unit.

Another former minister and member of the long-term committee agreed that the committee, and JASP as a whole, had had disappointingly little impact – but not because it was misconceived in principle. 'The essential means of (developing joint approaches) is to have separate financing for them over and above what is contained in departmental budgets. This should be in the hands of the Treasury ... Or it could be given to a body of a research council type ... The Committee was not futile. It simply had no resources.' It is ironical to recall the efforts made by the Odgers unit six or seven years before to develop a social services budget for the Social Services Committee; and also to note that, typically in Whitehall, these efforts appear by the mid 1970s to have been totally forgotten by all concerned.

Though views differed about the defects of JASP, it was widely agreed that these lessened its ability to survive in the face of ministerial indifference and departmental obstruction – two mutually reinforcing problems. It was widely felt that ministers had lost interest in JASP even before the end of the Labour government. Any progress in interdepartmental coordination, commented a former minister, requires the active participation of ministers, 'to bang heads together'; the difficulty was that this was very time-consuming for ministers. But without ministerial backing, and especially from the Prime Minister, JASP could have made no headway against departments which in the view of one official had 'ganged up' against the CPRS, nor against the weight of the vested interests, such as the professional associations, in both local and central government.

More generally, many felt that JASP was 'a creature of its time' – its time being the time of its gestation, the very early 1970s, when public expenditure was rising and expected to continue to rise, and when, in consequence, it seemed likely or at least possible that additional resources would be available for some of the needs identified by JASP studies. It was the time before 'the IMF visitation', that is the visit by IMF representatives in 1976 in response to the British government's request for a loan. The loan was made, but only on condition of major cuts in expenditure.

Moreover, ministerial outlooks and the spirit of the times had deteriorated hand in hand. The Thatcher administration, commented one official, was interested neither in social policy, nor in coordination, nor in the longer term, nor consequently in exercises such as JASP. 'People in Whitehall now have less time than I had in the mid seventies for this kind of speculative long-term thinking', said a DES official. A DHSS official was blunter: Whitehall had become 'much more brutal' than it was – too brutal for idealistic operations such as JASP.

Given all this, few people felt that the CPRS had been wrong to disengage itself from JASP. One or two did: a couple of officials felt that the CPRS could have 'forced the pace more', in the words of one, and that had it been less 'gentle' with obstructive departments, it could have achieved more at less cost to itself. One former minister felt very strongly that the CPRS had been wrong to end JASP. 'It could have got going again by 1978/79, as departmental budgets began to increase. It could have provided a valuable incentive to any departments willing to develop joint approaches.'

A former permanent secretary supported this view. The CPRS should have maintained its role: it could take as much as ten years to develop a genuine and workable joint approach. Meanwhile, the case for JASP was indicated in the waste of resources in ill-coordinated programmes such as housing and services for elderly people. If JASP had succeeded and become institutionalised, reflected Lord Hunt, the CPRS would have faced the difficult question of whether or not to keep such a large proportion of its own resources tied up in a coordinating capacity; it would almost certainly have been wrong to do so. (This would indeed have been a task more suitable for the earlier coordinating unit.)

It is hard to detect any longer-term impact of JASP. A controlled contrast is in fact virtually impossible, given the radical change in the whole climate of policy making which followed the arrival of the Thatcher government in 1979; the new 'brutal' Whitehall, with its lack of interest in 'speculative' thinking, would have been a deeply inhospitable environment even for a better-established activity. 'We had more time for research in those days', said Mrs Thatcher herself, looking back at the CPRS of the early 1970s shortly after her 1983 decision to abolish the CPRS altogether.[16]

A minority of those interviewed detected faint traces of JASP in working practices. Some DHSS officials felt that its principles had survived in the activities of the DHSS's cross-sector policy review group. Another believed that DHSS's working relationship with the Inland Revenue had improved as a result of JASP and related activities; the same was true of contacts with those responsible for Supplementary Benefits, the Department of Energy, and the Department of the Environment. But overall few people were prepared to claim that Whitehall now operated more interdepartmentally than in the past; nobody could identify major lasting changes in the policy making process brought about by JASP. The climate of the Thatcher years was not the only cause of the return to that 'departmentalism' which JASP and its predecessors had tried to modify, but it certainly did nothing to discourage it. Whitehall departments were still (1983) 'a group of warring baronies', commented a Scottish Office official from his Edinburgh vantage point. JASP had left no traces in the social services division of DHSS, said a DHSS official. 'The current (February 1982) briefing line in the department is to emphasise the total deadness of JASP.' 'Relationships between statisticians and policy-makers in departments are not now as good as they were at the end of the JASP period', said a senior statistician. 'There is a cultural tide at present against (close working relationships). There is a great temptation for administrators to say "Don't bother with the facts: this is a political issue." ' In the Whitehall of the 1980s that last comment resounds far beyond the working relationships between statisticians and administrators.

It is hard to disagree with these views. The student of the Whitehall policy making process in the mid 1980s can detect there few, if any, tangible traces of JASP. Whether in the relationships between departments, or Whitehall's relationship with local authorities, or in the repeated frenzied series of public expenditure cuts, little 'jointness' is visible. What remains is the short bookshelf of the published reports of the several JASP studies (including the later Social Briefs), and the feeling on the part of a good many people, inside as well as outside Whitehall, that 'there must be a better way' of making decisions about resource allocation in the social welfare field, and of interrelating the planning and administration of social programmes.

The history of JASP and its immediate forebears gives some pointers to what such a 'better way' might be, and how it may be made effective. The coordinating Secretary of State for Social Services, plus supporting unit, in what turned out to be a strangely isolated episode, early hit upon the importance for a would-be coordinator of an independent control over resources – as several participants in JASP were later to observe. But for the result of the 1970 election, the unit would also have had a chance to test the plausible hypothesis that only a sustained effort by a central non-departmental staff can offset the continuous centrifugal pressures of Whitehall. In terms of its own wider objectives the CPRS was probably right to abandon JASP in 1977, but the result was inevitable. The Rogers initiative demonstrated, negatively, the impossibility of managing a successful interdepartmental exercise from the base of one of the departments concerned. For the other departments involved, the cost-benefit equation was far too heavily weighted towards the DHSS. This episode also underlined the need for support from politicians at the top; Rogers' committee of permanent secretaries, chaired by himself, was not capable of 'knocking heads together' when individual departments declined to cooperate. Moreover Rogers, and his successor Nairne, seem to have underestimated the extent of scepticism about the value of jointness that existed even in their own departments.

JASP Mark I was both too transparently 'rational' in its approach, and too little concerned to develop consensus at the level of the permanent bureaucracy. Rothschild's interpretation of the mandate given to the ministerial meeting in early 1973 was not discussed with departments; when ministers came to discuss the CPRS 'client group' paper the same autumn their native lack of interest in this kind of approach was devastatingly reinforced by the hostile briefing which they received from their departments.

The short-lived ROSS was interesting in being, uniquely, the result of an initiative on the part of ministers themselves. Barbara Castle's comments indicate that she, at least, was satisfied with the outcome – viz. the demonstration that Britain was already well on the way to becoming the poor man of the western welfare world. But even ROSS illustrated the perennial problem faced by would-be coordinators in dealing with ministers. On the one hand ministerial interest and backing is essential if departments are ever to be dislodged from their trenches. Ministers clearly enjoyed the initial ROSS presentation. On the other hand it is exceedingly hard, and in the long run impossible, to sustain ministerial interest in the gritty detail of the necessary debates about, for example, the relative disadvantage of specific client groups and about the relevant programmes. In ROSS senior ministers who had literally applauded the original CPRS presentation proved reluctant, and perhaps genuinely unable, to master or to involve themselves in the arguments as to whether one of their departments' policy areas should be the subject of an interdepartmental study. But without a lead from senior ministers, departments who wanted to drag their feet were able to do so with impunity.

JASP Mark II incorporated some lessons learned from previous experience, especially from JASP Mark I. Though by this stage not overoptimistic about the likely contributions of ministers nor about the enthusiasm of their departments, the CPRS took care to build both parties into the JASP process. It also successfully built into the rules of the exercise the assumption that JASP reports would be published, thus alerting the relevant constituencies outside government, as possible sources of pressure for changes which departments left to themselves were often reluctant to make. (The outstanding case of the opposite approach had been the CPRS race relations report of 1974 which, unpublished and unpopular, was studiously ignored by all concerned until the disasters of which it had warned duly came to pass in the spring of 1981.) The weakness of this tactic in practice was that most JASP reports were published only shortly before or, in some cases, actually after the CPRS had disengaged from JASP and could thus not exploit any pressure thus generated.

Five years after the CPRS had disengaged itself from JASP it found itself once again, for the last time, commenting on trends and priorities in welfare spending. In the summer of 1982 Mrs Thatcher's Cabinet asked the CPRS to suggest some options for major cuts in public spending. On the basis of figures supplied by the Treasury, and after a rapid survey of the possibilities, the CPRS produced a summary list of options. Not many were likely to produce savings on the scale required. The few that did included the effective dismantling of the National Health Service and its replacement by a private insurance scheme. The political row generated by the leaking of the CPRS paper, and of this option in particular, in *The Economist* was to be a major influence on Mrs Thatcher's decision, less than a year later, to dismantle the CPRS itself. It was a melancholy ending to the history of the CPRS involvement in questions of social policies.

REFERENCES

1 Private information
2 Richard Crossman (1977) *Diaries of a Cabinet Member*, vol. 3, pp. 128–9, Hamish Hamilton and Jonathan Cape
3 Cmnd 4506 (1970) *The Reorganisation of Central Government*, HMSO
4 Central Policy Review Staff (1977) *Relations between Central Government and Local Authorities*, HMSO

5 Lord Hunt of Tanworth (1983) *Cabinet Strategy and Management*, paper given to RIPA/CIPFA Conference, 9 June 1983

6 Barbara Castle (1980) *The Castle Diaries, 1974–76*, p. 389, Weidenfeld & Nicolson

7 Central Policy Review Staff (1975) *A Joint Framework for Social Policies*, HMSO

8 Central Policy Review Staff (1977) *Relations between Central Government and Local Authorities*, HMSO

9 Central Policy Review Staff (1977) *Population and the Social Services*, HMSO

10 See Susan Crosland (1982) *Tony Crosland*, Jonathan Cape, pp. 306–7

11 Castle, *op. cit.*, pp. 669–70

12 Castle, *op. cit.*, p. 670, note 1

13 Central Policy Review Staff (1978) *Housing and Social Policies: Some Interactions*, HMSO; *Services for Children with Working Mothers*, HMSO

14 Private information: this and later quotations for which no references are given are drawn from interviews with serving civil servants and former ministers carried out between July 1981 and April 1982

15 Hunt, *op. cit.*

16 Discussion with author

5 ～ *Policy coordination: a view of Whitehall*

An enthusiasm for rational planning begot JASP, but by the end of the 1970s both appeared to have gone the way of the neap tides of administrative reform: consigned to the history books of modern government. Nonetheless, one might expect to find that some areas of administrative life were modified in a lasting way by the passage of these powerful ideas. It was with this thought in mind that we studied the problems and processes of coordination in the central government departments – the Department of Health and Social Security (DHSS), the Department of Education and Science (DES), and the Department of the Environment (DoE) – most closely involved with policies towards the two 'tracers' discussed in chapters 2 and 3.

A PARADOX AND AN ANALYTICAL FRAMEWORK

Our research, conducted in the early 1980s, revealed a paradox: policy coordination is pervasive and yet conspicuous by its absence. It is the bread and butter of life in Whitehall, yet it rarely grips the imagination, intellect or enthusiasm of key actors in the way envisaged by the architects of JASP. One explanation of this paradox is simply that coordination is a far from simple idea and phenomenon. It may be undertaken in a variety of ways and for a variety of reasons.

For example, the DHSS tried to develop strategic planning across the health and personal social services during the 1960s and 1970s, producing a unique priorities document during the period of 'resource shock' in the mid 1970s[1]. The department continues, albeit more narrowly, to try to link the policies and resource flows of these services[2]. It also attempts to examine fundamental questions, such as the broad allocation of resources between social security, health and personal social services.

Similarly, there have been instances of interdepartmental coordination – or attempts at it. Both our tracer groups have been the subject of jointly agreed policy statements since the mid 1970s[3]. In the case of the elderly, the White Papers *A Happier Old Age* and *Growing Older*[4] were evidence of this, as was the major expansion in specialist housing for old people involving increased cooperation between the DHSS and DoE. Interaction in respect of the elderly has consisted mainly of an interdepartmental working group, the circulation of draft papers, bilateral meetings between DHSS, DoE and DES, and similar meetings between these departments and the various pressure groups which comprise the 'elderly lobby'. Interest in policy for the elderly has been strong and growing, with policy coordination a goal in the days of both growth and retrenchment. It is the likelihood of major and beneficial developments in service provision which has changed – for the worse – as resources have diminished.

By contrast, the under-fives have been the subject of more fickle government interest. They were briefly the focus of interest in the mid 1970s and in recent years attention has again been focused on this group, although less intensively and with less optimism. During periods of strong interest, policy coordination – especially across departmental boundaries – was *the* issue in relation to the under-fives. Partly because of this and partly because the under-fives are more precisely identified as a distinctive client group by pressure groups than by government departments, the coordinative mechanisms have differed from those for the elderly. The need to create a public forum in which outside agencies and government departments could talk has been greater and attempts have been made to meet this need. More noticeably than with a major client group like the elderly, the initial interest in the under-fives depended upon hopes of growth with which to fuel developments. The subsequent resurgence of interest was an attempt, in the face of resource shortage, to counter-balance the marginality of the under-fives to established lines of policy making: an attempt to modify priorities by coordinated action rather than, as with the elderly, to coordinate priorities across major programmes.

As these brief sketches indicate, strategic coordination itself can take a variety of forms. However, we were also forced to recognise that a vast amount of coordination takes place as a matter of routine without producing the kinds of results, or even the broad perspectives on problems and issues, which JASP was designed to achieve. What we have just identified as routine coordination seemed to exist alongside and yet almost independent of what we have already described as strategic coordination. Indeed, we will argue that the former could even militate against the latter. To understand our topic we must therefore explain why so much coordination of one kind yields comparatively so little of the synoptic coordination which lies at the heart of the rational approach to planning public affairs. In addition, we need to trace the extent to which – if at all – the JASP era promoted a long-term shift in favour of synoptic or strategic coordination in the culture and machinery of the central government departments most closely involved in social policy matters.

In order to pursue further the elusive nature of coordination in Whitehall, we will outline our findings using the simple framework which is redeployed in later chapters. First, we will deal with barriers to coordination and the nature of the problem posed by them. Second, we will explore factors which facilitate coordination and increase the likelihood of its taking place. Third, we will note some of the key costs, benefits, incentives and disincentives which influence the actions of individuals, groups, sections, departments and whole organisations. Part of our purpose is to begin to trace the interlocking nature of structures, processes and action within administrative systems. Despite the problems involved, we clearly see the need for explanations which span these different levels of abstraction and analysis.

BARRIERS TO COORDINATION

The barriers to policy coordination are legion. They include incompatibilities in the basic division of labour adopted by different departments or sections: for example, the client group perspective at the heart of much DHSS policy compared with the functional pattern in the DoE and DES. More prosaic, but as important, can be the degree of correspondence between the pace of policy development in different sections or departments. 'It is very difficult', one civil servant noted, 'to keep our attitudes and theirs in step. This is not because we have different views, but because one has moved an inch forward before the other.'

Less prosaic is the question of departmental styles. These vary considerably, the differences often causing confusion and sometimes hostility. One such difference is departments' knowledge of and sympathy for local government. A spokesman for one of the local authority associations claimed that the civil service as a whole misunderstands local government. He spoke of a 'hierarchy of incompetence and misunderstanding', with the worst department being the Home Office which has key responsibilities but 'no idea or understanding of how local authorities are run'. In his view, the DoE, because it is so dominated by financial negotiations, finds it 'very difficult to relax and go out to find about local government' – with the exception of specialists such as those in the housing field.

In addition to department styles, ministerial styles differ substantially and change more frequently. Ministers can foster or stifle initiative in their civil servants. They can induce introspection and defensiveness or encourage imagination.

Underlying these various factors, however, are three fundamental barriers: policy ownership; policy streams; and policy implementation.

Policy ownership

Government depends on how a complex division of labour and policy issues, or territories, come to be 'owned' by departments, divisions, sections and even individuals. Respect for these territorial boundaries is culturally entrenched: it is the first law of administrative etiquette. For example, asked what would happen if he attempted active coordination, one civil servant replied that he 'would probably be told to mind [his] own business'. There was, he agreed, a sense in which discrete areas of policy are self-contained cells, or the property of the particular division or branch, unless the minister says otherwise. Clearly demarcated territories 'owned' by different groups may possibly be spanned by resource allocation issues, or by ministers, but not easily by other divisions or sectors. 'Anything else', he said, 'tends to happen when individuals are motivated and tend to chance their arm.' At his own level people were 'building their empire and keeping quiet. But at Under Secretary level if they were bright and pushy – they could start a minute by saying "it is not my business" but then carry on and get away with it, or not. They need to be motivated or have the time to do it, but the system does not provide for it.'

Such 'ownership' also has a strong interdepartmental dimension. Issues of particular sensitivity to one department can become 'no-go areas' for related departments. Ownership of policy territory can also extend to outside organisations which come to be seen as the 'property' of particular departments or divisions. Thus, the DES wished to encourage links between the Pre-School Play Groups Association and the schools; but 'to some extent this cut across the DHSS who saw them as theirs'. This despite the fact that DES gave them a grant.

Policy ownership can give rise to tunnel vision as well as to respect for others' territories. When asked who was doing the wider thinking on a particular issue, one interviewee replied that 'our thinking is limited to what we will pay for'. But policy ownership is of particular interest because it helps to explain the paradox outlined earlier. A division of labour implies the need for continuous and detailed coordination on countless mundane issues. Information has to be exchanged across boundaries so as to achieve any, even a minimal, sense of purpose and coherence. What we have described as routinised coordination is the essential lubricant in any specialised and complex administrative machine. Yet routine coordination, far from leading on automatically to more generalised forms of coordination, may become a key barrier to the kind of strategic coordination envisaged in JASP. Not pushing matters of strategic significance which cut across or challenge existing patterns of ownership is a price willingly and frequently paid in order to maintain good day-to-day coordination on routine matters. Routine coordination respects and depends upon the rules of administrative etiquette; strategic coordination almost inevitably threatens them.

It would be wrong, however, to imply that a species of chauvinism characterises the civil service merely for reasons of administrative convenience. The whole system is founded on 'policy ownership'; ministers may find it as difficult to overstep boundaries as do civil servants[5]. For all but the most bullish ministers, mutual agreement with colleagues or the sanction of higher authority are usually preferred to bruising conflict if sensitive boundaries are to be crossed. Conversely, for all but the most 'altruistic' ministers, and departments, the pressure on resources also ensures that budgets are spent on programmes at the core of the department's remit; normal levels of resource scarcity tend to reinforce the boundaries established by policy ownership. As was noted:

Naturally a DOE minister will be reluctant to use housing money for a responsibility which statutorily belonged to the DHSS. I expect this [the reluctance to take on expenditure outside the remit] becomes more pertinent when there is no money around.

The cabinet and cabinet committee systems may seem to offer a ready means of crossing boundaries; but 'generally cabinet committees get involved where there are disputes between ministers or only where final approval has to be given'. The cabinet system usually works within the system of policy ownership and affects only marginal adjustments to it; strategic overviews can be attempted only on a limited number of fronts at a time. The limits which 'policy ownership' place on a minister's ability to assess issues beyond the departmental remit was the main reason for creating the Central Policy Review Staff in the first place[6]. Central government simply does not naturally or normally operate as a corporate system. Moreover, because of the relatively low status of social policy, strategic coordination is less of an issue at the highest cabinet level in social than in economic and foreign policy. At times this 'natural pecking order' is reinforced by other political factors. One prescient interviewee claimed that:

the CPRS is petrified that if it offends the Prime Minister it will be cut out. She has her own policy advisors at Number 10 and the CPRS has had to be very good and take what is handed to it. Therefore it has worked mainly in the economic field.

The process of drawing boundaries around policy fields is one which involves parliament and the control of public expenditure as well as ministers and civil servants in policy divisions. Legislation embodies duties and powers which administrations can interpret either narrowly within the confines of traditional boundaries or more creatively. The steadily increasing need for supported living for old people which falls between sheltered housing and residential care (Part III accommodation) provides a good example. It has required DOE and DHSS jointly to create and maintain a hybrid form of care – 'part two and a half'. The attempt has been reasonably successful, 'But only up to a point. In the movement to "two and a half" there is pressure on us to accommodate people in marginal areas ... We are always bending the rules so far as you can bend them, but that's still at the margin. We cannot go "beyond legal powers or budgeting powers".'

One civil servant, referring to the joint finance proposals[7] – another boundary spanning programme (discussed in chapter 3 and below) – argued that the Treasury took a similar view to the DHSS Finance Division: 'they viewed it with suspicion; Parliament votes money for one thing and ministers want to use it for another. That was how they saw it.'

In many fields the basic structural and procedural barriers created by 'policy ownership' are exacerbated by professionalisation. The helping professions may sometimes work together enthusiastically for the good of the client, but different professions perceive problems differently and have divergent views about solutions. Moreover protection of professional paradigms can also be overlaid by the defence of status and salary differentials. Administrative civil servants can be crucial creators and arbiters of inter-professional discussion, but gulfs between professions may remain.

Policy streams

'Policy ownership' refers to specialisation within and between departments in relation to groups of clients and types of service. The existence of policy streams reveals a different pattern of divisions in the work of government: one which is also deeply entrenched. As we noted in chapter 2, Webb and Wistow have identified three principal streams: service, or output, policies; resource policies; and governance policies[8]. The first refers to policies about needs and services and is institutionalised in the professions and in the 'policy divisions' of the social policy departments. Until now we have been discussing the problems of coordinating policies *within* this stream. However, the second and third streams are just as important and coordination across them is as vital as coordination within the service stream.

This is obviously true of service and resource policies. There seems little point in committing the government to an objective and then not willing the means; but it happens – frequently. One way of trying to alleviate the problem is to develop a strategic plan which relates service policy objectives and matches them to resource flows. It implies a high standard of strategic planning. The introduction of programme budgeting, the PESC (Public Expenditure Scrutiny) system and the consultations about Rate Support Grant (RSG) were all intended to achieve such a strategic synthesis. In practice they have produced scant coordination between service and resource policies.

It was made clear to us that these strategic decision making processes offer only a very limited incentive for spending departments to coordinate their policies. PESC, for instance, operates on the basis of bilateral discussions between spending departments and the Treasury. As for contact between spending departments, the news from one department was that 'we would not see it in terms of putting our stalls out, we would not naturally see any merit in work in concert with DHSS'. This is partly because the processes are 'coarse grain' exercises dealing with major issues in the 'division of the spoils', partly because bilateral relations with the Treasury continue to be of prime importance (and reinforce rather than challenge 'policy ownership'), partly because departments which agree on a mutually advantageous pattern of resource flows cannot guarantee that the Treasury will support the bargain, and partly because the uncertainty of public expenditure control vitiates all such planning.

The latter point was made repeatedly and emphatically. Public expenditure processes have become increasingly supply-led rather than need- and demand-led. Consequently, resource policies dominate rather than complement service policies; this pattern of dominance provides little encouragement for strategic planning. One interviewee spoke of his department having to reconcile conflicting policy objectives:

For example, that the [most needy] should not be neglected at a time when local government is being told to hold down its expenditure. Ministers say there is a lot of fat and they may be right, but local authorities squeeze across the board ... Therefore, we're often in difficulties because messages coming down are contradictory in terms of clashes of ministerial policies and also as between the general and the particular.

Another senior civil servant held that the present government, in effect, said that it did not believe it worthwhile to forecast future need. 'It follows inexorably', he said, 'that this affects our strategic role ... Yet again this year local authorities have been told to have a second go at their budgets. There is little point in building a forward plan on such uncertain data.'

Finance is not, however, the only component of resource policies: the 'manpower watch' has been a complicating factor for all authors of service policies for some years. Our research suggests that the development of strategic expenditure planning machinery has promoted little detailed coordination between service planning and resource allocation planning. This is borne out, for example, by the apparent lack of relationship between the distribution of resources to health service districts, to local authorities through the RSG, and to localities through urban programmes. However, this lack of 'fine tuning' pales into insignificance alongside the growing dominance of supply-led expenditure control and its impact on policy coordination.

The significance of the governance policy stream is less immediately obvious but has been fundamental, especially since 1979: 'this is a government with a policy about government', and that policy has greatly complicated implementation. In particular it has complicated central government's relationships with local government at a time when implementation has become the major issue. As it was put to us, 'there is no great impetus to develop policies – the problem is to get the policies we have adequately implemented, given constraints on manpower and resources'. The basic philosophy of upholding local authority autonomy on matters of service policy – though not on aggregate expenditure decisions – has been reinforced by an enthusiasm for decentralisation. Quite apart from any philosophical attractions, the approach has the distinct advantage that it decentralises blame for service inadequacies.[9]

One of the basic tenets of this government – and of the last – is that government allocates and holds resources but that services ... are entirely a matter for the local authorities.

The unintended consequences of this policy about governance can best be illustrated by considering the complexities of policy implementation.

Policy implementation
In education, health, housing and the personal social services, central government can set broad policy aims and detailed specifications but implementation depends upon local statutory and voluntary agencies. The government's emphasis on 'decentralisation' as a principal approach to governance is therefore directly relevant to policy implementation. From the perspective of local policy coordination, central government can appear supportive or extremely unhelpful. Local authorities and voluntary agencies might be expected to coordinate their policies in either of two contexts: that of detailed, complementary and well-articulated central policies; or that of a laissez-faire regime which nonetheless removed or avoided the creation of barriers to local coordination.

Current government philosophy does not support the former, but interpretations of the philosophy vary considerably amongst and within departments. The DHSS, for example, has to operate its three services quite differently: the centralised social security system in which local discretion is limited; the partially centralised national health service in which professional autonomy is strong; and the decentralised personal social services in which local authority professionals nonetheless are managed. Despite such variations there has been a long-standing attempt to develop detailed policy objectives and guidelines, spanning the health and personal social services in particular. The commitment to this approach is reflected structurally in the department's client group system. On the other hand, DOE is not organised to develop strategies for client groups and appears to take a laissez-faire approach; but it regards itself as far more willing than DHSS to maximise local 'steerability' through the allocation of resources. The housing association lobby, we were told, had tried to persuade ministers that instead of relying upon local sources for 'topping up' there ought to be a central fund: 'the argument is that the DHSS should withhold some of their money [to create such a central fund], but it offends their theological ideas of local needs and local divisions'.

Such variations in 'steerability' and in the interpretation of governance policy, produce major barriers to coordination in both the centre and localities. In respect of DOE and DHSS 'there are two different feed lines down the departments ... They are mismatched systems for delivering the goods to customers. If the one gives out, then the other necessarily fails.' Given these problems, the prerequisite for effective local coordination is that central departments be cognisant of local circumstances and of their impact on local policy environments. However, the traditional lack of such monitoring is a fundamental obstacle to central support for coordinated local action. Inspectorates, regional offices and policy divisions are well used to monitoring the local provision of specific services but consideration of whether local *joint* working is being fostered seems exceptional. That it is not the rule was made evident by the interviewee who, when asked how far the department has responsibility for monitoring or promoting collaboration between education and the personal social services at local level, replied:

It does not do it. In a general sense the government attempts to promote corporatism [sic] but I do not know of any attempts to monitor what happens at the level of local authorities, though there is a close contact ... on identified issues on which coordination is essential, e.g. the Warnock Report. In addition, we separately – through our own links with the locality – try to foster it, but we do not have direct knowledge of how far it is developing.

The low priority accorded to policy implementation and to the impact of central government on localities reflects the civil service culture in which priority is given to supporting ministers in their policy making role. The system ensures that the workers dance attendance on the queen bee, but it does not guarantee the production of honey. One example was revealed in discussing the problem posed for DOE by the reluctance of elderly people to bear the disruption associated with housing improvement. Such people need support; social workers and home helps – for who the DHSS is responsible – are one source of such support. However, the potential role of DOE and

DHSS in jointly fostering such local collaboration seems not even to have been recognised.

Despite these barriers and implied governmental shortcomings, examples of policy coordination can be found. They may not be numerous or spectacular in relation to needs, but they provide evidence that – given certain opportunities and incentives – the major difficulties of structure, culture, personality and political philosophy can occasionally be overcome. In this section we discuss two such facilitating factors; others are discussed in the later section on costs and benefits. The first concerns the intellectual climate and values which can lend support to policy coordination and may even generate a culturally engrained belief in its importance. The second is that of organisational machinery: we consider which mechanisms in central government, if any, positively promote policy coordination and whether the JASP era led to their development.

Village life

One view of government which emerges from discussions with civil servants and which has been emphasised by academic observers[10] is that of close informal relationships and contacts comprising a 'Whitehall village'. This village is not strictly confined within the parish boundaries of Whitehall but includes voluntary organisations, bodies like the local authority associations, and innumerable other interest groups. To what extent might it foster coordination through personal contacts and communications?

Village life depends upon informal but patterned relationships and upon centres of social contact. For all but the most senior civil servants, however, informal interaction is increasingly confined to the most mundane settings – the office canteen, for example. Informal contacts take on greater significance and a different tone within the field of interaction between government and outside organisations, however. One interviewee from the voluntary sector said that, 'If I have any influence it is over lunch and the sort of meetings I have with X; we trust each other, we know the game and are sophisticated people ... The rules of the game are, first of all – to achieve any objectives – you must work both within and without the system.'

Informal relationships are important in their own right and also facilitate more formal relationships. Care is taken in managing informal contacts, and meeting on neutral ground is an important means of distancing people from their formal roles and freeing discourse: hence the importance of clubs and restaurants to this part of 'village life'.

Informal relationships with ministers are at least as important to bodies like voluntary organisations as those with key civil servants, but they depend upon a different and more prestigious social round. We were assured that one of the great strengths of a particular voluntary body director was that:

he has meetings with all ministers; he is involved in the post-5 o'clock circuit – the cocktail and dinner circuit. This has been facilitated by the past and present chairman ... The extent to which ministers take you seriously is whether they recognise your face.

It was even held that 'coordination works better on an informal basis, because we meet when we want to meet because there are things to discuss'. Yet neither the office canteen nor the Pall Mall club is an adequate substitute for the village pump. The very size of Whitehall – not to mention the rest of the policy-making system – falsifies the village life analogy. The major limitation to an informal approach to coordination is precisely that there are countless *small* networks, none of which matches the scale and complexity of the coordination task. The patterns and limits of these networks are set largely by conventional assumptions about the issues and roles which need to be closely related. Informal village life merely builds on and strengthens more formal approaches to coordination; it does not wholly displace them.

Keeping informed: the culture of consultation

Consultation comprises a more patterned system of interaction underlying informal contacts. It is essential to the business of government; knowing who to consult and when is a central characteristic of the good civil servant. Within the civil service itself one form of consultation – keeping people informed – is routinised at a very low level of formality. 'We do exchange a lot of papers' was a continuing refrain in our interviews. 'Photocopying has made this kind of joint working possible. A great deal of material is copied.' Additionally, there is 'a tradition of spreading information widely about departments.'

Coordination by Xerox (and telephone) is basic to work within and across departments, but it raises real problems of discrimination and also depends upon the openness of the source: keeping developments secret violates norms about consultation, but is comparatively easy in an informal system. The system also depends on the judgement, alertness and memory of the source: 'there is a lot of overlap and there is the problem that we may forget to keep them informed'. However, the demands and pressures of the flow of work help overcome some of these defects by creating networks between individuals and groups who might not work closely in a purely informal system. This may be especially important in strengthening contacts across departmental boundaries. It is important to stress – as a number of civil servants did – that 'a lot of ordinary departmental work is interdepartmental work'.

There's a tendency to assume that departments consult on policies and go away and work separately, but in practice policy is in a constant state of being made and remade. Therefore a great volume of work is day-to-day work which has a formative role in policy because it creates a common awareness of problems which each department handles.

Such routine contacts arise in response to a variety of stimuli, notably parliamentary questions and debates, pressure group action and comments from field authorities.

The diversity of reasons for 'keeping in touch' on issues was repeatedly stressed. Informal consultation to coordinate views was seen by all civil servants as a central and routine feature of their work. All departments must respond to parliamentary and ministerial stimuli, but those which are closely involved with 'service' professions (e.g. DHSS and DES) tend also to be alert to these professions' opinions, as expressed in conferences and the 'trade press' and by members of the professions working within the departments. DOE seems to be less affected by such external pressures. Nevertheless, like other departments, it maintains contact with the field through Regional Controllers, and this provides an 'external' source of issues which prompt informal consultation.

While routine work clearly generates much informal consultation, this guarantees neither cooperation nor a response. As one civil servant remarked wearily:

There always seems to have been some 'Jaspery' as part of my remit – always trying to see that others were aware of things which had implications for their services, and vice versa. But it was a total failure and when we even failed to get 'Social Security' to take an interest [in a particular issue], we just threw up our hands in despair and gave up.

Moreover, even if a response is obtained it is quite likely to be defensive and self-protective. 'Assistant secretaries', we were told, 'spend their lives considering services for their client groups and they were not anxious to let us have a free hand. Eventually we were ground down by their persistence – and some hostility.' One result is that 'you get lazy. If you have three days you know that you could go across and try and talk about housing or something, or you could spend those three days and really get something polished up within your own field. It is a picture of despair.'

However, structured attempts to promote policy are unlikely to depend wholly upon informal consultation. At some stage they will be formalised in the creation of an *ad hoc* working party or committee or in the circulation of a draft consultative document or white paper. The responses may be no more positive than those elicited by informal consultation, but some response is more likely because 'the stakes are higher'. This fact may also galvanise a formal group or working party into being as an effective system of consultation:

some committees serve an initial purpose in ensuring that particular people ... get a coordination function landed on them and [then] there is no need to meet. In theory there is an official committee on IYDP [International Year for Disabled People] but it has met about twice, though an enormous amount of paper has been distributed through the network and acted on ... We did much the same with *Growing Older* ... a steering committee ... settled the general scope of the document ... but it rarely met as a group because the work was handled bilaterally or through the distribution of drafts.

Formal consultation through the distribution of drafts has traditionally been at the heart of relations between government departments and outside organisations. It is an essential element in honing bright ideas down to implementable policies. For governments such consultation is often vital; for outside organisations it is often of little value because it is at the 'post-strategic thinking phase'. For many organisations these formal contacts may provide the basis for more informal and more useful relationships, but such contacts will be made only with organisations which departments trust.

It was the shortcomings of this traditional system and culture, in which coordination is routinised, which prompted the enthusiasm for rational planning in the 1970s. The basic criticism of the traditional approach was that strategic thinking and policy coordination were forgotten in the detail of daily work. It is important not to underestimate the importance of routine work and informal relations, nor their cultural milieu. In so far as the enthusiasm for rational planning has increased awareness of the need for strategic thinking, induced a commitment to a system-wide viewpoint, and encouraged a broad perspective on the costs and benefits of acting in different ways, it may have enhanced the capacity of the traditional system to handle strategic issues.

Coordination: culture or fashion?
One view of coordination is that it is a hallowed tradition embedded in the culture of the civil service, cabinet, government, and parliament. The informal processes described above fit neatly into this picture. A cogent summary of why coordination is culturally embedded was provided in the observation that:

the costs of not cooperating are so great one can't forge on regardless. Snags all the way would mean that the machine of government had collapsed. Administration is run by large departmental ships of state, one can't proceed on assumption, one has simply got to accept the ... need to collaborate.

What this argument does, quite aptly, is present an essentially defensive case for routinised coordination: government cannot afford the costs of disorganisation. However, the case for strategic coordination was presented in altogether more positive terms by the CPRS: a synoptic approach was intended to increase the likelihood of achieving ambitious goals. Has this vision been incorporated into the culture of Whitehall? The most 'pessimistic' thesis is that the heightened interest in coordination during the late 1960s and the 1970s was a purely temporary phenomenon. As described to us it was merely a changing fashion: 'Departments are too entrenched to change'. Collaboration, JASP, the Planned Programme Budgeting System (PPBS) and even the 'think tank' were all passing fashions: 'They are all sent to plague us ... coping with the plague is just another part of being effective in the job.' One version of this thesis associates the declining interest in systematic coordination with the rejection of rational synoptic planning after the Tories came to power in 1979. Throughout this administration coordination has been 'on the retreat ... and become associated with detailed planning ... which is anathema to the present ministers'. The CPRS, other central analytical units, and a concerted approach to social policy were also regarded as largely matters of fashion: such units, it was said, 'go up and down'; and with the CPRS 'on the wane, so are other similar units'.

However, it was not only rational planning and such units which were vulnerable after 1979. The emergence of a new political style was mentioned repeatedly in our interviews, as was its importance in shaping relations between the government and other agencies. One voluntary sector comment was that this government 'behaves strangely', outlining programmes without any prior consultation but with extensive consultation subsequently. One explanation for such behaviour and for changes in established procedures was that it does not occur to the government 'that the voluntary sector is part of the social and economic life of the country and that it can't operate locally unless it has sustainable relationships with local authorities, trades councils, etc.... wage levels are central to economic policy and there is an unholy alliance between that and thoughts about the voluntary sector as cheap labour.'

Other explanations of the government's style were the capriciousness of individual ministers and the poor relations with the civil service, described by one interviewee as worse than any he had known. In his view ministers spring policies that are 'way down the road' from where they want to be, then move back 'and end up with something further down the road than if [they] had worked in the traditional way of trying to move towards a consensus'. However, this strategy for defending radical change by circumventing the search for consensus was also seen to shade into traditional interdepartmental conflict.

To these outsiders' views of the impact of political change must be added the insider's experience of the impact of a minimalist philosophy. Public expenditure had been pruned by previous governments, but after 1979 reductions were to be one element in a broader move away from state provision and involvement. The number of civil servants was to fall and their involvement in and responsibility for social policy was to become more remote:

> As there is a closing in we are feeling our way towards new ways of working ... less work can be done, more work is spread wider, we spend more time on questioning how we are doing ... it is a bit like a sandcastle collapsing inwards. We are simply not operating on an expansive basis any more. [In] the heyday of setting up large-scale monitoring procedures, that was seen as a correct central government responsibility. Now the message is to leave it to local authorities to move away from the 'narrowing' role of central government ...

If these quotations convey an impression of an inchoate policy world in which consultation as well as more analytically elaborate approaches to coordination have been discarded, it is important to emphasise that it is a view from one standpoint in the early years of a government pursuing radical change. It is also important to note that the remarks refer only to the handling of new policy initiatives. Some areas of well-established policy were identified, such as the Urban Aid programme, where consultation was well developed and provided a good base for policy discussion. Nevertheless, the potential importance of government style cannot be doubted in general, nor can the sharp shift in fashion away from the more elaborate approaches to policy coordination.

Demands for strategic coordination have continued to surface. The problem has not gone away just because the rational, synoptic approach has become unfashionable. The new style of government ushered in after 1979 has espoused coordination by the assertion of political will. In many respects, the *status quo ante* has been re-established, albeit in a more dramatic form. This new intellectual climate has caused problems for the tradition of widespread consultation and routinised coordination, as we have seen, but its implications for JASP have been altogether more fundamental. It has counteracted the beliefs and values of the 'optimistic' tradition and prevented it from gaining a firm foothold in the culture of Whitehall. But what of the approach to the machinery of government favoured by the rational planners: the creation of think tanks, policy units and coordinating committees? Did the JASP era succeed in transforming the Whitehall method of working, even if it failed to implement new ways of thinking?

Beyond informality: departmental structures

We have already indicated the importance of routine patterns of work and conventional assumptions about which issues and roles should be brought together. The organisation of the work of government departments fundamentally reflects the second of these and determines the first. None of the departments we looked at had been restructured after JASP. Their structures varied considerably and reflected different approaches to the organisation of work and the coordination of policy.

The DHSS, reorganised in 1972[11], is an interesting example of the impact of structure on work routines and relationships. It faces an enormous task of strategic coordination because it spans a number of professions and semi-professions, incorporates the disparate roles of professionals and administrators, embraces three major functional areas, and is responsible for many client groups (e.g. the elderly in general, the mentally handicapped and the mentally ill). For us, a central and interesting feature was the system of client group teams within the Service Development Group. These were developed specifically as a coordinative device which would harmonise inputs from the various professionals, administrators and different functional specialisms relevant to each client group. Four principal client groups were delineated in this way: children; the mentally ill and mentally handicapped; the elderly and physically handicapped; and the socially handicapped (homeless people, substance abusers etc.). For each group the basic structure is similar. The team is led by administrative civil servants – usually an assistant secretary and principals – and includes designated social work, nursing and medical colleagues. Although nominally a team of equals, 'willy nilly it is *primus inter pares* with the administrators in the Chair because they have the line to the minister and they do the writing ... when a crisis comes [they] are usually in the firing line and [are] very often the only ones who know the implications' of what is being done. The team handles many matters reactively, but is also the focal point around which policy is developed and experience of the field synthesised: 'virtually any issue affecting the group will be discussed there'.

However, the teams do not necessarily provide a simple solution to the coordination of different inputs and perspectives. There can be confusion about hierarchies with, for instance, a senior medical officer regarding himself as the equal of both the assistant secretary (on account of equal pay) and the principal (with whom he works). There can also be 'very considerable tensions' from a variety of sources which underline the need for specific coordinative mechanisms. Such tensions arise from differences of professional interest and perspective (e.g. doctor/nurse) and the conflict between professionals and administrators. According to one administrator:

Professionals do not have to meet ministers at 10 minutes' notice and produce answers off the top of their heads ... They do not realise how difficult it is to persuade ministers to do things or that if we do certain things they have spin-offs across the board ... For us, on the whole, ministerial business takes priority but it is difficult for them to accept this.

The professional members of client group teams have external reference groups whose interests and expectations may conflict sharply with the prevailing political ethos in which administrators must work. Thus the merit of having professionals in the DHSS could be said to be that of representing their professions' values and perspectives; acting as a 'fifth column' and not merely a source of technical information. In that sense the client group team would seem to be the point at which this input should be reconciled with the political input. In practice it is the administrators who reconcile these tensions within the team, not ministers. The latter are likely to be given professional perspectives only by the Chief Medical Officer or Chief Social Work Service Officer. It is hardly surprising, therefore, to find differing opinions among administrative civil servants about the whole concept of team work and about the merits of the professional. It was an ex-civil servant who was the most scornful. 'What', he asked, 'have they got to do with it? It is usually the administrators who make the decisions and the team who rubber-stamps them. Quite honestly I could have lost my team and not noticed the difference, it would not have mattered if I never saw them again ... don't think I'm being arrogant but they are not really up to it. Their saving grace is that they also know they are generally not up to it.'

The client group teams are only one mechanism for coordinating the multiple interests and issues of a complex department such as DHSS. Before considering other mechanisms, however, it is worth noting the contrast between DHSS and a department like DOE. Despite the fact that the work of the latter embraces a variety of technical fields, there are comparatively few service delivery professionals – unlike DHSS and DES. Housing management, for example, is not organised in the way that medicine and social work are in DHSS. In DOE, again, unlike DHSS and DES, specialisation is by function not by client group: responsibility for housing is spread across three divisions. As a result, coherent policy for, say, the elderly in this field 'would only be created by working across the grain'. But is this systematically attempted in the case of the elderly for whom housing policies are crucial? Does DOE, even if not creating a policy for them, at least examine those policies which affect the elderly? In answer to these questions we were told that:

There are no organisational inhibitions on that, it is just that it has not happened in that manner. But there are other ways, especially in this department: ministerially – he likes to take a keynote subject and work it up, giving a paper to an elderly pressure group or lobby, this draws on an informal group ... There are benefits and penalties in working that way: the penalty is that it occurs at a hell of a pace; the benefits, that it concentrates the mind and obstacles get removed.

DOE depends upon the flow of work – and especially ministerial interest – to cut across functional divisions: in DHSS this route to coordination is *additional* to the structural provision for handling client group policy. In principle there are other mechanisms for promoting a coherent approach to the elderly in DOE: for example, the allocation of resources to special need groups. The PESC housing allocation is shared between new towns, housing associations and housing authorities. The latter's share is divided up between DOE regions using a generalised needs index (GNI). But it is a 'wholly mechanistic process'. The ministerial decision on the housing associations' share is followed by meetings with the Housing Corporation to agree a programme covering all aspects of housing association work in which 'there is always some earmarked money for the elderly'. In making regional allocations the corporation uses a modified GNI 'with a further nod towards the elderly ... as housing association tenures are heavily concentrated on the elderly'. In addition there is an inner city weighting. All this leads to an Approved Development Programme. DOE regions allocate housing authorities their share following meetings between regional controllers and each authority. The basis of the allocation is partly a localised GNI and partly a local discretionary element (LDE)[12]. The former is 'a set of indicators of general relevance', whereas the latter is there 'for local humpiness and lumpiness' – a balance which housing authorities favour.

This element of discretion has prompted some housing departments to consult with social services departments about special housing needs in order to present a good case to the regional controller. Unintentionally, therefore, the DOE system facilitates *local* contact across departmental boundaries; but at central government there is no strong incentive to develop a coherent set of service policies for the elderly. The strategic decisions about their needs are seen primarily as the distribution of housing programme resources between authorities and functions, rather than as ends and policy objectives. More-over, this predominance of resource allocation decisions has increased in recent years as public expenditure on housing has been cut severely. In evidence to the Select Committee, the department has said, in effect, that it does not believe that forecasts of future housing needs are worthwhile[13]. The ethos is overwhelmingly that of implementing resource decisions: allocating shares of what ministers and the government are prepared to spend.

Paradoxically, therefore, while DOE lacks a clear set of client group policies it has much more 'steerability' than DHSS or DES. It substantially influences what housing departments can do because of their dependence upon capital expenditure. Traditionally, central government has controlled the latter much more closely than revenue expenditure, which is so dominant in health, personal social services, and education. On the other hand, the central department's contribution is a mechanistic allocation by formula, with discretion appearing mainly at the level of regional and local interaction. Strategic thinking about policies for client groups depends upon the interests of ministers; it is not institutionalised in the structure of the department.

Returning to DHSS as our prime exemplar, let us now examine the extent to which mechanisms exist for handling strategic issues above the level of client groups.

Mechanisms for strategic analysis

Simple administrative mechanisms exist for dealing with the complexity inherent in large government departments: for example, regular meetings between permanent secretaries and under secretaries, working parties, and committees of inquiry. Large working parties are currently out of favour because 'they are slow and you get big reports and then have to consult on them'. Assigning a coordinative role to an individual may become increasingly attractive and the development of the proposals published in *Care in the Community*[14] suggests that ministerial backing can make this an effective mechanism for cutting across divergent interests. Nevertheless, working groups will continue to play a role and, as we have seen, they can be instrumental in promoting informal networks and between departments.

Over and above these traditional devices, departments developed two mechanisms in the 1970s which are of particular interest because they seemed to provide for strategic analysis of the kind envisaged in JASP: departmental strategic committees; and policy units. In addition, the coordinative potential of financial planning and management must also be considered. None of these were specific products of the JASP initiative, but their emergence did reflect the steady growth of interest in synoptic planning from the mid 1960s onwards.

At the time of our research there were three strategy committees in DHSS. The Health and Social Services Committee (chaired by the Permanent Secretary) and the Social Security Strategy Committee (chaired by the Second Permanent Secretary) reflected the basic functional division within the department. The Cross-Sector Policy Review Group (chaired by the Chief Social Work Service Officer) recognised the problems posed by this division and was intended to span it. Together these three committees mirrored, at a high level, the more informal and routine interactions seen at lower levels. They also appeared to provide opportunities for handling the most fundamental policy issues. We were told however that 'the members of one of the committees were all too high level to know what was going on or to pick up on things early on, or they were not prepared to go back and ask their chaps to do work which was not germane to them'. The members were described as defensive and 'very willing to criticise each other'.

Whether wholly justified or not, the situation conveyed to us of a lack of direct knowledge of problems among senior officials bears out Tullock's comments on the 'winnowing' of information when strategic issues are not germane to day-to-day work and when a defensive, self-protective attitude prevails (see chapter 2). It also implies that any real progress is achieved by more direct means. Work on the problems of the disabled, backed by a minister, was cited as an example. Nevertheless, some issues such as the allocation of resources between DHSS functions can only be handled at a very high level and for these the strategy groups seem the appropriate mechanism. The balance of spending between social security and health and personal social services is crucial to the elderly, for example, and the possible need to switch resources has been discussed intermittently for many years.

At this highest level, however, the really crucial barriers which emerged were the many forces of inertia, rather than the composition, will, or competence of the strategic committees. One of the civil servants involved claimed that:

There are very great problems because it is only possible to make switches from social security to services. Anything off services (and onto social security) would go nowhere ... but the opportunities are very few given the constraints of the uprating of benefits. It would be very difficult to justify such a switch to politicians unless it was taken from one client group and given to the *same* client group. For example, the over-80s addition has become fossilised. If that were to be taken away and used for specific services such as extra domiciliary help for the vulnerable elderly, then it might be justifiable. But in practice it is very difficult to ensure that the cash transferred would benefit the over-80s. It might be possible to make that kind of switch at a time when public resources are increasing ... But this kind of issue does not go by default in the sense that no-one thinks about it.

The forces of inertia do not necessarily render the strategy committees ineffective, but even apparently marginal strategic adjustments can be thought to impose disproportionately large political and administrative costs. Even if the key issues are addressed systematically, change may not be achieved (though inhibitions about fundamental change have not prevented major restructuring and cuts in the DHSS pattern of expenditure – especially on social security – since the period of our fieldwork).

It is worth asking whether the same constraints applied to the quintessential example of a JASP approach within DHSS – the Policy Strategy Unit (PSU). At the time of our research, the Policy Strategy Unit was the latest in a succession of such arrangements; the need for a central analytical capacity having been recognised for some years. The unit consisted of a head, three full-time principals and three part-time professionals ('a doctor, an economist and a social scientist') drawn from other sections of the department at assistant secretary/senior principal level. In addition, the unit had access to outsiders.[15]

The unit's work could be divided into five main categories: providing the secretariat for the strategy committees and for the annual one-day, 'end-of-term' meeting of ministers and senior civil servants; undertaking a strategic overview of the department's work and remit; providing advice on policy presentation; receiving and commenting on all major departmental submissions to ministers; and undertaking specific studies. The original intention was that the unit would devote approximately two-thirds of its efforts to the last of these and that the topics studied would include both long- and short-term issues approved by ministers. The unit was intended explicitly to increase ministers' opportunities for looking at strategic questions, especially those spanning the department. It was a 'departmental CPRS'. Its relevance to the elderly client group was especially clear: a number of its studies were addressed directly to their needs. Its contribution to policy towards the under-fives was less clear.

At the time of our research the unit was less than a complete success and its fund of ministerial support was draining away. It had some successes, such as liaising with key figures in the voluntary sector to study the problem of alcoholism, but they were limited in number and impact. The main explanation for this lack of impact is that analytical units with a general remit depend for their effectiveness almost entirely upon overt and unambiguous backing at the highest level. Specialist – one issue – units (concentrating, for example, on the monitoring and review of capital expenditure) may successfully and quite rapidly obtain expertise and credibility, and establish a good network of contacts and relationships. The problem for the staff of a generalist unit, however, is that they have to roam around; they risk alienating many rather than consolidating relationships with a few. Only the keen edge of authoritative support can overcome this incubus – at least as far as effective *analytical* work is concerned. Without such support the likely survival route is to become an extension of the minister's office and undertake speech writing and related activities.

Beneath this explanation of the precariousness of general analytical units lies the fundamental problem that they run counter to basic civil service traditions and attitudes. The defence of domain is an integral feature of policy ownership and the investment in one's own 'patch' can be especially strong at the level of assistant secretary and under secretary. Most under secretaries and many assistant secretaries can expect no further promotion; there is time, therefore, to 'dig in' and protect the integrity of their patch, thereby preserving control over their work environment. But it is precisely at this level that the generalist policy unit must, to be effective, cut across the departmental division of labour – a division which encourages caution and incrementalism and which limits synoptic and radical thinking. Such thinking would also pose the real threat that experience and accumulated wisdom would be lightly discarded. As one interviewee remarked:

Departmental feathers were ruffled by the thought that a free floating unit was going to take them on. It was worrying for them and not really without grounds, they were worried over whether such people had either the knowledge or experience to come up with anything sensible.

Policy units, like most other devices for affecting strategic policy coordination, can be relatively easily neutralised. Access to information is crucial to analytical success and a combination of starvation and overfeeding can rapidly disrupt the analytical digestive system. Policy units are not staffed so generously as to enable them to seek essential information on more than a few topics at a time and they are therefore dependent upon crucial papers (e.g. ministerial submissions) being sent to them. Unless they have unwavering and overt support from the top, or attractive benefits to offer policy divisions in return for cooperation, the likelihood of being by-passed at least some of the time is great. Even given overt support, the 'wheelbarrow' technique can be used to overload a unit with trivia and divert its energies into digesting material which the suppliers would be better placed to sift and select. Work on selected topics can also be subverted: by obstructionism, by charges of naivety and ignorance of the essential background and detail, and – at the last ditch – by ensuring that potentially attractive and apparently successful proposals for change are taken out of the policy unit's hands at the implementation stage, leaving the unit to move onto other things and the proposed change to run into the sand.

All these problems can be overcome if one or more conditions prevail: heads of divisions and sections have a strong commitment to a goal which transcends their sectional interests; policy units have incentives and rewards to offer those on whom they depend for cooperation; the leadership and authority of those in power are systematically and continuously used to support the synoptic, analytical viewpoint and task.

The first of these implies altruistic behaviour on the part of sectional interests or a recognition of common, superordinate interests. The personal interests of career and a good working environment are unlikely to sponsor such a viewpoint on their own. A corporate way of working at senior level is one way of trying to offset the centrifugal pull of sectional interests, but it is only weakly developed in most central government departments and it has delivered much less than it promised even in local government. The prevailing values and philosophy of senior staff are therefore a crucial determinant of the balance struck between sectional and synoptic thinking. In the case of DHSS, several senior civil servants claimed that the structure and style of the department promoted a generous breadth of vision. Our own glimpses of the department at work provided some evidence for this view, but also for the argument that a retreat into traditional policy ownership is the natural tendency when the going gets tough. Generally, there can be little doubt that attitudes in policy divisions are sufficiently wary as to necessitate additional sources of support for policy units.

The second possibility, that of inducements to cooperate, is of limited value to *generalist* policy units precisely because they are generalist and do not control many of the short-term rewards for cooperation – especially access to resources and specialist expertise – which operational divisions can often offer each other. The third possibility – support from the top – is therefore likely to be the prime determinant of the success of policy units in whatever department. The backing needed is that which can be provided only by permanent secretaries and ministers. The former are crucial, but they have been socialised into the civil service traditions and in some cases may be unwilling to make good use of analytical capacity, and policy units in particular. If their support is lacking, the position of policy analysis, synoptic thinking, and of policy units, depends almost entirely upon ministers.

Unfortunately, ministerial support is a volatile asset for two reasons. The first is that ministers, and political styles, change and sustained support is therefore unlikely over a long period. For example, the DHSS's PSU began with strong support: it 'had overt ministerial support, and I mean *overt*; if things weren't done properly they would ask the PSU to do it'. However, the general ebbing of enthusiasm for the CPRS, which tended to put other policy units on the defensive, was compounded by ministerial changes in the department. This vulnerability of analytical units is compounded by the dilemma that their analytical wisdom can easily conflict with the prevailing political wisdom. A unit which is unwilling to risk such a clash could as well be located in a political party's research department, but one which takes the risk jeopardises ministerial support.

Despite these inherent weaknesses, the potential role of the analytical unit in promoting coordination is not to be underestimated. Given support it can help cut across the fiefdoms of political ownership; even more important, perhaps, it can provide a focal point for those topics which because they span the interests of several policy divisions are central to the interests of none. Our research revealed several 'no home' topics of this kind which may not have been subjected to close study if the PSU had not existed in the DHSS. Precisely because they span boundaries, many of the most fundamental policy issues, like community care, fall into this category.

Financial coordination

The problem of policy coordination is inherent in the division of labour, but it is thrown into sharpest relief by scarcity:

While everyone has got plenty of money it does not matter if there is waste. On the other hand if you have resources there is also time for coordinating committees. The time when you need coordination most is when it is most difficult to do it.

the impact of the current crisis ... I see as throwing up quite positive results; it churns up the machine and makes people look at preconceived notions which are not questioned when you have 2 or 3% growth.

An obvious response to this challenge is to stress cost-effectiveness and ensure that its active pursuit, and not reactive decision-making, is the essence of financial control. We have argued that changes in financial control at the highest levels have provided only limited opportunities for, and incentives to, interdepartment collaboration. As regards financial allocation *within* departments it is debatable whether it is still primarily a reactive system of bilateral trading with individual policy divisions or whether the positive pursuit of cost-effectiveness has begun to provide a financial spur to policy coordination. Certainly the language of cost-effectiveness is pervasive and as one civil servant said of a particular policy, he was interested in promoting it only 'where it is cost-effective.' Several divisions would put forward bids for development and his staff would review them 'to see that they are presented as objectively as possible in terms of value for money against a background of containment of overall expenditure'.

A number of interviewees spoke of the changing financial role; from what was merely a restrictive controlling role ten to fifteen years ago to currently 'providing advice and analysis in support of ministers and different levels within the department'. There has been a development, encouraged by their terms of reference, of principal finance officers 'trying to move more in the direction of being positive advisers and analysts rather than controllers/storekeepers'. This development is, however, constrained by the paucity of finance officers. As one such officer admitted, 'we are pretty thin on the ground'. He also maintained that something had to be done on the training of finance officers 'to see if they can make a more positive contribution to the evaluation of projects and the development of initiatives which make better use of resources'.

Even if such barriers were removed a more active financial role would at present almost certainly be concerned with cost-cutting. One of the fundamental features of a preoccupation with short-term expenditure constraint is that it leaves little room for looking at the medium- to long-term. The coordinative potential of financial divisions appears to have been underdeveloped in the past and to be unduly constrained by short-term pressures in the present.

COSTS AND BENEFITS

In examining the barriers to and opportunities for policy coordination we have emphasised the importance of structures and processes. We now complement this by considering the costs and benefits to which individuals in central government respond by considering their motivations and how they perceive their interests. Currently we lack any well-researched understanding of how individual behaviour and motivation interacts with structures and processes in shaping policies[16]. Here we shall concentrate on the behaviour of ministers and civil servants and on just a few of the possible ways of generalising about their patterns of behaviour.

The most obvious explanation of ministerial behaviour is that it is determined by the pursuit of political success. Unfortunately for ministers, the opportunities for major political success in the social policy field are rare compared with economic or foreign affairs. Political success for several post-war decades consisted essentially of skilful defence of programmes and budgets in lean times, and rapid expansion – relative to other areas of 'expenditure' – in periods of growth. It was a strategy of 'maximisation' which accorded well with the dynamics of bureaucracy[17] and which became deeply rooted in government departments in the post-war years. Indeed, it still remains as a subterranean, though publicly repudiated, model for political success. Such a strategy reinforces rather than challenges 'policy ownership'. It offers little incentive to engage in policy coordination. It was, however, modified during the 1960s and 1970s when the re-appraisal of the performance of the major social services led to a greater concern with policy coordination.

The demise of JASP represented a failure to institutionalise this concern as a fundamental preoccupation for *ministers*. Policy coordination as a political objective has therefore continued to be conditional upon two factors: the extent to which party programmes and manifestos specify social policy changes which depend upon a high order of policy coordination; and the personal perspectives and values of individual ministers. The first has been well illustrated, for example, by the substantially frustrated attempts over several decades to bridge the taxation and benefits system. Linking health and local authority services in a policy of community care has obviously been another enduring, and bipartisan, pressure towards policy coordination. The more personal impact of ministers' interests and values is reflected in the emphasis given to particular client groups – especially to the mentally handicapped and the physically handicapped. The two 'waves' of interest in the under-fives also depended largely upon ministers who were willing to step outside the conventions of policy ownership and seize the opportunity, however limited, for positive action.

To these factors has been added a third: the search for 'value for money'. Although initially subordinate to maximisation as a route to political success it became a much more urgent pressure on ministers from the mid 1970s onwards. After the Tory election victory in 1979, political ideology – for the first time in the post-war years – favoured a decisive reversal of priorities: ministerial reputations would be made, in principle, by containing and reducing expenditure rather than by maximisation. In practice, however, this has not produced an overwhelming emphasis on cost-effectiveness, or on policy coordination to this end. Instead, as we have noted, the emphasis has been on short-term cost-cutting; the pursuit of cost-effectiveness in the medium-term has to survive as best it can.

Nevertheless, these 'resource stream' pressures have pushed some areas of coordination to the fore. Two examples are noteworthy: the linking more closely of statutory, voluntary and informal care systems; and joint finance. The first has yielded a generalised concern, but little effective policy coordination and very limited political success for ministers[18]. The main problems are that objectives are unclear and that informal care 'systems' are large, diverse and inherently difficult for the statutory sector to work with. The former is probably the decisive barrier to greater policy coordination in this field. In so far as cost-cutting in the public sector is the objective, unilateral action in the state services with little – or no – emphasis on coordination can be seen as sufficient. Alternatively, if a longer-term approach to cost-effectiveness is envisaged, the respective roles of and the interaction between the different systems are at stake and the way forward is therefore essentially problematic and unclear. Our research found little evidence of real progress towards a coherent strategy in this field and underlined the continuing confusion between cost-cutting and cost-effectiveness in thinking about 'value for money'.

Joint finance is a different case: although 'some people have been sceptical about it . . . it has been successful politically. It was one of the initiatives picked up enthusiastically (by Tory ministers) from their predecessors.' Moreover, it is an ideal issue for junior ministers to handle: it is relatively safe politically and 'the sums are relatively small'. The nature of low-key political success is well illustrated by joint finance:

It already commanded cross-party support in local government by the time of the election [1979]. It has been the kind of thing where ministers get instant feedback from the chairman of social services committees. They get a feel from them of where government initiatives are going well and this one came across very positively. There was some reluctance from the local authority associations and the financial end of local government was suspicious, but the Directors [of Social Services] have always been supportive. Thus from the point of view of a subjective evaluation, joint finance has come over well.

The great strength of joint finance as a politically rewarding approach to policy coordination has been that, apart from being comparatively inexpensive, it has been supportive of both a politically accepted service policy (community care) and the desire for cost-effectiveness. It has also helped to take some of the political sting out of local authority expenditure cuts. If Labour ministers had not invented it, Tory ministers would have been under great pressure to do so.

What this illustrates is the relatively high political returns needed from policy coordination; returns which are necessary to outweigh both the political costs of potential conflict and the time which is necessary in boundary spanning exercises. Issues which cross boundaries are subject to far more uncertainty – and therefore to a higher risk of failure – than those which sit comfortably within the established conventions. To make an investment worthwhile there has to be a good chance of a politically successful outcome, a deep and personal commitment by individual ministers to the particular cause or to the general principle of spanning boundaries; or just, perhaps, a temperamental disposition towards giving the system a shake.

Generally, active ministerial interest is concentrated upon getting policies accepted and started. Coordination at the implementation level is very much a matter for civil servants, whose motivations we examine below. Ministers, of course, become highly concerned with the details of implementation when 'things go wrong'. Departments of state are governed as much by the need to spare ministers any political embarrassment as by the need to promote their political success. One of the most obvious recent examples of *operational* coordination induced by politically unwelcome failure of implementation is that of the registers of children at risk of abuse and non-accidental injury. An example of operational failure feeding back via ministers into *strategic* policy coordination is that of the scandals in hospitals for the mentally handicapped[19].

Despite the potential impact of JASP, the concern with cost-effectiveness, and the problem of 'policy failure', it is difficult to see ministerial interest in policy coordination as other than sporadic and conditional. Are civil servants more or less consistently motivated? The obvious hypothesis is that civil servants are so closely attuned to serving ministers that their motivational graphs peak and dip in concert with those of their political masters.

The galvanising effect of parliamentary questions and of criticisms emanating from parliamentary committees, and implementing authorities, is one constant in civil service life. Ministerial support for a limited number of policy developments is another. Although it varies between departments, the effect of ministerial involvement was a persistent theme in our interviews: it is undoubtedly a factor in interdepartmental relations. According to one senior civil servant the interests of ministers 'are the main determinants of what departments do'. This, he said, was especially so in DOE where there is a tradition 'of massing their forces on things ministers are interested in. This has an impact. If there are five things that the Secretary of State wants and one thing that the DHSS wants this has an important impact on how much priority DOE gives to it [the DHSS issue].'

Typically, ministers' involvement will be in topics identified by party manifestos and policy documents, in fields of personal interest, in 'departmental issues' which represent a line of continuity in departmental policy and thinking, or in issues which have become pressure points: 'it was a combination of ministerial interest and pressure from outside that led the department to initiate action'. Whatever the source, ministerial interest has the same consequences for civil servants: it imposes priorities on their use of time; it at least partially dilutes the determination of other civil servants in the same department to defend their policy fields against intrusions and disruptions; and where coordination is needed it counteracts the reluctance to invest in boundary spanning activities.

However, many civil servants value continuity and some, at least, look for a genuine and personal impact on policy. Such personal preferences can affect attitudes towards the ministerial role and can reduce the impact of ministerial interests. This comes close to asserting that many civil servants favour, or are resigned to, an incremental approach to policy development. As one put it, 'a lot of work seems to ascend in some slow rising spiral. There are not many opportunities for sudden changes in direction.'

Beneath this, however, there can be quite contrary commitment to gradualism as the most politically secure and durable form of change.

We are more likely to do such policy development by evolution; something which is evolving is more likely to go on through a change in government. Therefore the civil service has the opposite motives to a minister; it does not want to let things get too closely associated with a minister or a particular civil servant . . . we tend to be trying to avoid peaks and troughs – especially where the objective is to improve services. Civil servants are bound to want to do that in a non-political way . . . Therefore there is a bit of resistance to strongly politically motivated things even if as an individual you strongly agree with it – because the ministers may move or if the other side [the Opposition] disagrees it becomes too much of a hassle to get the thing through.

This perspective reflects the importance of policy ownership within the civil service not merely as a systematically defended division of labour but as a commitment to particular 'lines' of long-term development. Ministerial support – if potentially volatile – is a threat to such continuity and this cost may outweigh the opportunities for more rapid change which ministerial support creates. Given a *continuity* of political interest, however, more rapid change – including the re-alignment inherent in policy coordination – may be highly rewarding to civil servants. It may be the highlight in what is often a frustrating career.

One interviewee, asked what benefit he derived from a successful coordinative exercise, replied: 'A lot of fun! I could', he said, 'spend the best years of my life on something which would not come off', whereas 'here was the possibility not only of some kind of achievement, but also of achieving it without additional expenditure. You couldn't say better than that!'

In so far as career prospects are the prime motivation for a civil servant, the dominant concern tends to be that of avoiding mistakes and embarrassments. Ministers' defensive needs are important; conformity with the expectations and codes of the civil service is also important. Both reinforce caution, incrementalism and an acceptance of the boundaries of policy ownership. The personal costs to civil servants of close involvement in policy coordination can therefore be high. Against this we have identified three other motivations which might support involvement in policy coordination: the need to provide ministers with political successes; the desire to feel a sense of positive personal achievement; and desire to develop services which are best suited to clients' needs. For some individuals these outweigh the more negative motivations and foster creativity and risk-taking. For the system as a whole, however, it is difficult to avoid the conclusion that only sustained ministerial pressure would tip the balance in favour of a consistently synoptic perspective. In practice, as we have argued, this pressure is applied sporadically rather than systematically: for most individuals for most of the time, the costs of policy coordination outweigh the benefits.

CONCLUSIONS

The explanatory framework we have outlined highlights the dearth of interlocking explanations of central government which span several 'levels' of analysis. The problem of 'policy ownership' provides an example of how such links can be made, at the level of structures and processes and of individual behaviour. For individual ministers and civil servants alike, the structures and processes of central government make the costs of strategic policy coordination high. The costs include transgressing the norms of a culture which regards 'territorial rights' so highly; conflict and loss of day-to-day cooperation; and blighting career prospects or wasting valuable time and energy on projects which are likely to become bogged down, to fail, or to be vulnerable to shifts in political support. Coordinative efforts may be a useful cosmetic to conceal lack of progress on a particular policy, but policy coordination which is intended to produce genuine results is inevitably a high-risk strategy for all concerned.

If the barriers can be outlined by tracing a connection between structures, processes and individual behaviour, then coordination should be explicable in similar terms. To return to our original paradox, however, policy coordination is both endemic and conspicuous by its absence – major successes are few. This is mainly because most coordinative activity is reactive and conservative rather than a creative search for change. One civil servant unconsciously developed three categories for us which encompass the field: coordination as 'routine courtesy'; coordination as a process of 'tying up loose ends'; and coordination as a means of 'being prepared for the unexpected' – which entails the creation and maintenance of a widespread network devoted to keeping people informed of impending developments. The first two depend on the mores and values of central government, the last also depends on a system of exchange between divisions and departments.

While all this activity is – on the whole – necessary and productive in a complex bureaucracy, it adds up to something very different from and less than the rational-synoptic optimism of JASP. It services incrementalism rather than formulating a critique of its limitations; it underpins – and is a corollary of – 'policy ownership', rather than challenging it. Moreover, the possibility of coordinating action on the larger and more complex issues is certainly sacrificed at times – perhaps routinely – in order to safeguard the day-to-day cooperation essential to this system of 'defensive coordination'.

This order of priorities is reinforced by the way in which public account-ability is structured. Failure within individual areas of responsibility may be heavily penalised, but imagination, risk-taking and breadth of vision are rarely rewarded. For example, the comparatively new system of parliamentary select committees reinforces narrowness of vision by being based on departmental boundaries. The logic of JASP in parliamentary terms would require a Select Committee on Social Policy. This does not exist and the incentives to cut across the boundaries of policy ownership remain limited for ministers and therefore for civil servants.

How then does fundamental boundary spanning occur? Because it is comparatively rare, the circumstances in each case are likely to be unique, but some generalisations can be attempted. One hypothesis is that ministers and political parties can alone transcend the routines of administrative life. However, as we have seen, ministerial involvement can be central but not always a wholly helpful factor. Moreover, civil servants can be willing, rather than reluctant, advocates of policy coordination. A more convincing argument must place the role of ministers within the broader context of the academic debates outlined in chapter 2.

We have argued that the 'rational-optimistic' approach to strategic coordi-nation depends upon several demanding conditions: the existence of a system-wide viewpoint; a well-developed capacity for policy analysis; and the presence of organisational altruism. We found only limited evidence of these conditions transcending policy ownership. System-wide thinking by ministers is spasmodic and the time and resources available for forward thinking – as opposed to day-to-day administration – are severely limited and may be diminishing. There is also only fluctuating support for analytical units. However, a countervailing and evident factor among many officials was a commitment to the well-being of clients. When asked what was to be gained by his colleagues and his department from collaborating with voluntary organisations, one civil servant replied: 'Nothing. We were doing it for the children. It was pure altruism.'

While the rational-synoptic view of policy change may be generally unrealistic, limited amounts of its various components can create a less dramatic but potentially productive mixture. In particular, they can foster 'learning by osmosis'. The injection of a challenging viewpoint may not produce a dramatic regrouping, but it may lead to a gradual modification of ways of seeing problems and of working across boundaries – providing those boundaries are not too rigidly defended, intellectually or organisationally. As one civil servant said in relation to a particular paper: 'things filter through: 20 or 30 Assistant Secretaries were coming back on every draft. Being forced to consult like that drove us bananas but I think it gradually achieved change. You gradually achieve some sort of consensus.'

This may seem a prosaic explanation, but it was certainly a factor in the few examples of active policy coordination which we identified. The source of such changes may be a minister and/or a paper produced by a policy unit, but it may also be evidence from external sources that a policy is failing or that unmet needs could be catered for by modifying existing policies. Whatever the source, however, the essential feature of 'learning by osmosis' is that attitudes and perspectives change in response to evidence and argument, and that this gradual process operates largely 'through routine channels of communication' – if and when it happens at all.

We would suggest that an explanation of change which posits a learning process as the core feature is the appropriate generic model to set against the emphasis within the 'pessimistic' tradition on power and bargaining. There are different sources and modes of learning and these enable us to identify variants, of which the pure case of change fostered by rational-synoptic planning is one and 'learning by osmosis' is another. We would argue that such learning can, in principle, lead to substantial and comparatively rapid policy change as well as to a slowly evolving incrementalism.

We found ample evidence of the centrality of power and bargaining, both as barriers and as facilitating factors. Conflicts, and especially the avoidance of overt conflicts – over policy and paradigms, the relative status and influence of service professions, and territorial boundaries – were a constant barrier to active policy coordination. Power was most evident in the form of ministerial authority and as pressure 'from below'. Both may provide a relatively gentle stimulus to a learning process, but they may also be powerful enough to impose change which proceeds against the grain of accepted perspectives and interests.

Bargaining is a pertinent but less overt factor. One example is the suggestion that a lack of bargaining power is a major weakness of policy units. Joint finance is also very interesting in this context. It appears to contradict 'pessimistic' models of bureaucratic life in which budget maximisation reigns supreme[20]; nothing could be more contrary to such models than a service giving its money away to others. Yet joint finance was specifically designed to be a good bargain. Policy coordination was to be 'bought' by offering a financial incentive to cross boundaries; the costs of collaboration were to be paid for from the health service budget. What joint finance tends to emphasise is that only when coordination is transformed into a positive sum game – when an implicit bargain is struck that both parties will benefit from working together – does collaboration become a real prospect. The real lesson to be drawn therefore is that resource incentives may be essential to boundary crossing; and yet central government exhibits relatively few examples of bargaining of this kind. One major barrier to the more widespread use of incentives is the continued dominance of bilateral relations between the Treasury and spending departments in the resource allocation process.

Having argued that the rational-synoptic approach to policy coordination survives in an attenuated form and that it is best seen as but one example of change through learning, we have now implied that a realistic view of the world would indeed see the exercise of power and the striking of mutually beneficial bargains as the predominant explanations of why the barriers to policy coordination are occasionally breached. In practice we are saying that these various explanations cannot readily be weighted, nor can they be rigidly opposed as mutually exclusive models. An active approach to policy coordination appears to be comparatively rare, but when it occurs it may be the product of learning processes, power struggles, or bargaining. Even more likely, it may be the product of two or more of these reinforcing each other.

REFERENCES

1 DHSS (1976) *Priorities for Health and Personal Social Services in England*, HMSO
2 DHSS (1981) *Care in the Community*, HMSO

3 See chapter 3 for a full discussion of joint policy in these fields
4 DHSS (1978) *A Happier Old Age*, HMSO; DHSS (1981) *Growing Older*, HMSO, Cmnd. 8173
5 Crossman's diaries reveal a number of examples, especially the struggle between the Home Office and the Ministry of Health for control over the Personal Social Services. R. H. S. Crossman (1977) *Diaries of a Cabinet Minister*, vol. 3, Hamilton
6 See chapter 4 and 'The Central Policy Review Staff: the first two years', a lecture given to the Political Studies Association Conference, 1973
7 Joint finance was introduced in 1976. It is an arrangement by which NHS monies can be spent on local authority or voluntary services providing such expenditure brings real benefit to the NHS. See G. Wistow (1983) 'Joint finance and community care: have the incentives worked?', *Public Money*, vol. 3, no. 2, pp. 33–7
8 A. L. Webb and G. Wistow (1982) *Whither State Welfare? Policy Implementation in the Personal Social Services, 1979–80*, Royal Institute of Public Administration
9 R. Klein, 'Health services', in P. Jackson (1981) *Government Policy Initiatives 1979–80: Some Case Studies in Public Administration*, Royal Institute of Public Administration, pp. 161–80.
10 H. Heclo and A. Wildavsky (1974) *The Private Government of Public Money*, Macmillan
11 M. Butts *et al.* (1981) *From Principles to Practice*, Nuffield Provincial Hospital Trust, ch. 2. See also S. Haywood and D. Hunter (1982) 'Consultative processes in health policy in the UK', *Public Administration* 60, 2
12 DOE regions 'perform what is in effect a localised GNI ... Outside London 60% is allocated through the GNI, 40% in London. The remainder is distributed, 40% outside London, 60% within, by the Local Discretionary Element or LDE.' (The percentages involved have changed since the time of our interviews.)
13 House of Commons (1981) *Third Report from the Environment Committee*, HMSO
14 DHSS (1981) *op. cit.*
15 J. James, 'Some aspects of policy analysis and policy units in the health field', in A. Gray and B. Jenkins (1983) *Policy Analysis and Evaluation in British Government*, RIPA
16 P. Self (1972) *Administrative Theories and Politics*, Allen & Unwin
17 See chapter 2
18 See Webb and Wistow (1982) *op. cit.*
19 Crossman (1977) *op. cit.*
20 See chapter 2

6 ～ Coordination at local level: introducing methods and localities

Central government has pursued improved social policy coordination at local as well as national levels of administration. While seeking to inject a more comprehensive approach into its own practice, the centre has also encouraged local agencies to cooperate in service planning and delivery. Consequently, our research at the national level was complemented by studies of inter-agency relationships in seven selected localities and as they affected policies for elderly people and children under five. This element of our fieldwork had the general objective of seeking to define the nature, extent and 'productiveness' of such relationships in a range of different contexts. Thus the approach adopted was to take three 'cuts' across local experiences of coordination: by *locality*, by *client group* and by *policy 'arenas'*.

Three such arenas were identified: the local authority (or corporate) arena; the health and local authority (or collaborative) arena; and the statutory/non-statutory (or inter-sector) arena. Each arena was found to be characterised by largely discrete formal arrangements for multi-agency planning. In this respect (and in the first two arenas, especially), they reflected the impact of successive national initiatives to strengthen local capacities for coordinated planning through approaches founded on the 'optimistic' tradition. In this sense in particular, therefore, the local studies were designed to be complementary to that of the JASP exercise at the centre. In addition they allowed us to consider whether social policy coordination had become more firmly established locally or nationally and, thus, whether the centre had been less successful in putting its own house in order than in encouraging local agencies to do so. The three arenas also provided the possibility of studying the experience of coordination at different stages in the development of inter-agency planning. Corporate planning, for example, had originated in the late 1960s, though it was not until the 1974 reorganisation that its structures were universally adopted. On the other hand, joint (collaborative) planning did not exist even as a concept until 1976; and there is still no nationally prescribed model for the inter-sector arena. Nonetheless, the optimistic litany of collaboration, comprehensiveness and consistency had been loudly echoed in successive prescriptions for each arena: from the earliest discussions of corporate planning[1] to the more recent advocacy of a formal basis for a partnership in planning between the voluntary and statutory sectors.[2] These planning initiatives also shared a strong emphasis on the need for formal liaison and planning machinery as essential vehicles for coordination locally.

Central government interest in policy coordination for the two tracer groups peaked at different times. In the case of children under five, the 'golden age' for coordination – in terms of its salience for national policy makers – was the period 1976–78. After that the issue fell from national prominence and re-emerged only briefly in 1981 through the joint DES/DHSS conference. In contrast, the equivalent national thrust of policy for the elderly came in the Green[3] and White[4] Papers of 1979 and 1981, with their emphasis on coordination as a key mechanism for securing national policy goals. At the same time, the tracer groups involved different groupings of local actors. The under-fives were primarily the province of the corporate and inter-sector arenas, with education and social services departments being the key participants on the statutory side. By contrast, health authorities make a major contribution to the provision of services for elderly people and the collaborative arena acted as the central forum for policy coordination. On the local authority side, housing rather than education departments impinged more significantly on policy making for elderly people, thereby introducing an additional category of actors in the shire counties where housing is the responsibility of district councils.

A final set of variations in the context for inter-agency relationships at local level arises from differences between local environments for policy coordination. Localities differ in many respects, including: local government and NHS structures; the relationship between health and local authority boundaries; resource bases and expenditure growth; service stocks; and levels of need/demand. Such factors are found in various combinations and would seem likely to create climates in which coordination may be a more or less demanding and successful exercise.

To summarise, therefore, our local fieldwork was designed to investigate how and if the experience of coordination at local level varied by arena, client group and locality. More specifically, it was concerned with the following questions:

(i) Did the nature and products of social policy coordination vary systematically between arenas as well as – or rather than – between localities or client groups?

(ii) Did experience on the ground reflect differences in the history and timing of national initiatives? For example, was corporate planning more firmly established and productive than formal planning procedures in either of the other two arenas? Was coordination for the under-fives more fully developed or had it slipped out of fashion leaving little to suggest that it had ever been attempted?

(iii) What was the role of formal planning machinery in attempts to improve social policy coordination? Did it provide a necessary forum for inter-agency planning or did less formal mechanisms prove to be effective substitutes for such formal approaches?

(iv) To the extent that variations were identified in arenas, client groups or localities, how might they be explained?

We seek to answer these questions in chapters 7 to 10. Before presenting our findings, however, a brief note is necessary on method and terminology. In addition, we provide an introduction to the seven localities in which the fieldwork was conducted.

DEFINITIONS AND METHODS: MACHINERY, PROCESS AND OUTPUT

The conceptual elusiveness of coordination (see chapter 2) initially posed problems of method. Two issues were particularly fundamental: where should we look for evidence of coordination taking place and how would we recognise it if we found it? The approach adopted was to distinguish between the machinery, the processes and the outputs of coordination. This provided two different starting points for our locality studies. The first was to focus upon the formal machinery for coordination around which so much of the national guidance centred. In essence, our strategy was to identify which kinds of formal machinery had been established, how it operated, what it produced and whether there existed a wider set of inter-agency relationships outside the framework provided by such mechanisms. Apart from providing a tracer for studying the process and output of interactions between service providing agencies, the study of formal machinery was important in its own right. Formal structures (coordinating committees, planning teams and the like) figured large in the prescriptions of the 'optimistic' tradition as the principal tool for promoting, nurturing and sustaining effective coordination. Thus an understanding of the strengths and weaknesses of such formal mechanisms seemed essential to an assessment of the strengths and weaknesses of rational planning.

Both of these considerations suggested the need for what was, in effect, a 'top-down' mapping of machinery and identification of its output. On its own, however, this strategy was too limited. Resting on an implicit assumption that the achievements of coordination were restricted to the products of formal machinery, it pre-judged one of our basic research questions: the relative importance of both formal and informal mechanisms for coordination. We hypothesised that many informal relationships might operate within the context of formal machinery and that such machinery would be a natural channel through which to process the outputs of informal mechanisms since it provided a means of legitimating and funding them. Yet we needed not only to test that hypothesis but also to chart any coordinating process and output which remained outside the formal machinery. Apart from any other consideration, the 'pessimistic' tradition suggested that individualistic entrepreneurial behaviour, relying on bargaining and networking, was more likely to be effective than more routinised and mechanistic formal approaches. Thus we adopted a 'bottom-up' approach to balance the top-down focus on coordination through machinery. This second starting point was organised around the identification of examples where agencies had combined, to a greater or lesser extent, to provide services. We then worked backwards from such examples to trace their origins, whether formal or informal.

These two complementary mapping exercises required the development of clear criteria for the categorisation of machinery and outputs to ensure, in particular, that the fieldwork teams, working separately and sometimes in widely differing localities, would generate broadly comparable data. As a result, we devised an experimental 'bureaumetric'[5] technique to supplement the qualitative methods of the traditional case study. Its purpose was to provide a quantitative tool which supplied both a check upon, and a context for, the more qualitative judgements formed in the course of observations and interviews. The approach we developed is described more fully in an appendix to this chapter. Here it is necessary only to note that our mapping exercise was confined to machinery and outputs in operation at some point in the three years 1979–81 and that the machinery 'count' was restricted to that which was:

(a) *formal*, as opposed to informal contacts by phone, letter or in person;
(b) *strategic*, i.e. included among its tasks responsibility for long-term planning;
(c) *locality-wide*, i.e. was not restricted in coverage to a geographical area smaller than that covered by a metropolitan district, London borough or shire county.

The machinery counts also categorised machinery according to whether its remit was exclusively concerned with one of two tracer groups or related to such groups as part of a wider remit (i.e. whether it was *tracer* or *cross-tracer* machinery).

Outputs were classified by their origin and type: those which had been produced by formal machinery (of any kind) and those which had emerged from informal processes of negotiation and agreement ('*machinery*' and '*informal*' outputs). In addition, we made a distinction between *tangible* and *intangible* outputs on the grounds that inter-agency relationships might not only produce new services but also less tangible processes associated with learning, such as the growth of understanding, diffusion of conflict and facilitation of communication. The tangible outputs were grouped into three categories:

(a) *policies* or plans for a service system as a whole or for its component parts (e.g. a comprehensive plan for services relating to the elderly/under-fives or for residential/day care services);

(b) individual *projects* which extended (or, less frequently, maintained) the range of service provision through the injection of *additional* resources (e.g. additional residential homes, home helps, childminders);

(c) modifications to professional *practices* or operational procedures which led to changes in the allocation or use of *existing* resources controlled by field level staff (e.g. multi-disciplinary assessment procedures, reservation of Part III/nursery education places for clients referred by hospitals/social services respectively, 'outposting' of nursing/teaching staff to Part III homes/day nurseries [or playgroups]).

These categories were interrelated. The implementation of individual projects, for example, might be part of some grander design agreed within or between agencies. At the same time, changes in professional practices might be associated with initiatives to increase the level of resources available to field staff as part of either a bottom-up or top-down process of developing individual service elements or the service system as a whole. We should emphasise, however, that these data are subject to certain limitations. First, they are incomplete: some small, localised outputs were probably not identified, especially in the larger authorities. Second, the origins of long established outputs could not always be established with certainty. Third, the counts excluded those projects and practices which had been agreed but had yet to become operational. They underestimate, therefore, the productiveness of the most recent coordinative practices. Fourth, there was a tendency for machinery to attract outputs, i.e. for projects and practices originating in informal processes to appear on the agendas of formal machinery purely as a matter of information rather than for substantive discussion. Wherever possible, we have taken this into account but there may still be some tendency for the counts to overestimate the contribution of formal compared with informal processes in the production of outputs. Nonetheless, the overall quality of the data is such that confidence may be placed on the broad trends and patterns revealed.

THE FIELDWORK SITES

Our conceptual framework identified a number of contextual factors which we hypothesised to be significant in shaping the nature and extent of coordination in local arenas. They were used to generate criteria for selecting fieldwork sites. The scope of the research meant that it was not possible to construct a large enough sample to be fully representative. Instead, the aim was to provide opportunities for studying coordination in environments where such factors were combined in different ways. They included:

(a) Structural complexity: this was the primary criterion reflecting the central importance accorded to enabling structures in the 'optimistic' model. Each of the major kinds of health and local authority structure were included among our case studies.

(b) Resource stocks and flows: the conceptual framework accorded a central role to financial resources and to study their impact both well and poorly resourced authorities were included among our case studies.

(c) Congruence within and between localities along both the structural complexity and resource dimensions.

(d) Experience of corporate planning: a reputation for corporatism was considered an indicator of intra- as well as inter-departmental planning capacity. It was also considered likely to be associated with systems-wide thinking and a potential for inter-corporate planning.

(e) Political control: providing a means of exploring the impact of political ideology and stability/change in party control on local environments for coordination.

(f) Demography: as an indicator of current and future levels of need. Coupled with data on service stocks this also provided a pointer to the likely pressures of demand (actual or anticipated) experienced by different agencies.

The criteria were drawn up on the assumption that each was important in itself in producing variations in patterns of interaction between agencies. At the same time, we anticipated that such patterns would vary according to the particular combination of factors within each locality. However, hypotheses about the outcomes of such combinations remained at best implicit at the time of locality selection and a major task of the research was precisely to explore the nature of such variations in local environments for coordination. Thus we were looking for localities characterised, among other things, by broadly similar patterns of structural complexity but different resource experiences – and vice versa. Our ultimate objective was to explore in a range of contexts the validity of our hypotheses about coordination and the factors which promote and impede it. In particular, we were seeking to establish the relationship, if any, between different groupings of our selected criteria and the extent of (a) machinery and (b) output.

Seven fieldwork sites were selected using these criteria: three shire counties (Cliffshire, Greenshire and Portshire); two metropolitan districts

Table 1 *Structural and political characteristics of the localities*

	Structure		Complexity score[a]		Corporate planning unit	Political control since 1974
	Local authority	Health authority	Elderly	Under-fives		
Cliffshire	Shire	Multi	15	7	No	Fluctuating
Greenshire	Shire	Multi	17	7	Yes	Conservative
Portshire	Shire	Multi	20	7	Yes	Conservative
Riverton	Met. District	Single	4	3	No	Conservative
Woodtown	Met. District	Multi	6	5	Yes	Labour
Fulborough	Inner London	Multi[b]	5	4	Yes	Labour
Templeborough	Outer London	Multi[c]	6	5	No	Labour

[a] Complexity score: number of statutory agencies with a potential responsibility for the tracer group.
[b] A multi-district AHA with two health districts relating to the London borough.
[c] A multi-district AHA with one health district coterminous with the London borough.

Table 2 *Resource characteristics of the localities*

	Resource stocks expenditure/capita 1978/79 (£s)			Resource flows percentage change 1978/79 on 1977/78		
	PSS[a]	Education[a]	AHA[b]	PSS	Education	AHA
Cliffshire	20	140	130	6.1	10.0	15.7
Greenshire	15	130	120	9.1	13.6	15.1
Portshire	15	115	140	6.4	25.5	14.8
Riverton	15	130	100	10.5	3.7	15.1
Woodtown	25	150	180	9.5	27.6	14.8
Fulborough	70	195	290	8.4	15.6	13.0
Templeborough	35	155	210	15.5	7.6	10.7
England	23	136	136	10.0	8.8	15.4

[a] Rounded to nearest 5.
[b] Rounded to nearest 10.

(Riverton and Woodtown); an inner London borough (Fulborough) and an outer London borough (Templeborough). Tables 1, 2 and 3 provide an overview of their structural, political, resource and demographic characteristics in relation to England as a whole. We provide below a brief introduction to each locality and the policy stances of their principal agencies towards the elderly and under-fives.

INTRODUCING THE LOCALITIES

Shire counties

Cliffshire

Cliffshire was a county of some geographic and socio-economic diversity, predominantly rural in the east and more heavily populated and urbanised in the west. Half its population lived in a former county borough and two neighbouring districts. Population growth was slower than the shire county average, both in total and for the under-fives (table 3). However, past and projected growth in the elderly was above average (30% compared with 7% nationally for the 60/65+ group between 1971 and 1981). Structural complexity was high with eight district councils, four health districts and overlapping health and local government boundaries, especially within the conurbation (table 1).

Table 3 *Demographic characteristics of the localities*

	Under-fives		Elderly: population 75 and over	
	Percentage of population aged 0–4: 1978/79	Projected percentage increase 1977–1986	Percentage of population aged 75+: 1978/79	Projected percentage increase 1977–1986
Cliffshire	6.1	6.8	5.0	25.9
Greenshire	6.4	12.8	5.4	21.9
Portshire	5.4	4.8	7.4	23.5
Riverton	7.2	4.5	3.0	42.6
Woodtown	5.6	2.9	5.6	15.8
Fulborough	4.3	11.1	6.2	22.5
Templeborough	6.6	13.9	4.9	20.7
England	6.2	9.8	5.3	19.6

Political control of the county council alternated at the three elections after 1973 and the successive majority groups adopted strongly divergent stances towards expenditure. The victorious Conservative manifesto of 1977 asserted that 'spending was out of control' and pledged to operate the rating system 'as fairly and as tightly as possible'. As a result, net per-capita expenditure fell from 13% to 1% above the shire county average and the county was in the minority of authorities which allocated to social services less than 2% annual growth recommended by DHSS (table 2). During our fieldwork period, the county's resource situation changed dramatically with the election of a Labour administration which immediately levied a supplementary rate and diverted substantial additional resources to the social services department while also creating a budget for a newly established joint social services, education and leisure services committee.

Expenditure considerations also influenced the parties' policy stance towards the balance of services for the elderly. The Conservatives were committed in 1977 to building no further residential homes and concentrating resources on domiciliary services (a stance subsequently modified). Labour favoured the expansion of both kinds of service but with the emphasis upon developing community-based provision. The parties' approach to the under-fives was even more distinct: Labour consistently favoured the expansion of day nursery, childminding and nursery education – and in 1981 proposed coordinating machinery to cover the overlap between the education and social services departments. The Conservatives, on the other hand, argued that provision for the under-fives could 'not be regarded with the same urgency as much of the remainder of social services work'. Nursery education and day nursery expansion came to a halt but pump-priming funds for playgroups were advocated.

Although the two parties initiated very different expenditure regimes, ideological differences were not a powerful factor in their policy stances toward the elderly and under-fives. Moreover the Labour group remained largely immune from the national ideological turbulence and remained solidly moderate. The anticipation of change in control was more important than ideological difference since it militated against long-term planning beyond the date of the next county elections.

The AHA (a teaching area) was an underfunded authority in an underfunded region and in 1977/78 was 88% below its Resource Allocation Working Party (RAWP) target. Its major financial difficulty was the insufficiency of its revenue allocation to commission major capital projects planned a decade earlier. Despite concentrating development monies on such developments – largely in the acute sector – some 700 beds remained unopened in 1982. Its own bed provision for the elderly fell far short of DHSS norms but it placed considerable emphasis on the SSD's deficiency in this respect. In essence, both authorities were grappling with the consequences of increasing pressures on services for the elderly without adequate resources, though joint finance was used to provide additional old people's homes. In this context the SSD tended to be defensive and avoid relationships which might involve commitments it could not meet. By contrast, services for the under-fives were relatively well provided. Nursery school places approached twice the national level and, although day nursery provision was cut between 1977 and 1981, the numbers of childminders grew rapidly after 1980.

Greenshire

Greenshire was a large shire county with both rural and urban dimensions. Largely prosperous, population growth had resulted from inward migration for employment as well as retirement. Overall, the existing and projected proportion of elderly was close to the average (table 3) but this concealed wide variations with some SSD areas estimating the proportion of elderly as between 30% and 50%. The proportion of under-fives was also then in line with national trends (table 3). An influx of high-technology industry had slowed the rate of job losses and kept unemployment levels below average.

Administrative complexity was a strong characteristic of the county with boundary coterminosity rare below the county level. Particular features included the large number of district councils, some of which, as former county boroughs, did not readily cooperate with the county. In addition, while the abolition of the AHA brought about administrative decentralisation in the NHS, social services was increasing centralised controls through the removal of its divisional tier.

Political control remained with the Conservative party in each of the elections after 1973 but district council elections had been marked by an increase in ratepayers' representation. The financial concerns of the electorate which supported such trends were reflected in the county's majority group in a dominant policy stance towards budgetary control and an emphasis on: the search for savings; maximising charges; seeking additional sources of income; and the optimum use of voluntary effort. Social services spending was low compared nationally but administrative base expenditure was close to the average (table 2). Spending constraint was less pronounced in the NHS. The AHA was a RAWP-gaining authority, though per-capita expenditure remained below the norm. Services both in general and for the under-fives and elderly fell below national norms. Within social services some contraction of services had taken place in absolute terms as well as and relative to the increasing elderly population. High profile non-statutory developments for the under-fives contrasted with below average provision by the education and social services departments.

Portshire
A predominantly rural county, half of whose population was concentrated in three urban areas, Portshire was relatively isolated both externally and internally. Rural decline and depopulation was being compensated for by inward migration to retirement areas and an above average growth in the elderly population was projected (table 3). By contrast, the projected growth among under-fives was projected at half the national rate. Geographical scale and isolation were reflected in the county council's long established preference for administrative devolution. However, its area boundaries were not coterminous with NHS or local government district boundaries and a considerable degree of structural complexity and overlap existed. Identification and loyalty with local areas were stronger than with the county.

Politically, Portshire had been characterised by long and stable patterns of Conservative control and expenditure constraint. Support for the voluntary sector reflected both of these features as did spending and service levels. Local authority expenditure generally fell below the average (table 2); social services experienced real cuts between 1977/78 and 1980/81 and had the lowest growth rate of all our localities. In contrast the AHA was relatively high spending but, against the national pattern, increased the hospital share of expenditure over this period. While the provision of old people's homes was reduced and geriatric bed levels were substantially below the norm, dramatic increases took place in private and voluntary homes for the elderly. Some improvements in domiciliary service levels were achieved in the late seventies but overall services remained below the national average. The pattern of low provision of direct services coupled with reliance on non-statutory development was also a feature of service for the under-fives and the county had a national reputation in this field.

Metropolitan districts

Riverton
Divided into two politically, economically and demographically distinct geographical areas, Riverton's dominant self-image was nonetheless that of a prosperous middle-class suburb. Yet some 40% of the population lived in large overspill estates built and originally administered by a neighbouring authority and containing high levels of social need and unemployment. The borough had the fastest growing elderly population of all our localities but the smallest projected increase in under-fives (table 3). Administrative complexity was apparently minimal – a single district AHA, coterminous with the

borough – but many acute and long-stay health services were in practice provided by neighbouring authorities.

Conservative control of the council was deeply entrenched. Antipathetic towards public 'bureaucracies' and sceptical of the need for social services, the over-riding concern of the ruling group was with holding down the rates. Theirs was a fundamental belief in the virtues of low government expenditure and self-reliance. This was reinforced by the history of the borough as an affluent suburb and a failure to recognise or accept its changed social and economic composition following its incorporation of the overspill estates in 1974.

Local authority expenditure reflected the influence of member ideology. Total local authority expenditure per capita was among the lowest of all metropolitan districts, as was spending on social services. Rate fund expenditure on housing was also very low though education fared better and was politically favoured. Nevertheless, over the four-year period 1977/78–1980/81 growth in expenditure on social services was well above average, primarily at the expense of education. Expenditure on health services was the lowest of our localities, reflecting the paucity of provision within the area, though growth over the period was above average (table 2).

Despite the council's overall low expenditure base, education provision for the under-fives was close to the national average. By contrast, social services made no day nursery provision until 1978/79 and proposals for a sponsored childminding service were rejected by members. Both AHA and social services provision for the elderly was low in relation to national levels and was under increasing pressures from the growth in the elderly population. Low staffing ratios combined with increasing dependency levels produced particular pressure on old people's homes and this led the SSD to initiate contacts with the housing department about the provision of very sheltered housing. However, this came to nothing, a victim of personalised and conflictual relationships between chairs and chief officers which apparently then characterised the authority. There was also a history of mistrust between health and social services though a new Area Administrator had begun to invest considerable efforts in re-establishing the joint planning machinery and SSD officers recognised that demand pressures were driving them towards closer cooperation with the NHS and other agencies.

Woodtown

An industrial city with a strong sense of civic identity and pride, Woodtown was to some extent in demographic and economic decline. Total population fell by 6% between 1971 and 1981 and a similar fall – twice the average for metropolitan districts – was projected for the next decade. With the lowest projected increase in the under-fives of all our authorities and an above average increase in the elderly (table 3), Woodtown had an ageing population structure. Although the city had a significantly above average proportion of households in the public sector, and a low level of car ownership, it had traditionally been prosperous: but, since 1979, its unemployment rate had run ahead of the national average. Structural complexity was relatively low, though the AHA – a teaching authority – had two districts.

Labour control for most of the last half century meant, as a former committee chairman recorded, that 'rates could be raised with impunity' and high levels of expenditure tended to be equated with effectiveness. In 1980, however, control passed to a new generation of Labour councillors, interested in community development and participation, and critical of the paternalistic Labourism of the past. The new leadership was also concerned to look at social policy as a whole rather than at each service in isolation. Both strands in this approach were expressed in the group's policy stance towards the tracer groups through the establishment of coordinating machinery and policies aimed to enhance independent living and individual autonomy. This was supported by expenditure policies which aimed to defend and improve the city's services without seeking confrontation with central government for its own sake. The shift in member paradigms also affected the non-statutory sector. While traditionally associating voluntary action with middle-class charity and believing that 'if a job needs doing, the council will do it and do it properly', a new emphasis was being placed on community resources, as the following extract from a party document illustrates: 'A socialist approach to social services aims not to replace but to sustain and build on the networks of family and community support systems.'

Local authority base expenditure was above the norm for housing, education and social services and the AHA was also well resourced (table 2). However, the commissioning of a new general hospital absorbed most of its development monies in the late seventies. Both the health and local authorities provided high levels of residential services and the SSD was providing new specialist homes for the elderly mentally infirm. Home help services were well developed and, against the national trend, per-capita levels increased between 1977/78 and 1980/81. Provision for the under-fives by both the SSD and education was also substantially above the average. One consequence of high spending and provision was that individual local authority departments and the health and local authority collectively rarely perceived heightened demand on service as a pressure to cooperate. Historically the city's departments were operated as independent political and administrative empires better able than most to absorb service pressures with continuing resource growth. While the politicians were critical of the undemocratic nature of the health service, the health authority was wary of any closer relationship threatening political control. When member pressure led to a joint review of services for the elderly mentally infirm, a separatist solution emerged, with each authority clearly defining its own sphere of operation. Similarly, within the local authority, education and social services ultimately agreed on a division of responsibility for the under-fives (under-threes to the former and threes-to-fives to the latter) when proposals for a joint service fell apart.

London boroughs

Fulborough

A compact borough containing areas of both urban decay and prosperity, Fulborough saw itself – and was widely seen – as a 'market leader' in both spending and policy development terms. In common with other inner city areas, the borough experienced considerable population decline with a loss of about 20% over the decade to 1981. However, above average increases in the under-fives and elderly were expected into the mid eighties (table 3). On almost all socio-economic indicators, the borough's residents were in greater need and risk than the population nationally: levels of unemployment, basic amenities, receipt of free school meals and single parent families all suggested above average patterns of disadvantage. Housing tenure patterns also differed markedly from the national pattern with a high proportion of privately rented accommodation and lower levels of owner occupation.

Administrative complexity was high: the AHA covered two local authorities; the borough was split between two AHAs; and education was the responsibility of the ILEA. NHS reorganisation, if anything, exacerbated this fragmentation when one of the two health districts took in part of a neighbouring borough. Political control had been exercised by the Labour party since 1974 but the stance of the ruling group had changed. Younger, more avowedly socialist, with community work roots and a higher proportion of women than its predecessors, it had particular commitments to: service decentralisation and control over decision-making at local level; the role of women as carers and workers (with particular reference to the under-fives and elderly); collaboration with statutory agencies; and a high valuation of the voluntary sector. The latter was highly articulate and operated as a quasi-political force with legitimacy in member eyes as a representative of consumer interests.

The locality was well resourced combining very high per-capita base levels of spending with continuing incremental growth, though there had been some reduction in social services share of the local authority budget. The AHA was under some pressure, however, as a RAWP-losing teaching authority. At the same time its geriatric bed provision was below DHSS norms. By contrast, social services provision exceeded such levels and the department was seeking to shift the balance of its services from residential to day and domiciliary care. Statutory provision for the under-fives was at a high level and was wide ranging in type. Specialist and innovative facilities were expected in the voluntary sector but in recent years the Preschool Play Association (PPA) had struggled to survive in the face of statutory competition.

Templeborough
Bounded by parkland and merging into suburbia, the borough nevertheless contained a number of identifiable and established working-class communities. The locality experienced a more than 10% fall in population over the seventies but its proportions of under-fives and elderly were above the national average, though only marginally so in the former case (table 3). Ethnic minority groups formed a substantial proportion of the total population and accounted for 40% of the under-fives but only 3% of the 75+ age group. The socio-economic status of significant proportions of the population was also indicated by above average levels of unemployment, low car ownership, a higher proportion of unskilled manual workers and many households lacking the exclusive use of a basic amenity.

Administrative structures were relatively simple: social services, housing and education shared a common boundary. However, in the case of the NHS, this was provided by a single district of a larger AHA being coterminous with the borough, though the district assumed authority status in 1982. Until the 1982 election, political control was vested in a traditional Labour group with extensive personal networks and an emphasis on statutory provision. The voluntary sector was supported only to the extent that it conformed with the statutory departments' models of care and was not actively critical of the council and its policies. Just prior to the election of a new and younger Labour group in 1982, voluntary agencies were invited to a series of policy discussions which formed the basis for a more overtly socialist manifesto.

Net local authority expenditure was consistently above that for Outer London and nationally (table 2), though the loss of RSG in 1980/81 necessitated an across-the-board savings exercise. Of the service departments, social services retained a high expenditure ranking in the late seventies but education experienced some reduction in its share of the council's spending. Expenditure on the NHS was complicated by the locality being an underfunded district within an overfunded teaching area. The establishment of a new general hospital also tended to siphon away growth from the community services. Geriatric and psychiatric provision were well below normative levels, with no geriatric out-patient places or long-stay beds within the district. On the local authority side, social services provision had been unable to keep pace with growth of the elderly population and both residential and domiciliary services had fallen on a per-capita basis – the latter to a lesser extent thanks to an aggressive commitment to community care. Provision for the under-fives had high base levels thanks to pioneering work by health and education. The SSD was also able to sustain service levels with increasing emphasis on childminding. Playgroup provision had declined, however, in the face of competition from education and problems in maintaining parental interest in a period of economic decline and increasing unemployment.

Conclusion

Brief pen pictures inevitably tend to some over-simplification and omission. Nonetheless, the above descriptions do present the essential features of the financial, administrative, demographic and political environments within which inter-agency coordination took place within each locality, arena and client group. Our task was to explore whether differing combinations of such contextual factors produced different patterns of interaction between agencies. In the next chapter, we describe the kinds of interaction we found and identify its outputs. In succeeding chapters, we seek to account for such findings by relating them back to the basic environmental factors outlined here and also to more subtle interpersonal influences located in the values and interest of key participants.

APPENDIX: NOTE ON A 'BUREAUMETRIC' APPROACH TO THE
STUDY OF MACHINERY AND OUTPUT

As we have previously indicated, there were two starting points for our locality studies:
(a) the 'top-down' mapping of formal machinery and its outputs;
(b) the 'bottom-up' mapping of outputs and tracing of their origins back to both formal and informal mechanisms.

The study of machinery was a central element in our fieldwork for two reasons: first as a means of tracing inter-agency process and outputs and, second, because an understanding of the role and effectiveness of such machinery was integral to an understanding of the strengths and weaknesses of the 'optimistic' model's prescriptions for coordination. But which machinery was to be studied? The world of bureaucracy which we were proposing to enter is covered with what, to the uninitiated, might appear to be a jungle of committees, sub-committees, working parties, planning teams and task groups, all more or less permanent and more or less formally established. Moreover, for our locality studies to be comparable, it was necessary to develop criteria which could be applied as consistent measures across them all. Ideally, we needed to compare not only the type and quantity of machinery in each locality but also its relative effectiveness. Ultimately, we were interested in the quality of 'jointness' in machinery, process and output. At the local level, previous work in this field had been largely confined to case studies relying primarily on the traditional methods of observation and documentary analysis. At the central government level Hood and Dunsire[6] had developed a quantitative approach to the comparison of the characteristics of government departments, which they termed 'bureaumetrics'. Goodin[7] had used a somewhat similar technique in exploring variations in the policy making capacities and practices of selected central government departments. Our need, however, was to combine the essential elements of qualitative and quantitative methodologies. In particular, we needed to devise measures of machinery and output which would enable us: to make consistent comparisons across the seven localities; to locate these within the national context; and to explain, on the one hand, the relationship between machinery and output in individual localities and, on the other hand, similarities and differences between localities. In practice, we do not pretend to have more than begun to develop a quantitative element to set alongside the more traditional case study approach. However, we record here both the method and results of our work as a possible starting point for further comparative work.

Criteria for study and comparison of inter-agency machinery

Four criteria were adopted for identifying and 'counting' machinery in each locality: that it should be *formal*, *strategic*, *locality-wide* and with a remit which either encompassed one of two *tracer* groups or had *cross-tracer* responsibilities. Formal machinery was distinguished from less formal processes (such as one-to-one contacts by phone, letter or in person) and informal or unstructured meetings of officers and members. It was defined as meetings at which a common record of the proceedings was agreed and circulated to all participants. It excluded, therefore, meetings at which no records were made or at which participants made separate notes for their individual purposes.

Strategic machinery was that formal machinery whose terms of reference included responsibility for presenting options, or making decisions about long-term planning issues such as the development and balance of service provision within or between agencies. This criterion, like the first, was dictated by the emphasis in the 'optimistic' model's prescriptions that formal coordinating machinery should be established with a long-term strategic perspective.

The criterion that the machinery should have a *locality-wide* role rather than be confined to smaller geographic areas also flows from the emphasis on strategic planning and its comprehensive perspective over a whole field of responsibility. In the present case, the locality was defined as the area covered by Local Social Services Authorities and thus generally coterminous with the territories of Local Education and (until 1982) Health Authorities. We hasten to add that our concentration upon formal, strategic machinery did not imply an assumption that decision making would in practice accord to a synoptic, top-down model of policy making and implementation. Indeed, our study of outputs was specifically designed to identify cases where outputs originated from localised initiatives at operational rather than policy levels. On the other hand, we hypothesised that, for such local examples to be systematised and placed on a more universal basis, they would ultimately appear on the agenda of formal, locality-wide machinery. In other words, the commitment of resources or approval of procedures implicit in extending such initiatives would require legitimation at the locality-wide level. This factor contributed to our decision to include within our counts not only machinery specifically relating to our tracer groups (the elderly and the under-fives) but also that with responsibilities extending across client groups (the *cross-tracer* machinery). Such machinery, for example, JCCs, JCPTs and general committees bringing together representatives of the voluntary and statutory sectors, provided potentially important channels for the diffusion and extension of locally developed initiatives.

It was recognised that the adoption of those criteria would mean excluding, for example, locality-wide machinery with responsibility for day-to-day liaison and operational matters and also strategic machinery with a sub-locality remit – for example those Health Care Planning Teams which, in practice, had been accorded a strategic rather than the formally prescribed operation planning role. It was necessary to do this to ensure that the machinery counts were restricted to machinery at a comparable level across the seven cases. Our discussion of the states of play within each arena does, however, take into account the role played by machinery below the locality-wide level. Such machinery tended to be particularly extensive in shire counties and multi-district health authorities, where, if nothing else, it represented a significant additional administrative cost for coordination.

To recap, therefore, we identified and examined the operation of a wide range of machinery whose field of responsibility included the two tracer groups. However, for the purposes of comparison between authorities, we concentrated upon that machinery which met the criteria of being formal, strategic and locality-wide. More informal mechanisms and processes were identified through a complementary bottom-up process whose starting point was the identification of outputs. Finally, it should be noted that the machinery was categorised as *intra-agency* or *inter-agency*. Our primary concern was with machinery through which inter-agency relations were conducted. However, since we hypothesised that the quality of inter-agency planning would be directly related to the quality of intra-agency planning, it was necessary to identify the planning machinery of individual agencies. The definition of inter-agency machinery presented some difficulties since at least two possible models appeared to exist on the ground:

(a) machinery composed of members from more than one agency and with terms of reference from and accountability to more than one agency;

(b) machinery with terms of reference from and accountability to only one agency but containing invited representatives from other agencies.

The latter appeared at best to be consistent with concepts of parallel or mutually sensitive planning rather than the integrated planning of the 'optimistic' model. Consequently, and for the purposes of the machinery count alone, the first definition was adopted for the inter-agency category. Inter-agency machinery was defined, therefore, in terms of both its composition and accountability.

REFERENCES

1 R. Greenwood and J. D. Stewart (1974) *Corporate Planning in English Local Government*, Charles Knight
2 Association of Metropolitan Authorities (AMA), Association of County Councils (ACC) and National Council for Voluntary Organisations (NCVO) (1981) *Working Together*, Bedford Square Press
3 DHSS and Welsh Office (1978) *A Happier Old Age*, HMSO
4 DHSS, Scottish Office, Welsh Office and Northern Ireland Office (1981) *Growing Older*, Cmnd 8173, HMSO
5 C. Hood and A. Dunsire (1981) *Bureaumetrics: The Quantitative Comparison of British Central Government Agencies*, Gower
6 *Ibid.*
7 R. E. Goodin, 'Banana time in British politics', *Political Studies*, vol. 30, no. 1, pp. 45–58

7 ~ Coordination at local level: state of play

In this chapter we present our findings on the extent and nature of coordination across the seven localities. In the first instance our objective is to provide a flavour of the state of play in each of the three arenas of agency interaction: the corporate, collaboration and inter-section arenas. The extent and operation of both formal and informal mechanisms are analysed, together with their achievements. In so doing, we draw upon, and contrast, two kinds of evidence: quantitative data collected through our 'bureaumetric' mapping of machinery and outputs (see chapter 6); and qualitative materials provided in interviews with local actors. The two sources are found to generate broadly – but not wholly – consistent findings. We conclude by highlighting similarities and differences between arenas, client groups and localities, thereby addressing the basic research questions set out at the beginning of the previous chapter.

THE LOCAL AUTHORITY ARENA

The rhetoric of rationality first began to take root locally in the local authority arena, where the 'optimistic' model became established in the particular form of corporate planning and management. The need for coordination was, by definition, at the heart of the corporate approach to local government. As early as 1967, the Maud Report criticised a situation in which there was 'unity in the parts but disunity in the whole'[1]. Its response was a blueprint for reorganising local government committees and management structures to promote coordination of both policy and administration. The Bains Report[2] of 1972 elaborated upon this blueprint and ensured that it became enshrined in the management structures of the reorganised local authorities which came into being in 1974. Underpinning these structures were four elements of formal organisation: the Chief Executive; the Chief Officer Management Team (COMT); the Policy and Resources Committee; and the Central Planning Unit (CPU). The first three were all but universally established but only a minority of authorities adopted the CPU [3,4]. The most recent evidence shows this pattern persisting into the early eighties[5]. However, research has consistently shown that the corporate approach has had substantially less

159

impact upon the planning and management processes of local government than its structures[6,7,8,9].

Given this background, we sought to establish how far a corporate approach had been undertaken towards the authority as a whole, and towards the elderly and under-fives in particular. Our findings were largely consistent with that suggested by the national pattern. Each authority had established a core of 'corporate machinery' but a number had never attempted to develop corporate processes. Where there had been an initial enthusiasm for such processes in other authorities, this had been dissipated by the late 1970s. Whether regulated by 'gentlemanly agreement' as in Greenshire, or polarised by competition, distrust and conflict as in Riverton, the corporate arena was one in which departments largely went their own way with little apparent regard to the wider local authority context. Such inter-departmental contacts as took place tended to be bilateral rather than multilateral and, in general, departmentalism reigned.

Formal corporate structures made little positive impact. COMTs rarely acted as planning bodies. In Cliffshire, for example, it was said the COMT meetings tended 'to get bogged down with fairly mundane issues. To exaggerate a bit, they tend to be issues like what sort of notepaper the authority should use or about telephone systems.' This experience was not untypical. In Templeborough, meetings were used primarily for 'mutual back-scratching', not for 'corporate interrogation or control'. In Portshire, where the COMT had a stronger role, the balance of its interest was strongly towards resource issues (such as personnel, land holdings and budgetary matters) rather than towards service policies.

There was little inter-departmental planning machinery for individual client groups. Three authorities had no machinery at all for the elderly and the same was true of the under-fives (table 1). Nor did corporate planning units (CPUs) act as the focus for inter-departmental policy making for the tracer groups. Although all but three authorities (Cliffshire, Riverton and Templeborough) possessed such units, they were rarely vehicles for policy development and initiation. In Woodtown, the core responsibilities of the CPU included servicing the COMT, population projections and coordination of the urban programme, while in Fulborough it was involved in consumer research and capital programme coordination. The overall Woodtown unit was described in terms which were of a general applicability: '[the unit] has not really been involved on the policy side, exploring issues and problems in depth but merely on the information side ... It's a bit of a ragbag, taking on responsibilities which don't fall elsewhere.'

A number of authorities had sought to establish a policy oriented corporate approach during the 1970s in which the CPU played a pivotal role. However,

Table 1 *Amount of machinery in the corporate arena (1979–81)*

	Machinery			Total
	Cross-tracer	Elderly	Under-fives	
Cliffshire	2	0	2	4
Fulborough	3	0	1	4
Greenshire	2	3	2	7
Portshire	3	0	0	3
Riverton	2	1	0	3
Templeborough	2	1	0	3
Woodtown	6	2	1	9
Total	20	7	6	33

as enthusiasm for the corporate idea waned, so too did the position of the CPU. In Fulborough the 'all singing and dancing' approach to planning was abandoned early on and the work of the CPU became that of 'using the strengths of departmentalism to occasionally get a corporate view', concentrating on specific *projects*. Corporate planning had been most fully developed in Greenshire where the CPU adopted a three year policy planning system with a continuous programme of policy analysis and review (PAR). However, as expenditure pressures grew, central planning became preoccupied with budgetary control and the role of the CPU diminished. The formal planning process was abandoned in 1980 although PAR was retained and used on a more selective and reactive basis. Woodtown conducted a comprehensive corporate objectives exercise in the mid 1970s but this was a one-off event, said to have no obvious impact on departmental policy and practice. Elsewhere, comprehensive corporate planning had never been attempted. By 1981 there was little evidence of chief officers anywhere retaining commitment to it. Benign coexistence rather than good-willed coordination was the hallmark of inter-departmental relationships, though even peaceful coexistence proved difficult to attain in Riverton.

In both Fulborough and Woodtown, member resistance was seen to be a factor in the demise of corporate planning. In Fulborough 'there was no corporate political will. The chairs tended to run their own show.' Similarly, in Woodtown, there was a reluctance to 'look with favour at a system of giving power to officers rather than themselves – which is what the corporate model implies'. More recently, however, the ruling group had strongly advocated a more coordinated approach to policy in selected policy areas, including the elderly and children, and member level machinery was associated with new inter-departmental initiatives. Officers emphasised that 'a great deal of the credit' for improvements in inter-departmental working between both housing and social services and also education and social services 'had to go to members for making sure it works by setting up joint sub-committees and the under-fives coordinating committee'. A less broadly based member initiative in Cliffshire produced a joint sub-committee of education, leisure and social services, inter alia, to develop more coordinated services for the under-fives. Such initiatives were comparatively rare, however.

The elderly

Housing and social services were the main actors with the contribution of leisure, libraries and education being small in comparison. Education was a growing provider through, for example, the attachment of teachers to day centres in two authorities; the use of school premises as luncheon centres in one locality and as an Age Concern centre in another; and also through pre-retirement classes, which were widespread. Nonetheless it was on the relationship of housing and social services departments that the coordination of services for the elderly was primarily dependent within the corporate arena. In the metropolitan districts and London boroughs, such coordination was a matter of one-to-one relationships between departments within the same authority. However, in the shire counties, where housing was the responsibility of up to 13 district councils, coordination had a more complex, inter-authority dimension.

A tradition of separatism
In six of our seven localities there was traditionally little interaction between housing and social services. This was reflected in the paucity of machinery for the elderly in the corporate arena (table 1) and in the lack of informal contacts for anything other than individual problem cases – an area of high potential conflict. Only in Greenshire had productive relationships been long established: for the rest insularity and separatism were the norm, or had been so until recently. The metaphors used in Fulborough where the two departments were described by one chief officer as 'paddling their own canoes' and by the other as 'driving their own steam rollers' were broadly applicable to the other five. Relationships in Woodtown were improving but were historically typified as: 'a case of the pot calling the kettle black which didn't get us anywhere. The amount of time and energy that was spent writing long and tedious memos proving that everyone else was worse than you, and how bad they were, is nobody's business.' Similarly, in Riverton, joint working was a very recent development in a context characterised by mistrust and antagonism between respective chairman and chief officers.

Table 2 *Amount of output for the elderly in the corporate arena*

	Machinery output[a]			Informal outputs[b]	
	Policies	Projects	Practices	Projects	Practices
Cliffshire	o	o	o	o	1
Fulborough	o	o	o	o	1
Greenshire	o	4	2	3	o
Portshire	o	o	o	o	1
Riverton	o	o	o	o	o
Templeborough	o	1	o	o	1
Woodtown	1	2	1	o	o
Total	1	7	3	3	4

[a] For counting purposes projects and practices were only included if they had originated in the formal machinery and implemented in the period January 1979 – December 1981.
[b] All informal outputs in operation 1979–81 whenever implemented.

The only locality where there was evidence of prolonged success in collaboration between housing and social services was Greenshire. Indeed one respondent described it as: 'joint planning at its very best – relations with the housing department are unique, I don't know of any other authority with such good ones'. Provision for the elderly included: support for extra care sheltered housing cost yardsticks; and the upgrading of sheltered schemes. Significantly, Greenshire had half of all the outputs recorded for the elderly in the corporate arena (table 2). Although many were provided through joint finance (as well as resources from the SSD main budget), the housing/social services inter-relationship largely operated outside the joint planning arena. Indeed the health districts resisted such joint finance spending. The relationship was mainly due to the entreprencurial activity of an assistant director in the SSD and his ad-hoc informal links with the Chief Housing Officers' Group (CHOG) which brought together all the district council housing authorities. Formal machinery between the SSD and CHOG had also been established, comprising a Working Party on Housing for Special Needs and its sub-group on Housing for the Elderly. Although this machinery was important, the most significant forum for collaboration was the CHOG. Not only did this bring together a large number of separate authorities (which the SSD would have found difficult, if not impossible, to deal with individually) but it also had an interest in achievement and in improving its status through association with the more prestigious caring service. Thus informal relationships proved to be the foundation on which a county-wide approach was subsequently developed through formal machinery, with the latter proving to be the source of twice as many outputs as informal processes (table 2).

A new impetus

Attempts were being made to establish closer working relationships between housing and social services in four of the remaining six localities, however. Only in Cliffshire and Portshire were there no signs of improved relationships. Much of the impetus behind the shift towards closer interaction elsewhere came from the housing departments, though social services were not necessarily unwilling participants. Historically, housing authorities in our localities had been reluctant to allocate housing on the basis of social rather than housing need and, thus, to accept a social care role; sheltered housing was not conceived as accommodation for the dependent and wardens were not expected to provide care. In Riverton, for instance, we were told:

In the past housing directors just sat there and thought it was good to provide housing schemes and to accommodate nice ladies who gave them no problems.

More recently a number of factors had combined to change that perception. The introduction of the Housing Investment Programmes (HIPs) alerted departments to the problem of the elderly and at the same time provided the information base necessary for more comprehensive planning. As one officer in Woodtown commented:

We were actually asked on the [HIPs] form how many elderly people we thought needed sheltered housing – it was the first time we were asked that and it was a very difficult thing to measure, but we had to look at issues of that nature.

This was reinforced by the shift in the building programme to a concentration almost entirely upon special needs housing. In Fulborough the requirement to quantify special needs in order to shore up the HIPs submission stimulated overtures from housing to the SSD. The SSD in turn used the opportunity to underline its claims for housing resources. The increasing frailty of tenants in sheltered housing and the shortage of SSD and hospital residential provision was also slowly forcing housing departments to accept that some change of approach was necessary. Thus, in Templeborough, for instance, the housing department was, after some years of inactivity and isolation on the elderly policy front, making tentative moves towards engaging with other agencies and sectors. Their perspectives on sheltered housing and the role of wardens was being reconsidered:

We are conscious we cannot stick rigidly to the 'good neighbour' definition, we don't want people to be transferred out of sheltered schemes as soon as they become too difficult to manage, they would know the next stop is the last stop ... the role of wardens will change as there is more longevity and as the old people's homes are not really what some people want ... I am planning a whole series of discussions with social services on sheltered schemes ... It's long overdue.

It was too early to say whether this approach would be successful but social services had long been outwardly oriented and were anxious to change a situation wherein, as they saw it, 'one needed to be an Olympic champion to currently qualify for sheltered provision'. In Fulborough, changes in outlook were much more tentative but evident nonetheless. Piper and Cass alarm systems were being considered by the housing department and a 'supported housing officer' appointed. Even in Riverton there appeared to be a major breakthrough when plans for a very sheltered housing scheme were developed by housing, social services and the AHA. The appointment of a new deputy director of housing as well as the factors outlined above facilitated this as did an increased openness within the SSD. However, longstanding and sometimes highly personalised antagonisms remained strong at chief officer and member level, and the scheme became the victim of a clash between the departments over a completely different issue.

It was in Woodtown that relationships between housing and social services looked most likely to be productive: apart from Greenshire, this was the only authority with more than one output for the elderly in this arena and the only one to agree an inter-departmental policy (table 2). Again housing took the initiative with member interest, HIPs and the appointment of an energetic deputy director with entrepreneurial skills all being important factors behind this. Social services were initially cautious but professional member interest in alternatives to institutional care led them to accept a new planning relationship with housing. The development of this more productive policy-oriented relationship was facilitated by the strengthening and redirection of a number of existing forums and the creation of new strategy groups. The Joint Housing and Social Services Sub-Committee met more frequently and assumed a stronger policy role. An informal meeting between deputy directors also shifted its emphasis from individual cases to broader policy issues. A 'Strategy for the Elderly' group was established in 1981 serviced by a working party drawn from the two departments' recently established Development Units. Without the planning capacity provided by those units (and especially that in the SSD) it is unlikely that the initiative could have developed so far. By early 1982, when our fieldwork ended, a broad strategy had been accepted and two schemes were already under construction to provide resource centres and associated very sheltered housing units.

Summary
A clear association was found between formal machinery and output: two-thirds of all machinery was in the two localities (Greenshire and

Woodtown) which produced the bulk of housing/social services outputs (tables 1 and 2). But machinery did not guarantee output, as the Riverton experience illustrates. The minimal levels of output in the three localities without machinery (Cliffshire, Fulborough and Greenshire) does not suggest that informal networks will readily fill the gap in localities without machinery. Indeed, in Greenshire and Woodtown the complementarity and mutual reinforcement of formal and informal processes were a striking feature of their achievements. Thus, in the case of the elderly, at least, formal machinery appeared to be an essential, if not necessarily sufficient, pre-requisite of the higher levels of output. Whether this was also true of the under-fives is an issue to which we now turn.

The under-fives

Within the local authority arena, coordination for the under-fives was primarily a matter for social services and education, the major service providers. Relationships between them varied considerably across our seven localities. At one extreme stood Riverton with neither machinery nor output (tables 1 and 3) and a history of acrimonious communication. At the other was Portshire with a national reputation for innovation and collaboration in the under-fives field and liaison procedures said to be 'inbuilt as a way of working'. An extensive network of coordinative machinery coupled with an ease of informal relationships produced substantial outputs, though many were in the inter-sector arena. Between these extremes was a wide range of interaction but a number of common themes emerged. First, formal relationships between the two local authority departments tended to take place within the wider inter-sectoral context. Outputs within the local authority arena were correspondingly limited. Second, education departments were generally reluctant to interact with other agencies: joint working was accepted as only a second best to the development of their own services. Finally, and not unrelated, informal relationships between education and social services were poorly developed in most localities.

Machinery and outputs

Very little machinery had been established for the under-fives in this arena (table 1). Indeed, in three localities there was no machinery at all, while there were only six forums in total across the seven localities. However, much of the formal interaction between education and social services took place within a wider arena involving the health authority, the non-statutory sector, or both. Multilateral machinery of one kind or another had been established in six of the seven localities by 1981. Only in Woodtown, however, was there a member level under-fives coordinating committee involving the education and social services committees, the AHA and the non-statutory sector: but in four others (Greenshire, Portshire, Templeborough and Fulborough) officer coordinating groups were in operation. In Riverton there was no collaborative machinery of any kind between the two departments (other than the Area Review Committee) while that in Cliffshire was not established until late 1981 and comprised solely of the education, social services and leisure departments. This picture appears broadly representative of the national experience presented by Bradley[10]. His findings suggest that in a sample of seven localities we would expect to find one or two coordinating committees and three or four officer groups. Our localities did seem to have rather higher levels of voluntary sector involvement than Bradley found nationally but the general pattern of multilateral coordination is broadly similar.

The lack of machinery in Riverton and (prior to 1981) Cliffshire was symptomatic of the lack of interaction between education and social services in these two localities. However, the mere existence of machinery did not necessarily mean that purposeful and productive relationships had been established. In Templeborough, for instance, a bilateral forum was first established in 1976 but needed re-establishing in 1978 and again, through wider membership, in 1980. Officers there considered that even 'continuing to meet is success', though the earlier two groups may have done more harm than good. They produced little beyond a joint holding report to the separate local authority committees and engendered a degree of mistrust, acrimony and despondency among participants:

We met and wrangled and jangled; there were no big blow-ups but it was one of those meetings you come out of and thought 'we just didn't get anywhere'. What eventually happened was people just didn't turn up to it.

Although the machinery in Woodtown had been more productive than in Templeborough (table 3), it was also suggested that the more the two departments came into contact the more distrustful they became. Furthermore, the machinery was also a function of the failure of bilateral relationships. A Programme Review Panel, a corporate body chaired by the head of the Corporate Planning Unit, was established because bilateral negotiations seemed unable to further collaboration. It was hoped that progress could be made by taking discussion out of the bilateral context. In the event, the barriers to productive bilateral discussions proved just as powerful in the corporate forum. Indeed, the Programme Review Panel had to overcome the further obstacle of a general absence of support for corporate processes. In Portshire similar barriers existed. Education and social services had endeavoured to produce a joint policy statement. However, this failed to secure the approval of the Director of Education who suggested that, rather than there

Table 3 *Amount of output for the under-fives in the local authority arena*

	Machinery output[a]			Informal outputs[b]	
	Policies	Projects	Practices	Projects	Practices
Cliffshire	0	2	0	0	4
Fulborough	0	0	3	6	2
Greenshire	0	0	0	0	0
Portshire	0	4	2	2	2
Riverton	0	0	0	0	0
Templeborough	0	0	0	0	2
Woodtown	0	3	0	0	2
Total	0	9	5	8	12

[a] For counting purposes projects and practices were only included if they had originated in the formal machinery and implemented in the period January 1979 – December 1981.
[b] All informal outputs in operation 1979–81 whenever implemented.

being a commitment to a joint approach, it would 'be more realistic to say that we believe in diversified provision'.

Even where formal relationships were well established and suffused with commitment and good-will, the machinery tended to develop a liaison and communication rather than a policy or planning role. This was equally true of officer and member machinery, joint planning machinery and wider coordinating groups in the inter-sector arena. For instance, in Greenshire the JCPT children's sub-group, the central focus for education and social services, was described as a 'useful talking shop' but an 'otherwise lacking forum – the only place where health, education and social services people can meet to talk about mutual concerns on a regular basis'. Similar sentiments were expressed about the officer coordinating group in Fulborough and, more sceptically, about the coordinating committee in Woodtown.

More concrete achievements of the formal machinery included joint training schemes, jointly appointed advisers, the provision of teachers for day nurseries, low cost nursery provision, pre-school advisory teachers for the handicapped, and combined nursery centres. However, outputs of the formal machinery predominantly operated at the inter-sector rather than the education/social services interface (see below). In the local authority arena itself no locality had produced a strategic plan for services for the under-fives; in only four (Cliffshire, Fulborough, Portshire and Woodtown) had any projects or practices been established through the formal machinery. Furthermore, a number of these were single service outputs routed through inter-departmental machinery. In Riverton there were no outputs at all while in Cliffshire, Templeborough and Fulborough machinery output was low and tended to be of the least demanding kind such as joint training or the production of booklets on service provision. 'Informal' outputs were particularly evident in Fulborough, and in Cliffshire informal, entrepreneurial activity by the under-fives advisers and operational level staff had also reaped some benefits (table 3). Combined centres – the height of good practice, as defined by central government – were at one time or another on the agenda of five of our localities, the availability of urban aid helping to stimulate interest. Only in three, however, had such centres been built and only in Portshire were the attendant operational problems overcome. In Cliffshire, the difficulties experienced in running two centres, built in the early 1970s, were such that in 1976 education assumed all managerial responsibility for them both, though in 1981 proposals for another combined centre were back on the agenda.

Outputs bridging the nursery education/day care divide were, on the face of it, more strongly developed by Woodtown's joint education and social services sub-committee. However, experiences there of joint working in a combined centre and a day nursery attached to a nursery school, coupled with severe problems encountered in developing additional joint services, were such that the two departments were retreating from joint working. Plans to build a second combined nursery centre were at an advanced stage when they were rejected by the education department, ostensibly on cost grounds. Eventually an alternative package was proposed involving extended day and extended year nursery education for the three to five year olds and sponsored childminding for the under-threes. The former was to be provided by education and the latter by social services. It was suggested that dividing the client group up in this way might, as a general principle, be the best way for the two departments to proceed.

Perhaps the most radical attempt to foster closer working in the corporate arena through the establishment of coordinative machinery was in Cliffshire, where, historically, formal relationships had been distant and largely unproductive. A joint sub-committee of the education, leisure and social services was set up in 1981, with one of its three working parties being primarily concerned with the under-fives. The sub-committee was given its own budget to stimulate and facilitate joint working. However, while this budget undoubtedly provided an incentive for departments to engage in a heavy programme of meetings, it also served – at least in the first instance – to drive out a more strategic, policy-oriented approach. In its first year the pressure to spend money was such that, as one officer put it:

There was no strategy to it. It rather smacked of mainstream service provision. It was a case of chief officers using it as a fund to tap into.

Thus, outputs comprised solely of funding for sponsored childminders and for equipment for childminders – both of which are mainstream social services provision. At the time of our fieldwork, it was not clear whether the committee would be able to work towards more fundamental issues such as the appropriate balance between education, social services and voluntary provision.

Coordination: a valued goal?

Reservations about joint working were expressed in every locality we visited. Education in particular was sceptical of the benefits of collaboration. Even in Portshire, where coordination was seen 'as very much the thing to do', there was some ambivalence in education's stance. Coordination had been pursued largely on pragmatic grounds, as a case of 'making the best situation of what we've got'. The education department in Greenshire felt itself to be in a similar position and considered collaboration very much 'second best compared to the hoped and planned for nursery education programme'. In Riverton, on the other hand, far from being second best, collaboration with social services was perceived as a real threat to the integrity of education itself, potentially leading to the dilution of the distinctive and superior contribution made by teachers. As one respondent indicated:

the worry we would have is with the idea of setting up a little independent department where nursery units were going to be controlled by non-professionals – I mean non-professional teachers. The bomb would really go up.

Nowhere else were reservations expressed so strongly but similar, albeit muted, sentiments were still to be heard.

It was not only education who were unsure of the virtues of collaboration, however. Thus, the joint sub-committee established in Cliffshire was a member initiative supported by officers from all the service departments involved (and the chief executive's department) only because of pressure from members. In Fulborough the social services department concentrated on day care for children under three, leaving ILEA to provide for older children – a similar division of responsibilities as proposed in Woodtown, though executed unilaterally and less explicitly. In part this may have been because working with ILEA was so difficult. As one respondent commented:

ILEA is the biggest bureaucracy there is: it's like a swamp, you don't know whether to surround it or drain it. It is impossible to get them to move in any direction.

Nevertheless, the idea that education was reluctant to become involved and 'the hardest department for anyone to get into' was one of the strongest themes uniting our localities. There were exceptions: in Greenshire an informal coordinative network had been built up around the formal structure whereby it was possible to 'have a chat over a pint'; while in Portshire good informal relations and considerable good-will were apparent at every level but especially between the chief education officer and director of social services. Elsewhere there were examples of similarly good informal relations and communication lower down the hierarchy, particularly among specialist advisers.

Summary

In contrast to the elderly, coordination for the under-fives was less completely focused within the formal machinery, as is indicated by the level of 'informal output' being almost as high as 'machinery output' (table 3). Significantly, however, informal outputs consisted largely of what we termed 'practices' (i.e. changes of working within existing resources), rather than projects (the setting up of new schemes), perhaps suggesting a limitation on what can be achieved informally, particularly by operational and advisory staff. In all, coordination for the under-fives in the local authority arena was poorly developed. Relationships were often poor, commitment low and outputs limited. However, to the extent that the relationships between education and social services also took place within the statutory/non-statutory arena, the above is only a partial view of the state of play for the client group as a whole. The success of the relationship in Portshire, and to a lesser degree Greenshire, for instance, is perhaps most clearly seen in the level of output for the under-fives at the statutory/non-statutory interface, where the possibilities of low cost provision provide an added incentive for joint working (see below).

THE HEALTH AND LOCAL AUTHORITY ARENA

As we noted in chapter 3, national guidance gave emphasis to the creation of joint machinery with a strategic planning role. In addition, the programme of joint finance was initiated by DHSS as an incentive for health and local authorities to collaborate. The coordination of local policy planning and service development for the elderly was a key task for the collaboration machinery but under-fives' services were a less central focus. Nonetheless, our fieldwork was designed to identify, for both tracer groups, the contribution to inter-authority coordination of joint planning, joint finance and less formal mechanisms. In addition, we were conscious that NHS restructuring[11,12] might be casting a shadow over collaborative planning during the fieldwork. It was necessary, therefore, not only to pursue the implications of structural change in the health service for collaboration but also to ensure that our findings were historically grounded and not merely a reflection of what might prove to be only temporary administrative disruption. The bureaumetric mapping of machinery and outputs over time was particularly important in this context.

Joint planning machinery

Cross-tracer machinery primarily consisted of the Joint Consultative Committees (JCCs) which authorities were statutorily required to establish and the Joint Care Planning Teams (JCPTs), which the 1976 joint planning circular had envisaged would be the keystone of joint strategic planning for priority client groups (DHSS 1976). This category also included a number of specialist groups dealing with joint finance. *Tracer group* machinery included bodies with remits covering the whole or defined parts of service systems for the elderly or the under-fives, and also those whose central concern was with other fields or issues (such as mental illness or child health services) but which impinged upon the two tracer groups.

JCCs and JCPTs had been set up in each locality. In two of the three shire counties separate JCCs with county and district councils had been established. Greenshire had originally adopted this model but subsequently combined them into a single JCC, in common with four other English shire counties[13]. Cliffshire was unusual in being one of the only four shire counties nationally to possess a district council JCPT. Considerable variations existed in the extent to which the core joint planning machinery was used, however (table 4). The average number of meetings nationally over the three years 1979–81 ranged from 0.7 to 4.3 times a year in the case of JCCs and from 0 to 8 times a year for JCPTs. The mean number of meetings per year across the seven localities was 2.8 for JCCs and 3.4 for JCPTs compared with 2.9 and 4.9 respectively in England as a whole. Thus, formal interaction between officers through the JCPT was somewhat less frequent in our fieldwork localities than nationally. The three year averages did conceal some important changes over time, however. For example, in Greenshire, during 1978–80 a period of 18 months elapsed between meetings of the combined JCC before a more regular round of meetings was re-established. The Riverton JCC and JCPT met on only seven occasions from 1974–80 and 1976–80 respectively, after which the AHA took over responsibility for the Secretariat and initiated a quarterly cycle of meetings for each body. Generally speaking, however, there was a marked reduction in meetings from late 1980 onwards as the NHS became increasingly preoccupied with the mechanics of restructuring. We return to this issue at a later point.

Tracer group machinery was less fully established: in only two localities had JCPT sub-groups for the elderly been set up compared with 62% nationally though a number of other planning groups had more limited

Table 4 *Frequency of meetings per annum: JCCs and JCPTs*

	JCCs	JCPTs
Cliffshire	2.3[a] 0.7[b]	3[a] 0[b]
Fulborough	2	8
Greenshire	2	6
Portshire	3[a] 1[b]	1
Riverton	2.7	2.3
Templeborough	3.3	4
Woodtown	4.3	3
All fieldwork localities	2.8[c]	3.4[c]
England[d]	2.9	4.9

[a] County councils JCC/JCPT
[b] District councils JCC/JCPT
[c] All JCCs/JCPTs
[d] Based on 70% response rate to survey of all English AHAs[14]

remits. Four of the localities possessed JCPT sub-groups relevant to the under-fives but their primary concern was with child health. Indeed issues surrounding the implementation of the Short Report on maternity services[15] commonly occupied a considerable amount of agenda time during the period preceding our fieldwork. Only in Greenshire were the full range of services for the under-fives a defined focus for the joint planning machinery. There, the JCPT sub-group for children effectively became the implementation arm of the Under Fives Steering Group, a county-wide forum for senior representatives of statutory and non-statutory agencies. This JCPT sub-group was also unusual in including within its active membership officers from the education department and corporate planning unit. In general, however, such systems-wide approaches to services for the under-fives took place outside the health and local authority arena and in contexts where the NHS tended to act as onlookers rather than full participants.

Table 5 summarises the amounts of joint planning machinery with a strategic role and a locality-wide remit. It reveals a relatively wide range of experience with Woodtown having some three times as much machinery as Fulborough and Riverton. While all localities possessed a basic core of cross-tracer machinery, there were significant variations in the amounts of tracer group machinery within and between each of the client groups. Overall, there was over twice as much machinery for the elderly as the under-fives. But the amount of machinery for the elderly varied widely.

Table 5 *Amount of cross-tracer and tracer machinery in the health and local authority arena (1979–81)*

	Machinery			Total
	Cross-tracer	Elderly	Under-fives	
Cliffshire	6	5	0	11
Fulborough	3	0	1	4
Greenshire	3	2	2	7
Portshire	3	5	3	11
Riverton	3	2	0	5
Templeborough	5	3	1	9
Woodtown	3	8	3	14
Total	26	25	10	61

Fulborough had none; Cliffshire and Portshire five groups; and Woodtown eight.

The table does not, however, include all the planning machinery in the collaboration arena. Health care planning teams existed in most localities and included local authority representatives among their membership, though generally of a senior practitioner rather than management rank. However, they were not included in table 5 for three reasons: they were established by and responsible to NHS management teams rather than JCCs or JCPTs; they were given operational rather than strategic planning remits; and in multi-district areas had localised rather than locality-wide roles. Nonetheless we did seek to establish whether in practice they contributed to inter-agency planning for the tracer group.

Collaboration in practice

Thus far we have done little more than expose the bare bones of health and local authority collaborative planning. We now attempt to flesh these out by examining the practice of joint planning in our seven localities. In particular, we identify the players and the products of joint planning: who participated in the machinery and what did they achieve? What channels of interaction existed outside the formal machinery and what was produced by them? We also studied the contribution of joint finance together with impact of *Patients First*[16] and the administrative upheaval which followed.

The players

In practice, the collaboration machinery provided an essentially bilateral forum in which active local authority involvement from the service departments was largely confined to social services. Housing, education and environmental health were at best onlookers and at worst non-participants. This reflected, in part, the apparently more extensive nature of service interdependencies across health and PSS boundaries. However, it also reflected the more subtle influence of joint planning's DHSS parentage, a factor both symbolised and reinforced by the limitation of joint finance to the social services during the period covered by our fieldwork. This restriction was perhaps most keenly experienced in housing departments which felt they were increasingly being called upon to accommodate the more dependent elderly as a result of shortages in hospital and residential provision. It was particularly influential in Cliffshire where district councils had been encouraged by the AHA to bring forward sheltered housing schemes in the early days of joint finance, only to find DHSS clarifying the terms of the programme to exclude all but SSDs from direct access to its funds. Thus rebuffed, housing authorities saw little incentive or purpose to their participation in the joint planning machinery. That this ruling need not necessarily exclude housing departments from receiving joint finance was demonstrated in Greenshire. The SSD there explicitly used joint finance to draw housing authorities into a programme for providing very sheltered accommodation. However, this was achieved in the first instance on a bilateral housing/PSS basis outside the collaboration machinery with the NHS (see above). Indeed, housing departments tended to be poorly represented on the joint planning (and especially the tracer) machinery across all seven localities. Their attendance levels at both cross-tracer and tracer machinery was also considerably lower than that of NHS and PSS personnel. Among several contributory factors to this situation was the strong tendency of NHS officers to reflect the emphasis in DHSS guidelines on residential care rather than alternatives based on sheltered or 'ordinary' housing. The quality of housing/ SSD relationships was a further important factor. Traditions of departmental insularity in metropolitan authorities and of domain sensitivity in county/ district relations were unfertile ground for joint planning in the wider collaborative arena.

The participation of education authorities was, if anything, even more limited. Education departments saw no practical reasons for attending meetings apparently concerned with issues on, and often beyond, the margin of their responsibilities and interests. This position was highlighted by the Director of Education who emphasised that 'relationships with the health service, if they are not non-existent, are certainly of no significance'. In another locality, this attitude led the JCPT to issue 'a three line whip' to the education department's nominal representative. For their part, education officers tended to see the interface of their services with the NHS as a

Table 6 *Amount of output for the elderly in the collaboration arena (1979–81)*

	Machinery output[a]			Informal outputs[b]	
	Policies	Projects	Practices	Projects	Practices
Cliffshire	0	9	1	0	1
Fulborough	0	3	1	1	3
Greenshire	0	0	0	3	2
Portshire	0	4	3	0	0
Riverton	0	4	0	0	1
Templeborough	1	1	0	2	2
Woodtown	1	10	0	0	0
Total	2	31	5	6	9

[a] For counting purposes projects and practices were only included if they had originated in the formal machinery and implemented in the period January 1979 – December 1981.
[b] All informal outputs in operation 1979–81 whenever implemented.

Table 7 *Amount of output for the under-fives in the collaboration arena (1979–81)*

	Machinery output[a]			Informal outputs[b]	
	Policies	Projects	Practices	Projects	Practices
Cliffshire	0	0	0	0	2
Fulborough	0	0	0	0	0
Greenshire	0	0	0	0	1
Portshire	0	0	0	0	0
Riverton	0	2	0	0	2
Templeborough	0	0	1	1	1
Woodtown	0	0	0	0	3
Total	0	2	1	1	9

[a] For counting purposes projects and practices were only included if they had originated in the formal machinery and implemented in the period January 1979 – December 1981.
[b] All informal outputs in operation 1979–81 whenever implemented.

relatively low level area of operational liaison. JCPT agendas all too often contained no items which justified absenting themselves from more pressing departmental matters. At best, therefore, education officers attended joint planning forums simply to maintain a watching brief.

Achievements of collaboration

(a) Policies

During the period 1979–81, no locality produced within the collaboration arena a comprehensive joint plan for the provision of services to the elderly or the under-fives client group as a whole (tables 6 and 7). Nor had the compilation of any such document pre-dated our study. Only one locality, Greenshire, jointly prepared base line data on service provision and gaps, a step generally considered to be an essential early stage in strategic planning. However, the exercise got no further: the relevant JCPT sub-group effectively ceased to exist after only one meeting and the provision of a verbal report to the JCPT. In two other authorities, Woodtown and Portshire, interest had been expressed in the balance of care model, which potentially offered a route to the creation of a joint information base. In Woodtown investigation of the model was still at an early exploratory stage, and in Portshire the authorities had made little progress in applying it. Comprehensive client group planning was similarly rare for the under-fives although, in Greenshire, an earlier corporate planning analysis and review exercise had formed the basis for subsequent implementation activity in the collaborative arena.

We identified only one successful example of coordinated planning on a formal and comprehensive basis. This was in Woodtown where, in 1977, the JCC established a working party of members and officers to make recommendations on the future development of services for elderly mentally infirm people. Thus its remit covered an identifiable sub-population of the client group and one for whom the lack of provision had aroused a great deal of adverse publicity locally. The working party's report, which took only some six months to prepare, specified a development programme for both health and local authority services. These programmes were agreed by both authorities and subsequently implemented with the aid of both joint finance and main budget resources. This example conformed closely to the joint planning model contained in the DHSS circulars[17]. It was, however, the only example of health and local authorities jointly seeking to construct, let alone implement, a coordinated programme of action for a defined client group population.

Plans for the tracer groups were not entirely absent from the collaboration arena. However, such plans were prepared within individual agencies, on a largely or wholly independent basis, and subsequently entered the arena for information and discussion. Each of the AHAs, for example, had prepared strategic plans which included services for children and elderly people. However, these were essentially health service documents to which local authorities generally made little, if any, effective input. Their contributions were largely limited to the provision of demographic data and details of existing and proposed levels of local authority provision. The strategic plans, themselves, varied widely in how far such provision was taken into account when making proposals for future health services. The Woodtown plan, for example, contained almost no mention of local authority provision but that in Cliffshire identified specific roles for such services and also included a costed development programme to bring them up to DHSS norms. Neither the separatism of Woodtown nor the Cliffshire approach of appearing to plan on behalf of the SSD, provided the most obvious or fruitful route to joint planning.

There was also a considerable amount of planning activity within SSDs for the tracer groups. For example, the Cliffshire department had invested a substantial amount of planning time in the development of a coordinated social services strategy for elderly people. Fulborough and Woodtown had also sought to secure a more coordinated and, in the latter's case, highly innovatory approach to the provision of services for this client group. However, as with the NHS, such plans tended either to be largely separatist in their approach or to make assumptions about the kind of provision that health authorities would make to the overall balance of care. As a result, therefore, the collaboration arena was characterised at best by *parallel* rather than *joint* planning, though in some localities there was little planning at all. Indeed, the quality of intra-agency planning was extremely variable and there was also a lack of congruence between the planning methodologies adopted by the NHS and local government, respectively. Thus, in the final analysis, the absence of joint plans was due not only to the tendency towards parallel planning but also to inadequacies and incompatibilities in the internal planning arrangements of health and local authorities. We discuss these issues more fully in the following chapter.

(b) Projects

Projects for the under-fives were only one-fifth the number of those for the elderly (tables 6 and 7). However, the great majority of projects were 'joint' only in the sense that they were jointly financed: of the 33 projects produced by machinery, 27 were joint financed. In the absence of comprehensive joint plans, individual projects were not integral elements of jointly agreed client group strategies: nor could they be selected within a comprehensive and jointly agreed framework of priorities. Indeed, an essential characteristic of joint finance projects was that they emerged from internal SSD processes rather than from a joint process of planning. The role of the collaboration arena was, therefore, largely to endorse and approve the allocation of funds from the joint finance programme to schemes which had been separately rather than jointly conceived.

In the case of services for elderly people, individual schemes ranged from the small to the large scale: from, for example, the employment of a single occupational therapist to the building of 50-place old people's homes. In between came support for home help and meals services; day centres; hospital discharge schemes; transport services; upgrading and staffing sheltered housing schemes; expansion of hospital social worker services; street warden and Good Neighbour schemes; specialist day and residential units for the elderly mentally infirm. These projects almost invariably emerged from within social services departments and were primarily designed to extend or prevent reductions in SSD provision. As such they were largely responses to actual or anticipated pressures on local authority provision rather than contributions to an agreed balance of care across the service system as a whole. This is not to say that they were without benefit to the NHS, since pressures not absorbed by the PSS might emerge within the health service. Certainly this was the case advanced by SSDs and largely accepted by health authorities, if only because it was impossible to prove it either way.

Projects emerging from the collaboration arena for the under-fives were very much fewer in number, partly because they were less eligible for joint finance. (In fact only 3 of the 27 joint finance projects in this arena were for the under-fives.) Consequently, there was no obvious reason to route projects through the joint planning machinery. Thus, the discrepancy between numbers of projects for the elderly and under-fives should not be considered as necessarily indicative of different levels of effectiveness in relationships between authorities. Rather, it tended to reflect the differential extent to which joint finance had been instrumental in attracting to the collaboration machinery for funding purposes projects which had originated elsewhere.

(c) Practices

For elderly people, changes in professional and/or operational practice involving existing resources were primarily concentrated around multi-disciplinary referral and assessment procedures for admission to residential care, sometimes taking place within short stay units in Part III homes. Such procedures were also, though less commonly, found in day care services. Their purpose was essentially to ensure a better match between need and resources, the involvement of specialist health personnel implying not only a more accurate assessment of need but also the allocation of health rather than SSD resources to those for whom this was most appropriate. Three other examples in this category of output were: the clarification and redefinition of the respective roles of home helps and domiciliary nurses; the input of health staff to old people's homes (for example, physiotherapists and nurses); and the inclusion of local authority care assistants in training programmes for nursing auxiliaries. Outputs for the under-fives followed a similar pattern: multi-disciplinary assessment panels at a child guidance clinic and for the allocation of day care provision; joint training of professionals; and the linking of health visitors with playgroups and mother and toddler clubs.

Thus, the dominant feature of outputs in this category was some measure of joint working between field level practitioners. Such interpersonal professional cooperation largely took one of two forms: the pooling of professional expertise to enhance assessment and allocation procedures; or the provision of specialist skills by one agency to another to extend the range and capacity of the latter's provision for clients. Such outputs tended to stem, at least in the first instance, from informal rather than formal processes, such as meetings between geriatricians and SSD managers or contacts between individual professionals. Where they involved the redeployment of existing staff resources on a localised level, these outputs could be effected simply through the one-to-one agreement of those responsible for such staff. Where, however, they implied the modification of working practices across a locality as a whole – or especially where additional resources were necessary to effect such agreements – more formal procedures were required. Thus, for example, individual initiative might secure a limited number of physiotherapy sessions in a residential home. However, an extension of this practice would require additional staff and, probably, the submission of a project for joint finance. Such developments were not common but did illustrate the potential of bottom-up, one-off initiatives to secure a wider coverage through the formal machinery.

Effectiveness of collaboration: assessment by participants

The mapping of outputs provided some kind of 'objective' data to set alongside the qualitative and subjective assessments of our respondents. The former suggested that the joint planning machinery had achieved little except to approve joint finance schemes and that initiatives in joint working had been initiated by practitioners outside the formal machinery. More specifically, the number of informal outputs was almost twice that of the machinery outputs which had not been joint financed (tables 6 and 7). How compatible was this finding with the views of actors within the collaboration arena?

Our respondents were, in fact, almost entirely negative in their assessment of the formal machinery, at least in terms of the three categories of output described above. Moreover, there was little variation in viewpoint by type of locality or by the amount of machinery it possessed. Thus there was broad agreement in Portshire (a shire county with a high level of machinery) that 'the official face of collaboration had been of minimal usefulness' and that 'we had the JCC because we had been told that we had to, but we could have managed well enough without it. It had been largely ineffective.' This view was echoed in the London borough of Templeborough which had a level of machinery close to the mean:

We have all the required organisation put out in papers and guidelines by the government. But in reality we tend to do what we are doing independently of each other and tell each other at some stage or another. I don't see, I don't feel any influence of the health service in what we do. I don't see much influence from us in what they do.

A review by officers of the collaboration machinery in Riverton produced a similarly comprehensive indictment, arguing that there was

no overall coordination of activity resulting in a lack of drive and progress on matters of common interest or concern, a degree of confusion about who is doing what, which not uncommonly leads to no activity at all ...

Despite – or perhaps because – Woodtown had more joint planning machinery than anywhere else, there was widespread scepticism about its ability to 'actually deliver the goods' and criticism of the establishment of machinery as an alternative to action: 'often a working group will be set up to look at a planning team's advice and even a working group to look at the working group'. A respondent suggested that this situation had become 'ridiculous. Dickens couldn't have done better with his Department of Circumlocution.'

These universally critical viewpoints applied both to the cross-tracer and tracer group machinery. JCCs were commonly dismissed as 'talking shops' and as 'bodies without teeth'. The following statement could be applied with little modification to almost any of the JCCs in the localities studied: 'always superficial ... meetings where they would rubber stamp the recommendations of that group'. JCPTs were equally criticised as being 'clumsy and ineffectual' and as bodies which had 'never done any joint planning'. Thus it was not uncommon for meetings to be cancelled for lack of business or for agendas to be dominated by joint finance rather than strategic planning and operational matters. Without such agenda items, however, the collaboration machinery might have withered even more completely. Not untypical was the view that 'joint finance was the only thing which kept the JCPT machinery alive – here were matters for discussion'. Nonetheless, there was also a concern in most localities that joint finance had been an overly dominant element in the world of JCCs and JCPTs, acting as a substitute for joint planning rather than a means of financing jointly planned services.

The tracer group planning machinery was no more highly valued, the following statement being not unrepresentative of opinion in our localities:

the planning teams get laughed at and are of pretty low esteem, probably justifiably. They produced papers which were seen as producing papers and regarded as a nuisance.

Weaknesses which were particularly identified included: the lack of analytical support for planning teams; inappropriate membership; tendency towards operational planning; and the absence of realistic strategic or resource guidelines. As one critic noted, 'if you ask them what they want, they go for the moon'. Many planning teams appeared to operate without any clear guidance and direction from above: team members were uncertain about their role and experienced a sense of purposelessness which was reflected in their work. Thus, for example, a respondent suggested that

to start with we had great difficulty in finding a proper identity for the planning team ... From a planning point of view we were not quite sure where we fitted in.

Another respondent emphasised that operational planning

dominates because there is an inclination to think about the shopping list and a lack of guidance about what [the team] should be doing ... we just wandered around and picked on things [to discuss].

At the same time, the isolation of planning teams from effective decision-making processes was underlined by the failure of their bids for joint finance. Thus it was exceedingly rare for meaningful joint finance proposals to originate from the tracer group machinery, unless social services routed a proposal through them in order to be able to report to the AHA that the relevant planning group was aware of this project.

These views did not, however, extend to all tracer group machinery. Rather they were concentrated upon the numerically dominant standing machinery (both JCPT sub-groups and Health Care Planning Teams (HCPTs)). Such machinery tended to have been established on a mechanistic basis in accordance with national guidance to establish a comprehensive set of planning groups. As a result such groups were, as the comments above demonstrate, cast adrift and looking for a role. There was, however, in addition to such *problem-seeking machinery*, a smaller amount of *problem-solving machinery*, i.e. planning groups established with a limited life and a clearly specified task. Such machinery, established in response to identified (or anticipated) problems, had a clear job of work to perform and appeared to be both more highly regarded and productive. An example of the latter category was the Woodtown working party on services for the elderly mentally infirm (EMI). A senior officer contrasted it with the JCPT sub-group for the elderly:

I have thought of killing off the [JCPT sub-group] because it is non-productive and time wasting ... [However] the EMI is a sub-group where we were able to use ...

machinery in a fairly formal way to develop a fairly full action plan, where we set precise targets for both sides of the services, where both authorities agreed and worked towards it.

A similarly productive use of machinery was identified in Cliffshire where a joint group was established specifically to review the overlap of roles between health and local authority domiciliary staff. This led to the amendment of job descriptions and to joint training. In Riverton, the need for problem-seeking machinery was also becoming clearly recognised. Recommendations that the standing planning teams should be scrapped and replaced by ad-hoc groups with a limited life and defined purpose were to be discussed after NHS restructuring had been completed.

Despite this lack of success, mistrust and conflict were rare. Thus good personal relationships and a 'marvellous' spirit of cooperation were credited to such machinery in Cliffshire while, in Riverton, more regular meetings were said to be promoting better relationships. 'We have made progress in that people are talking to each other and there is less mistrust' – or, rather, as another respondent expressed it: 'the mistrust is that of a different authority rather than of individuals'. Apparently good relationships could, however, be seen to reflect the weakness of formal coordinative mechanisms. Thus, a respondent in Greenshire noted that at meetings of the collaboration machinery, 'nobody does anything to rock the boat – keep up friendly appearances and why not? There is nothing else at stake, no planning or policy making. So what is there to get hot under the collar about?' At the same time, however, the promotion through machinery of personal relationships and understanding were seen as the *prerequisites of output* in collaborative planning.

Good personal relationships and a proper understanding of the roles and responsibilities of the authorities and agencies involved are essential preconditions of success in any joint planning exercise.

To be able to collaborate, you have to know the other organisation and its system, their services and the key people – know where to plug in ... you have to ... have that level of understanding before you can collaborate effectively.

Joint finance was particularly credited with the promotion of learning. In Greenshire, the joint finance sub-group was accepted as a forum where 'participants do actually learn through the discussion of projects what collaboration is all about'. A similar group in Riverton was held to have promoted trust and understanding after its establishment in 1980 in an environment where such features had been notably underdeveloped. At the same time, however, joint finance could lead to less than harmonious relations as was indicated by disagreements over specific issues in Cliffshire, Portshire, Riverton and Greenshire.

Nevertheless, there was evidence that mutual understanding and learning had taken place in Greenshire, Cliffshire, Riverton and Woodtown. In addition, there was agreement in all localities that levels of interaction had been enhanced since 1974 by the requirement that authorities establish machinery and meet together. However, such machinery's output had been at the intermediate level of the *prerequisites* of effective collaboration: inter-authority planning ultimately remained a 'fringe activity' as the following response illustrates: 'How could we possibly claim we are properly discussing and planning services together? We aren't. There are two systems in parallel.' A similar image was used in another locality where collaboration was seen to be taking place 'only at the margins'.

It is an uncovenanted mercy rather than something which springs from routine working. It is like two vehicles travelling down the same road: at times, certain protuberances mesh, and then they move apart again.

Inter-agency policy coordination was, therefore, a marginal area of work for health and local authorities. To the extent that coordination of provision for elderly people and children under five was a live issue, the perceived priority was to coordinate within the boundaries of individual agencies rather than across a service system. As a result, policy and service coordination was at best a parallel, rather than a shared, goal and activity for agencies within the collaborative arena.

The impact of NHS restructuring

It seemed unlikely that the evolution of inter-authority relationships would remain unaffected by the administrative upheaval entailed in the implementation of *Patients First*[18]. Our findings confirmed this view: the joint planning machinery effectively ceased to operate in five of the seven localities during 1981 and was, at best, only beginning to be reactivated in the first half of 1983. Only in the two metropolitan districts, where the AHAs were, in effect, reconstituted as new DHAs with the same – or largely similar – teams of chief officers, was a cycle of JCC and chief officer meetings maintained. In Riverton, where relationships had been difficult and the machinery slow to develop, restructuring provided a new stimulus for collaboration. The new DHA took over responsibility for a mental handicap hospital previously managed by another authority. Lacking experience in this speciality, its officers initiated a regular round of informal meetings with the Director of Social Services who had a specialist interest and expertise in this field. It was hoped, on both sides, that these discussions would generate trust and lessen misunderstanding across a wider field, including services for the elderly. In Woodtown, on the other hand, while the JCC also took forward a planning initiative in the mental handicap field, no movement was discernible in the case of the elderly. Indeed, health service staff indicated that they had been positively discouraged from bringing formal agenda items to the planning machinery.

I've had a hint that we should not produce papers for the JCPT, and was told not to spend too much time on that but to deal with other things that are more urgent. I don't think anyone is going to make a name for themselves by having a very active planning group – not here, not at the moment.

In London and the shire counties, the disruption of inter-authority relationships was all but total. Meetings of cross-tracer and tracer groups machinery petered out and inter-authority planning contacts came to a standstill. Area-based officers were seeking new posts. Responsibility for establishing new collaboration arrangements fell, in the main, to officers with little experience of working with senior SSD managers and who, not infrequently, felt they had been excluded from such contacts, in their previous district-based roles, particularly in relation to decisions about the expenditure of joint finance.

The distance between NHS officers at district level and headquarters staff of SSDs was a common feature of both the London boroughs and the shire counties in the period before restructuring. One director of social services, for example, explicitly refused to conduct any negotiations with the district administrators, insisting instead on relating to the area administrator whom he saw as his opposite number. In another locality, district staff expressed continuing frustration at the refusal of the director and his senior staff to participate in 'their' Health Care Planning Teams. In a third locality, when the new DHA invited an SSD area director to join a joint finance group, it was swiftly informed that responsibility for such matters lay at headquarters and not area level. This did, however, mark a rare – albeit unilateral – initiative to establish any kind of new collaboration machinery within our localities in the period up to the summer of 1982. Indeed, the following view, expressed in mid 1982 by a District Management Team (DMT) member in one of our localities, was not untypical of the wider situation:

It is all a bit of a mess and a bit vague; it worries me that this year is flying past and we still haven't got a JCC or a JCPT.

A further twelve months elapsed before at least one JCC held its first meeting. A local authority officer in that locality described their situation as being one of 'drifting in neutral with the engine switched off'. That description, however, suggested a degree of continuing momentum not readily apparent to the outside observer in the majority of localities studied. In short, collaborative planning was effectively in abeyance during 1981 and

1982 and was apparently only beginning to get underway by 1983. The short-term impact of restructuring was, therefore, much as predicted and our experience suggested that there was much work to be done in re-establishing contacts between authorities.

Joint finance seemed a potential early source of difficulty with DHAs resisting local authority proposals for a pooling of their allocations. Having been in a position of minimal influence over the spending of joint finance and, from a distance, perceived the situation to be one of excessive SSD influence, district officers were disinclined to surrender any degree of control over 'their' joint finance monies. SSD officers, for their part, were maintaining the need to allocate development monies in accord with their view of priorities across the local authority as a whole rather than in response to the vagaries of NHS allocation formulae. Thus, the opening negotiating positions and the delay in establishing formal contacts suggested that progress in collaboration would be by no means certain or smooth in the new structural context.[19]

Summary

The perceptions of individual actors about the 'productiveness' of collaborative planning largely coincided with the data obtained through our outputs mapping exercise: within an overall pattern of limited output, the funding of individual projects through joint finance was the clearest tangible attainment. Little progress had been made in the production, still less the implementation, of joint plans and output had been concentrated at the 'projects' and 'practices' end of the output continuum. The joint planning machinery was generally lacking in effectiveness, at least when measured against DHSS intentions (see chapter 3). Participation in the machinery tended to be ritualised rather than real with the inter-authority coordination occupying a marginal position in the work programme of decision makers. To the extent that we were able to identify a practical commitment to policy coordination, this was primarily rooted in a concern to enhance intra- rather than inter-agency coordination. Indeed, a preoccupation with the former drove out the latter (at least in the short to medium term). The tangible outputs of health and local authority relationships were overwhelmingly joint finance projects, though in many cases NHS involvement in these was limited to the all-but-automatic approval of proposals prepared within social services departments to bolster up their own service systems. Examples of innovation in joint working were encountered but these tended to be small-scale, highly localised and the outcome of entrepreneurial rather than planning skills. At the less tangible level, the joint planning machinery promoted understanding and, less frequently, generated conflict.

Nonetheless, some of our respondents had identified an additional level of achievement: the importance of inter-agency learning as a prerequisite for collaborative planning. In this category of intermediate output, some progress was apparent, though not universally so. Moreover, it resulted from the slow accretion of understanding at the level of individuals. It was, therefore, a fragile base for the future in the context of widespread disruption to personal contacts and networks caused by restructuring in the majority of our localities. That the promotion of understandings of the structure and culture of another agency's administrative and service systems constituted an achievement in the collaboration arena was in any case a clear indication of the gulf to be bridged between health and local authorities in the late 1970s and early 1980s. We should, however, enter one caveat to the conclusions about the state of planning in the collaboration arena. The findings of the national survey of collaboration do indicate that the seven localities studied here may not be representative of the full range of experience nationally[20]. Meetings frequency in the seven localities was below the nationally reported norm and this was also true of the average number of all JCPT sub-groups (3.5 in six of the seven localities against 4.4 nationally). A similar discrepancy between the case study localities and the national pattern is revealed by comparison of scores on a composite variable constructed by combining frequency of JCC/JCPT meetings and numbers of JCC/JCPT sub-committees/sub-groups. The mean score for six of the seven localities was 11.4 on this variable compared with the national mean of 12.8. Thus, none of our localities were significantly above the mean (the highest individual score being 13) in terms of quantity of machinery and frequency of its use. It would appear, therefore, that the seven localities were biased towards low achievers in the sense that, collectively, they represented a group at or below the national mean for the extent and utilisation of collaboration machinery.

THE STATUTORY/NON-STATUTORY ARENA

Within the statutory sector, liaison with the voluntary and private sectors was seen as largely the role of social services. The health authority and education department had far less contact, particularly at the planning level. Nor were non-statutory agencies equally involved. For the vast majority of organisations, contact with the statutory sector was confined to registration and grant aid applications. Beyond this the private sector was almost wholly excluded. The role assumed by, and expected of, voluntary organisations varied from actor to actor and the nature of interaction was diverse even within individual localities. Nevertheless, there was little evidence anywhere of effective non-statutory sectors. At best agencies from the two sectors worked together on individual schemes.

No single voice: relationships within the non-statutory sector

Interaction between the two sectors was, in part, shaped by the nature of relationships within the non-statutory sector itself. These were largely marked by separatism and independence. A voluntary sector respondent in Woodtown acknowledged:

No we don't do much with other voluntary organisations, we don't present a [common] line or anything like that. A couple of years ago the women's liberation group did have a jumble sale and did let us have a stall for a percentage of our takings. But we don't fight campaigns together.

A respondent in one of the statutory agencies in Cliffshire made a similar point, though perhaps with more regret:

The voluntary sector is very diverse and disaggregated. An attempt to organise itself is very difficult so it is not as if there is an organised voice anywhere for the voluntary sector. It is very difficult to get the voluntary sector to speak with one voice.

The rather parochial outlook of many voluntary organisations posed problems for any attempts to achieve greater integration. In Fulborough, for instance, moves towards the unification of diverse organisations into borough-wide 'umbrella' structures, most notably through the Council for Voluntary Service (CVS), were made in the face of considerable opposition. There was also resistance to the establishment of an Age Concern in Woodtown. In Woodtown and Fulborough, particularly, the general fragmentation of the voluntary sector was overlaid by a more distinct divide between the traditional middle-class philanthropic organisations and the smaller, self-help and community activist groups which had been springing up more recently. Although, in Woodtown at least, the CVS had, in assuming an enabling role, sought to bridge this gap, for many councillors it was still tarred with the paternalistic brush and lacked legitimacy.

The private sector was even more fragmented than the voluntary sector. Branches of the Association of Child Minders were being established in a number of our localities often with the help of social services. In Portshire, however, where private residential homes were assuming a growing role in the care of the elderly, even this level of coherence was lacking. The ad-hoc nature of the development of private care, seen largely as the response of hoteliers to changing economic conditions, militated against the emergence of an organised voice for the sector, though an Association of Proprietors had been formed in one social service division.

Statutory/non-statutory relationships

(a) Styles of interaction

Given the range of participants, styles of interaction between statutory and non-statutory agencies varied enormously both within and between our localities. A number of common themes can, nevertheless, be identified. Within the statutory sector, relationships with the voluntary sector tended to be much less well developed by education and the health service than by social services. Education, pre-eminently concerned with the defence of its own boundaries and reluctant to get involved in collaborative activity generally, tended to see even less need to talk to the voluntary sector than it did with statutory agencies. Even in Portshire and Greenshire, where inter-sectoral relationships had been constructive: 'involvement of the voluntary sector is seen very much as second-best compared to the hoped and planned for nursery education programme'. The PPA recognised that they were only seen as important: 'so long as we are doing what the Education Committee wants us to do'. In Cliffshire the education department tended to regard playgroup provision as an inferior form of occupation rather than education, little more than a useful stopgap. Thus it saw consultation with PPA over the siting of new nursery units as totally unnecessary.

Health service involvement was even more limited, particularly at the planning level. In a number of our localities health service planners had little understanding of the voluntary sector, conceiving it solely in terms of fund raising, volunteers, or 'that thorn in the flesh', the Community Health Council (CHC). For instance, in Woodtown, a senior planner had no contact with the CVS which, he told us quite erroneously, was not very active, and he dismissed Age Concern with the comment, 'I wouldn't even know where Age Concern hangs out'. At operational levels, contacts were stronger, as evidenced by the fact that hospital discharge schemes had been established in five of our seven localities. However, at this level broader issues were likely to be lost in the discussion of day-to-day problems.

On the voluntary side attitudes towards greater coordination with statutory agencies ranged from an easy acceptance of a subordinate, co-opted and supplementary role to a vigorous protestation of independence and separatism. In general, however, voluntary organisations were concerned to remain their own people. As one respondent in Fulborough explained: '[The voluntary sector is] not madly keen on ever becoming too closely in touch with the local authority. I think that a lot of things wouldn't get done.' While in Portshire it was suggested:

Ours is quite a difficult role to play: we want to be involved, to be not too far away, but not too close either – you get sucked in and if we appeared to be representing the county council our constituent bodies would run like hell.

Some organisations saw a certain distance as vital if they were to retain their capacity for innovation and criticism and were to be able to provide an alternative to statutory services. A Fulborough respondent argued that: '... we are there to dream dreams, have visions and take risks; to find new ways and possibilities of doing things – at the margin'. The financial dependence of many of the more major voluntary agencies upon the statutory sector was seen as particularly threatening though there was little evidence that statutory agencies actually used this relationship to extend control. Some voluntary agencies, however, accepted their dependence completely. The Old People's Welfare Association in Fulborough, for instance, all but enveloped by the SSD and totally reliant upon it for financial support, played an uncritical passive role: 'we work parallel to, and as an alternative to, the local authority; as supplementary to them and as agents for them'. Other voluntary bodies within the borough regarded this as a model to be avoided.

Relationships between the sectors were rarely difficult. If not well-developed they were simply distant or non-existent. Yet, while many voluntary organisations were trying to stand their distance, they were not usually antagonistic or overtly critical. A number explicitly stated that it was their policy to try 'to work within the statutory sector', preferring a 'back door' approach to 'banner waving'. Both the CVS and CHC in Templeborough chose this route, not without some success, particularly in the latter case. Templeborough's Age Concern, on the other hand, was far less circumspect. Concerned about the dependence of voluntary sector influence upon informal, and therefore vulnerable, channels, it engaged in sniping activity from the sidelines in an attempt to chip away at the departmentalism of the local authority.

(b) Channels of interaction

While formal machinery was not the most frequent point of contact between the two sectors it provided the only real means of systematising the relationship. But inter-sector relationships were primarily focused on grant aid applications and registration, for which formal machinery was inappropriate and which rarely generated more broadly based discussions. As one respondent in Woodtown commented:

We have good relations with social services who register the premises and ensure we have the right number of (square) feet per child etc., and the local social worker pops in once a term just checking to see if we've had the right x-rays etc. From then on we are out of their hands.

The concentration of registration criteria upon physical rather than caring dimensions was of little help in promoting a more policy based relationship, though it was rarely apparent that the statutory sector was fully committed to such a development. In Portshire one officer did suggest that the role social services would have liked to assume was less one of

inspection, like the TV licence man [than] providing a support service to the private homes, but we are largely prevented by manpower.

However, more normally the approach adopted was a laissez-faire regulatory one.

The two sectors also inter-meshed through cross-representation and 'multiple hat wearing'. Social services were frequently represented on the management committees of major voluntary organisations. Officers and councillors were sometimes also involved in voluntary organisations in a personal capacity and in a number of our localities officers in the voluntary sector were beginning to be elected to the local councils. Thus a CVS in Cliffshire told us:

We've got county council representation through the area director [social services] but not a councillor. There is a move that we should have a county councillor though actually we employ a county councillor who is on the social services committee.

The potential of such linkages was not always exploited but there were a number of occasions when they provided an opportunity for influence, even in localities where formal interaction between the sectors was extremely limited. In Riverton, for instance, one voluntary trust was persuaded to build an old people's home, with local authority help. The officer responsible commented:

The previous trustee from the local authority was not going along to meetings. So I took over and saw how much money they'd got ... I said let's work together and suggested that they build a home ... This is not the result of a conscious policy of going out and finding people or organisations to help, it was more of an opportunistic situation once I saw how much money they had got.

In Cliffshire these semi-formal and informal linkages were put to greater use by the voluntary sector than the statutory sector. Officers in the voluntary sector, through their activities in the Labour party, were able to shape its manifesto and include a commitment to support the voluntary sector, allowing 'the voluntary sector influence which it would not otherwise have'. In Fulborough and Woodtown there was a particularly close relationship between the Labour borough councillors and the growing numbers of small and highly vociferous, radical self-help and community action groups. In Fulborough we were told:

the members' attitude is that they are jolly good organisations and their membership is drawn almost exclusively from activists in the Labour Party.

Machinery and outputs

Although cross-representation and 'multiple hat wearing' could provide useful channels of communication and influence between the two sectors they did not present a real opportunity for systematic and continuous dialogue. Potentially this role could be better fulfilled by formal machinery established between the two sectors. The document *Working Together* stated:

Most fundamentally, there is a need to take a broad view of all statutory and voluntary services which impinge on the social services area. There needs to be machinery for ensuring services can be looked at as a whole, whether across the personal social services field, or client group by client group, or both.[21]

However, as it went on to say:

Consultation arrangements which facilitate an effective form of joint planning are still relatively rare. We consider such arrangements to be essential to effective liaison.[22]

Certainly, such machinery was poorly developed across our localities. More machinery was in operation in the inter-sector than the local authority arena (table 8) but its coverage was patchy and it was rarely used for the discussion of policy. General or cross-tracer machinery was particularly lacking. In three localities there was no cross-tracer machinery at all while that in Woodtown and Templeborough was only narrowly focused. Only in Portshire and Cliffshire was there a general forum linking the two sectors: in Portshire officers from the AHA and SSD met twice yearly with the voluntary sector; while in Cliffshire an advisory committee established between the social services and the voluntary sector met five times a year. Both groups were seen to be of limited value at that time however. In Portshire it was suggested that meetings were 'all a bit circular' and functioned primarily as 'an exchange of news and views'. Views in Cliffshire were mixed: one voluntary sector member felt the Advisory Committee had given the voluntary sector 'real credibility with the county council' though an officer in the SSD was more sceptical:

I would look at it cynically as one of those classic bodies that co-opt the opposition to quieten it in such a way as to say they are consulting and in such a way as to provide no opposition and at no cost to the authority.

A weakness in the formal arrangements, identified by both voluntary and statutory respondents in Cliffshire, was the absence of an officer support group for the Advisory Committee which could meet regularly and progress issues which might otherwise 'become lost in its minutes'. At the time of our fieldwork, such a group was being established under the leadership – on the statutory side – of the deputy director and an assistant director of the SSD. On paper at least, this suggested a commitment to move inter-sector relations away from tokenistic consultation to a more effective and ongoing partnership. Outside Cliffshire and Portshire the formal machinery tended to be client group specific but the voluntary sector in Woodtown lamented the

Table 8 *Amount of machinery in the inter-sector arena (1979–81)*

	Machinery			Total
	Cross-tracer	Elderly	Under-fives	
Cliffshire	3	0	1	4
Fulborough	0	2	2	4
Greenshire	0	1	4	5
Portshire	3	1	6	10
Riverton	0	2	1	3
Templeborough	1	2	3	6
Woodtown	1	2	4	7
Total	8	10	21	39

Table 9 *Amount of output for the under-fives in the statutory/non-statutory arena*

	Machinery output[a]			Informal outputs[b]	
	Policies	Projects	Practices	Projects	Practices
Cliffshire	0	0	1	0	4
Fulborough	0	0	0	1	1
Greenshire	0	1	12	1	2
Portshire	0	10	4	0	2
Riverton	0	0	1	0	1
Templeborough	0	0	2	1	0
Woodtown	0	2	2	1	2
Total	0	13	22	4	12

[a] For counting purposes projects and practices were only included if they had originated in the formal machinery and implemented in the period January 1979 – December 1981.
[b] All informal outputs in operation 1979–81 whenever implemented.

absence of a wider forum where they could 'sit down together and kick ideas about'.

Tracer group machinery

Machinery for children under five was far more extensive than that for elderly people: 21 under-fives groups compared with only 10 for the elderly (table 8). These groups often provided a standing forum for the exchange of ideas about service developments. Only in Riverton and Cliffshire had an under-fives coordinating committee or officer group involving the voluntary sector as well as the statutory agencies been established. In some localities (especially Greenshire and Portshire) such groups provided the major forum for inter-agency discussion for the client group within the statutory sector as well as across the sectors. Their effectiveness is reflected in table 9 which shows that 27 of the 35 machinery outputs were in Portshire or Greenshire. Outputs from the Greenshire machinery reflected the inclusion of the non-statutory sector and were primarily centred around joint training. In Portshire the locality-wide forum was only part of a multi-disciplinary county, area and divisional based coordinating and joint training structure which provided a comprehensive structure for top-down and bottom-up interaction. It is perhaps evidence of the greater commitment to coordination in Portshire that unlike Greenshire the majority of outputs were projects rather than practices (table 9).

Woodtown's under-fives coordinating committee and Fulborough's officer group were less well integrated into the policy arena and outputs were correspondingly low. They were confined, in the case of Woodtown, to a booklet on services for the under-fives (the other outputs revealed in table 9 related to Non-Accidental Injury (NAI) procedures and were produced by the ARC), while in Fulborough the outputs were even less tangible. As the chair of the officers' group in Fulborough remarked:

It has never seen itself as a policy making body but the opportunity to exchange topical information and discuss a variety of issues has greatly facilitated formal contacts as and when the need arises.

Comments about the committee in Woodtown are somewhat less positive:

It is my impression that neither of the two city council departments [social services and education] – and it might also be true of the health authority, but that's guessing – actually regard the coordinating committee as of any importance. Any policy issue which is of importance the department will take to its own committee and would not contemplate taking it via the coordinating committee.

Nor did the committee provide a forum for informal liaison and exchange of information because its formality as a committee of the borough council intimidated many voluntary sector representatives, one of whom said:

The committee is very awe inspiring; it's around an enormous table and I think it's very off-putting. When I went I didn't open my mouth.

Similar comments were made about a formal committee in Cliffshire linking the voluntary sector with one of the district councils:

They're mostly formal and take place in the Council House. So it is difficult for the voluntary sector to contribute – men arrive with silver teapots and the councillors know how the committees work.

Table 10 *Amount of output for the elderly in the statutory/non-statutory arena*

	Machinery output[a]			Informal outputs[b]	
	Policies	Projects	Practices	Projects	Practices
Cliffshire	0	0	0	0	1
Fulborough	0	1	0	0	1
Greenshire	0	5	0	0	2
Portshire	0	0	0	0	3
Riverton	0	2	1	0	0
Templeborough	0	1	0	0	0
Woodtown	0	3	0	3	0
Total	0	12	1	3	7

[a] For counting purposes projects and practices were only included if they had originated in the formal machinery and implemented in the period January 1979 – December 1981.
[b] All informal outputs in operation 1979–81 whenever implemented.

In Woodtown, ad-hoc machinery established around a specific issue such as the Home Start Steering Group was more constructive. Informal liaison groups established at a more localised level were also able to act as forums for the real exchange of information and ideas, albeit over operational issues. Indeed there was evidence in every locality that informal processes could be productive. Table 9 records 16 informal outputs in all, though in common with the pattern of output for the under-fives in the corporate arena, these were primarily changes in working practices rather than setting up of new projects.

There was far less locality-wide inter-sectoral machinery for elderly people than children under five. The disparity in the amount of machinery in the two client groups revealed in table 8 was mirrored in the amount of output. As table 10 shows there was very little formal output for the elderly in this arena, though it was supplemented by a number of informal outputs. Greenshire's five projects were the biggest exception but were actually produced by the collaboration machinery and informal links between participants in that arena.

In the statutory/non-statutory arena, the machinery in Greenshire consisted solely of twice yearly divisional conferences organised by Age Concern and attended by statutory agencies. In Cliffshire there was no machinery specifically for the elderly. Nor was the machinery in Portshire and Templeborough of any account, informal linkages playing a far more important role in the latter than formal structures. In both Riverton and Woodtown ad-hoc machinery had been established around specific issues, though in Woodtown much of this was practitioner and sub-locality based. These groups were relatively productive, resulting in the setting up of a number of individual projects such as a street warden scheme in Riverton and in Woodtown a hospital discharge scheme and, perhaps most importantly, the foundation of a local branch of Age Concern. The only group in Fulborough, the Elderly Person's Liaison Group, was very similar in nature. It functioned largely as a consumer group for elderly people in the borough and gave them an opportunity to question housing and social services officers.

Summary

There was little indication that the inter-sector arena was in any sense a planning arena. Certainly no strategic plans had been developed for either client group. Only in Greenshire and Portshire was there evidence that the voluntary sector was accepted as an equal partner in policy discussion, and there only in relation to the under-fives. Elsewhere the assessment made by one respondent in Woodtown was universally applicable. As he put it:

It would be quite inaccurate to say ... that the voluntary sector has any say at all on policy. It is still very much in the position of fighting its own corner.

At best there was what was described as a 'tremendous rapport' between Age Concern and the SSD in Portshire which nonetheless did not extend to invitations to discuss policy for the elderly; and at worst there was the total non-interaction between sectors in Riverton in relation to the under-fives such that in the AHA a number of respondents failed to recognise the term 'non-statutory sector' while officers in the SSD noted:

maybe we could stimulate the voluntary sector, but we haven't the least idea how.

ARENAS OF INTERACTION: CONTRASTS AND COMPARISONS

Our accounts of the states of play within each of the three arenas provide a summary of the level and productiveness of interaction in the seven localities studied. A number of variations by locality and client group have already been identified. We shall now draw these findings together by examining patterns of variation across the arenas and considering what light they throw upon the extent to which the 'optimistic' model had been successfully implemented at the local level.

Participation through bilateral or multilateral processes?
The 'optimistic' model sees planning as a comprehensive process in which the range of participants fully reflects the range of interests within the

boundaries of a given planning arena. The objective is to secure a systems-wide agreement on the range and scale of services to be provided and the respective contributions of each agency. In none of our arenas was participation sufficiently comprehensive for such a perspective to be taken. Indeed, inter-agency relationships primarily took place on a bilateral rather than a multilateral basis. Thus, in the collaboration arena, relationships were largely limited to the health and personal social services, with neither housing nor education making an effective contribution. The corporate arena was similarly dominated by bilateral relationships between housing/social services and education/social services. The comprehensive, corporate viewpoint rarely emerged leaving the field, in most cases, to departmental isolationism or competition. In the inter-sector arena, this pattern was partially relieved in the case of the under-fives where a wider spread of interests was represented: education, social services, health and voluntary agencies. In practice, however, the general pattern was for health to make a limited output and for bilateral relationships between the other parties to take place within a multilateral setting. Questions about the overall balance of provision did not find a place on the agenda, therefore.

Machinery and outputs

We began the previous chapter by identifying questions about variations in the extent and productiveness of inter-agency relationships and also whether experience locally would bear any discernible relationships to the history of national initiatives to promote coordination. Underlying these questions was a further issue relating to the role and value of formal machinery. Would the development of formal machinery, in accordance with the prescriptions of the 'optimistic' model, produce high levels of output compared with the contribution of less formal approaches?

To answer these questions we attempted not only to gain a 'feel' for the dynamics of inter-agency relationships but also to chart amounts of machinery and output through our 'bureaumetric' tools. These quantitative measures were, of course, statistically unsophisticated and experimental in their design. Nonetheless they proved a useful aid in making comparisons, however crude, between localities, arenas and client groups. A summary of the findings which emerged from those comparisons is provided below.

(a) Arenas
Nearly half the machinery identified was located within the collaboration arena, with the remainder being almost equally divided between the corporate and inter-corporate arenas (table 11). This suggests a higher level of

Table 11 *Machinery totals: all areas*

	Arena			All arenas
	Corporate	Collaborative	Inter-sector	
Cliffshire	4	11	4	19
Fulborough	4	4	4	12
Greenshire	5	7	5	17
Portshire	3	11	10	24
Riverton	3	5	3	11
Templeborough	3	9	6	18
Woodtown	9	14	7	30
Total	31	61	39	131

interaction through formal policy machinery *between* health and local authorities than *within* the latter authorities. In particular, client group machinery was all but non-existent in the corporate compared with the collaboration arena. Thus the corporate planning machinery was less fully developed than that for joint planning even though the former approach was historically longer established and required the establishment of mechanisms across the boundaries of agencies operating within a common administrative and financial framework. It might be argued that in such circumstances formal machinery was unnecessary: inter-departmental planning could more easily be conducted through less formal processes. Such a view would not be consistent with our experience, however. As our interviewees revealed, relationships between local authority services were typically characterised by insularity and competition rather than by high levels of informal interaction. Moreover, those informal contacts which did exist tended to deal with operational matters and individual cases rather than planning issues.

A number of fundamental questions remain, however. Did the differences in machinery levels really matter? Were corporate relationships really any less productive than those in the collaboration arena? Table 12 suggests that, for the elderly (who had a substantially higher priority in joint planning than the under-fives), the higher level of collaborative machinery was associated with very high levels of output compared with the levels achieved in the corporate arena (53 and 18 outputs respectively). However, the great majority of machinery outputs in the collaboration arena were independently planned SSD projects which entered the collaboration arena solely in search of joint finance. Indeed our respondents were generally no less sceptical of the value of collaborative machinery than they were of the corporate machinery, at least

Table 12 *Output totals by arena*

	Machinery outputs			Informal outputs	
	Policies	Projects	Practices	Projects	Practices
Elderly					
Corporate	1	7	3	3	4
Collaborative	2	31	5	6	9
Inter-sector	0	12	1	3	7
All arenas	3	50	9	12	20
Under-fives					
Corporate	0	9	5	8	12
Collaborative	0	2	1	1	9
Inter-sector	0	13	22	4	12
All arenas	0	24	28	13	33
Both client groups					
Corporate	1	16	8	11	16
Collaborative	2	33	6	7	18
Inter-sector	0	25	23	7	19
All arenas	3	74	37	25	53

so far as the production of tangible outputs was concerned. The main exception to this was in respect of that group of machinery which we have termed 'problem-solving' rather than 'problem-seeking'. (Significantly, it was this category of machinery which also tended to be most productive in the corporate arena.)

Despite their reservations about the utility of such formal machinery as a vehicle for producing tangible output, many respondents in the collaboration arena emphasised its considerable contribution in providing contexts for promoting informal relationships and learning, especially about the other party's planning and financial systems, organisational structures and services. This is the kind of knowledge which actors operating within a common (local authority) framework might be expected to share. It is, of course, impossible to measure the extent and consequences of such learning and informal relationships. However, the fact that the number of informal outputs recorded was broadly equivalent to the two arenas (table 12) is significant. At the least, it would appear that, starting from a base of very limited interaction in the years before NHS reorganisation, informal relationships in the collaborative arena had been as productive as those in the corporate arena, despite the latter's common organisational framework and longer history of formal inter-agency planning. The broad conclusion to be drawn from our comparison of the corporate and collaboration arenas, therefore, is that policy coordination had apparently been pursued more frequently and, at least as successfully, through joint planning than through corporate planning.

The inter-sector arena was unlike the other two in lacking a nationally prescribed structure or model for cooperative planning. Somewhat surprisingly, therefore, we recorded more planning machinery in this than the corporate arena (table 11). Also, surprisingly, we found that the level of machinery output in the inter-sector arena was about twice as great as that in the corporate arena and marginally higher than in the collaborative arena (table 12). On the other hand, there was little variation between arenas in the level of informal outputs. However, the data must be interpreted with caution and particularly the machinery output totals. Our fieldwork showed that many outputs in the inter-sector arena were relatively small-scale and had minimal resource implications. This is reflected in the disproportionately large numbers of 'practices' (i.e. outputs which did not incur additional financial costs) found in the machinery outputs category (table 12). Nonetheless, the overall number of outputs in this arena does bear out the view of our respondents that, generally speaking, this had been a field in which inter-agency relationships were of growing significance and productivity. In addition, the view that the statutory sector had been an important source of finance in the growth of the voluntary sector is supported by the relatively large number of project outputs. Earmarked funds (especially urban programme monies) had played a significant role here but they were less dominant in funding projects than was joint finance in the collaboration arena. Moreover, and in contrast to the all-but-automatic allocation of joint finance to SSDs, voluntary agencies generally had to compete for earmarked funds in the inter-sector arena, both among themselves and also with statutory agencies.

Despite the apparently productive nature of interaction between statutory and non-statutory bodies revealed by our output counts, some respondents criticised the absence of an overall framework for the development of a partnership between the two sectors. This led, they suggested, to a tendency of such relationships towards a reactive and ad-hoc approach which precluded the prioritising of new initiatives within a broad development strategy for the two sectors. The absence of formal machinery capable of developing such a comprehensive perspective was particularly noted and this gap is reflected in the relatively small amount of cross-tracer machinery which we identified in this arena compared with the other two. Much of the cross-tracer machinery in the corporate and collaboration arenas was charged with the task of developing and coordinating a strategic approach to inter-agency policy making and planning (JCCs, JCPTs, COMTs and Policy Committees). However, as our interviews made clear, such bodies tended to degenerate into talking shops or handle relatively low level operational issues. They played a more constructive role only when backed by more specialist, problem-solving machinery capable of conducting detailed planning. Thus, the broad pattern of outputs in the collaboration and corporate arenas was not dissimilar to that in the inter-sector arena in the sense that the emphasis was almost exclusively upon individual projects and practices rather than comprehensive plans or policy statements covering the whole or even a defined sub-population of a client group (table 12).

In none of the arenas were formal (or for that matter informal) processes an effective vehicle for policy coordination at the strategic level. However, in the very few cases where comprehensive planning had been productive, our experience was that formal machinery had played a central role. Indeed, table 12 suggests that, in general, more output was produced through machinery than informal processes. While not wishing to underestimate the importance of formal machinery, we would nonetheless wish to enter two caveats. First, machinery tended to attract outputs which had been initiated elsewhere. Though not requiring endorsement from the formal machinery, such outputs might appear on its agenda for information or to provide a substantive item for discussion. Second, in the collaboration arena, the role of machinery was generally restricted to the allocation of joint finance. For both these reasons, therefore, there is some tendency for the output counts to overestimate the productivity of formal machinery. However, as we have noted previously in this chapter, this tendency could be set alongside the opportunities for learning presented by membership of formal machinery.

(b) Client groups

Overall there were similar amounts of machinery and output for each of the client groups but a number of differences emerged within these overall totals (table 12). Machinery for the elderly was particularly concentrated in the collaboration arena while that for the under-fives was most strongly represented in the inter-sector arena. The corporate arena had roughly equal – and low – totals of client group machinery. These figures were entirely consistent with the reports of our respondents and, to some extent, reflected the distribution of responsibilities for service provision and the relative scale of statutory and non-statutory roles. For example, the non-statutory sector continues to be one of the major providers of day care for children under five while services for elderly people have traditionally been higher cost and professionalised.

Table 13 *Output totals by client group*

	Machinery outputs			Informal outputs	
	Policies	Projects	Practices	Projects	Practices
Elderly	3	50	9	12	20
Under-fives	0	24	28	13	33
Both client groups	3	74	37	25	53

	Machinery outputs	Informal outputs	All outputs
Elderly	62	32	94
Under-fives	52	46	98
All	114	78	192

It was, however, less clear that the distribution of machinery by client group in the corporate arena reflected so closely the distribution of responsibility for service provision. The under-fives have been the subject of DES and DHSS initiatives to promote coordination which have no equivalent for the elderly at the DOE/DHSS level. Despite this, machinery totals were broadly similar. Output totals, on the other hand, were more consistent with what might have been expected, that for the under-fives in the corporate arena being about twice that for the elderly (table 12). However, our interviews with key actors and review of documents revealed that a significant proportion of such outputs originated in contacts between education and social services departments which took place in the inter-sector arena. In other words, relationships between statutory bodies could be more productive on 'neutral' territory than in the context of their own authority.

Differences between client groups also emerged in respect of types of output: while there were almost twice as many machinery as informal outputs for the elderly, the respective totals were more nearly equal in the case of the under-fives (table 13). At the same time, there were almost twice as many projects for the elderly as for the under-fives with the proportions being reversed for practices (table 13). These findings suggest two conclusions. First, new resources were apparently more readily available to fund 'joint' projects for the elderly than the under-fives. However, since the great majority of such projects were 'joint' only in the sense of being funded by joint finance, 'genuine' joint working was arguably more strongly developed for the under-fives in the shape of inter-professional cooperation to modify operational practices and procedures. Second, the relatively larger number of informal outputs for the under-fives also suggests that interaction took place more freely and was more productive for this group than for the elderly. Our own experience confirmed that, while outputs for the under-fives were often modest in scale, relationships between agencies tended to be more strongly developed for the under-fives than for the elderly and that this was particularly the case where such interactions took place through the inter-sector arena. To this extent, therefore, the push given nationally to coordination for the under-fives appears to have borne fruit locally, if only in comparison to what has been achieved through the more recent emphasis on coordination for the elderly. Indeed, it raises questions about whether the emphasis on the dissemination of good practice, in the DHSS/DES 'letters'[23,24] particularly at the operational level, might profitably be replicated for the elderly. At the strategic level, and with the particular exception of Greenshire and Portshire, however, planning was little if any further advanced for the under-fives than the elderly.

(c) Localities

The distribution of machinery by arenas within individual localities largely reflected the overall experience (table 11). Thus no locality possessed more machinery in the inter-sector or corporate arena than in the collaborative one. Only one locality, Woodtown, had more corporate than inter-sector machinery, a finding consistent both with the Woodtown ruling group's espousal of a client group approach to policy and also their relative reluctance to include the organised voluntary sector within such an approach. However, the majority of our localities had identical or broadly similar amounts of machinery in both corporate and inter-sector arenas. Indeed, the discrepancy between total amounts of machinery in those arenas was largely accounted for by one locality, Portshire, which had ten pieces of inter-sector machinery compared with only three in the corporate arena.

The total amount of machinery in individual localities varied widely, from 30 in Woodtown, where many respondents had suggested that the locality was top heavy with machinery, to 11 in Riverton, where formal mechanisms were considered weak or unnecessary. In four localities the pattern of machinery across arenas was strongly consistent. Thus machinery totals for each arena were consistently low in Riverton and Fulborough and consistently high in Woodtown, while Greenshire occupied the median position in each arena. The discrepancy between arena totals in Cliffshire was largely accounted for by the fact that three pieces of machinery in the collaboration arena never met. In Portshire and Templeborough, there was significantly less machinery in the corporate arena than the other two, suggesting that within the local authority, there was no room for even the tokenism which characterised the collaboration arenas in those localities.

Although there was a wide variation between individual localities in

Table 14 *Output totals by locality*

	Machinery outputs			Informal outputs	
	Policies	Projects	Practices	Projects	Practices
Elderly					
Cliffshire	0	19	1	0	3
Fulborough	0	4	1	1	5
Greenshire	0	9	2	6	4
Portshire	0	4	3	0	4
Riverton	0	6	1	0	1
Templeborough	1	3	0	2	3
Woodtown	2	15	1	3	0
All localities	3	60	9	12	20
Under-fives					
Cliffshire	0	2	1	0	10
Fulborough	0	0	3	7	3
Greenshire	0	1	12	1	3
Portshire	0	14	6	2	4
Riverton	0	2	1	0	3
Templeborough	0	0	3	2	3
Woodtown	0	5	2	1	7
All localities	0	24	28	13	33
Both client groups					
Cliffshire	0	21	2	0	13
Fulborough	0	4	4	8	8
Greenshire	0	10	14	7	7
Portshire	0	18	9	2	8
Riverton	0	8	2	0	4
Templeborough	1	3	3	4	6
Woodtown	2	20	3	4	7
All localities	3	84	37	25	53

machinery totals, they were not clearly related to variations in locality type and degree of complexity. Thus both the highest and the lowest machinery counts were made in the two metropolitan districts, localities with low degrees of complexity. The scores in the two London boroughs were 12 and 18 respectively while totals for the shire counties ranged from 17 to 24.

The distribution of outputs by locality is shown in table 14. However, those data should be treated with particular caution in making comparisons at the level of individual localities. For example, the number of projects may be expected to vary both with the size of a locality's joint finance allocation (which is broadly related to population size) and also with decisions on how joint finance should be allocated – between the elderly and other client groups and between small numbers of expensive projects or large numbers of low cost ones. Similarly outputs may vary in the extent of cooperation implied (low and one-off in the case of many joint finance projects but high and continuing in the case of joint management) and also in the extent of geographical coverage (highly localised/authority-wide). For all these reasons, therefore, it would be misleading to compare the 'productiveness' of coordination in our seven localities simply on the basis of the crude outputs contained in our tables. Equally, and for the same reasons, it would be misleading to compare them on the basis of similarly crude machinery/output ratios. Nevertheless, it proved useful to place the output totals alongside the findings which emerged from our interviews, if only as a check on their mutual consistency.

Thus, for example, Riverton and Fulborough were reported to have relatively small amounts of machinery which achieved little, a view which is fully consistent with our machinery and output counts. At the same time, informal relationships in Riverton appeared very poor and often conflictual: what interaction there was seemed to take place almost exclusively through formal machinery. In Fulborough, on the other hand, there appeared to be a more highly developed (though by no means locality-wide) network of informal relationships and a conscious attempt in some quarters to sustain and to take advantage of them. Again the output counts largely support these judgements: Riverton has the lowest number of informal outputs while Fulborough not only has four times as many but, more surprisingly, has the highest score of all the localities.

Whereas Riverton is a low machinery/low output locality and Fulborough is a low machinery/low machinery output (but high informal output) locality, Greenshire offers yet another variation: 'average' machinery/high output (in both the machinery and informal categories). Yet Portshire (like Greenshire an administratively complex and poorly resourced shire county) appears as a high machinery/high output locality (in both output categories). Neither of these findings would definitely have been predicted from our interview materials in which the machinery of coordination, in particular, was widely criticised for its ineffectiveness. Both localities had, however, a national reputation in the under-fives field and this is reflected in almost half of all identified machinery outputs for the under-fives being located within these two localities. Yet, there were important differences between the pattern of outputs within these two localities which our interview materials go at least some way in explaining. In particular, Greenshire's outputs for the under-fives were overwhelmingly in the practice rather than the project category, i.e. of a kind which implied modification to existing practices/procedures and which could be accomplished within *existing* resources. Portshire, on the other hand, had almost twice as many projects as practices, implying that joint working had been accomplished through the injection of new resources rather than changes in the use of existing ones. The latter pattern is not inconsistent with the reported emphasis on investing in low cost day care in Portshire while the former reflects the influence of resource scarcity in Greenshire. It also draws attention to the extent to which joint working had developed in the absence of additional resources to oil the wheels of cooperation. This finding is, of course, contrary to the argument advanced in respect of the elderly in Greenshire where the injection of additional resources by the SSD was said to be a necessary incentive for the promotion of joint working between it and the housing authorities. There are important differences between the client groups in that the joint objective for the elderly (very sheltered housing) could not be met within DOE cost yardsticks and thus without the parties finding a source of additional resources. Nonetheless, the contrast between the Greenshire experience in respect of each of the tracer groups does raise the question of whether there was a higher value commitment to joint working in the under-fives field and, if so, whether the processes of its emergence have any lessons for the elderly.

Conclusion

This brief review of our locally based findings illustrates, inter alia, the contribution which a form of bureaumetrics can make to the study of coordination. In particular, it can provide a useful tool for making a more systematic comparison between localities, and with a greater degree of consistency, than would be possible using the more qualitative techniques of traditional case studies. Thus it has enabled us to highlight with a greater degree of confidence than would otherwise have been the case variations in patterns of machinery and output. It also provided an additional check on the accuracy of actors' accounts of the states of play within their localities. However, the meaning and significance of such variations emerges more fully when they are set alongside the insights into the dynamics of inter-agency relationships which our interview materials provided. For example, our fieldwork experience suggests that the barriers to coordination vary with the type of outputs which it is hoped to achieve: whether responsibilities are being demarcated or shared; whether they involve cooperation between actors of broadly equivalent status using existing resources or actors of unequal status and additional resources; whether implementation of inter-agency agreements depends upon single agency, bilateral or multilateral action; whether outputs are localised or authority-wide. In other words, some weighting of outputs to take into account such factors, among others, would strengthen the contribution of our bureaumetrics approach.

Within these limitations, however, we may draw two conclusions from our review of coordination for the elderly and under-fives in the seven localities we studied. First, systematic rational planning was poorly developed across localities, client groups and arenas. Second, the degree and productiveness of interaction between agencies varied considerably: levels of machinery varied in apparently similar kinds of locality. Enabling structures, therefore, are not enough. Common boundaries and organisational structures do not necessarily generate high levels of coordinative output and they are associated with different levels of interest and endeavour in the coordination of social policy. Similarly, the micro level of structure – formal machinery – is also associated with variations in perceived levels of utility and recorded levels of output. In other words, machinery is not a sufficient condition for effectiveness in coordination. However, it does appear to produce higher levels of output than informal processes alone. More particularly, the design and utilisation of formal machinery (and especially problem-solving machinery) appears to have been a necessary condition for systems-wide, strategic planning and thus for the production of projects and practices within an agreed framework of priorities rather than on an ad-hoc basis.

Taken together, these findings are not insignificant since they mean that we are called upon not to explain blanket failure, or success, but to explain degrees of success and failure. In other words, we need to identify and account for those factors which, in differing contexts, make for differing degrees of success and failure in coordination. However, the variations we have encountered between apparently similar types of locality suggest the need to be sensitive not only to the impact of particular variables in isolation but to their combined effect in particular situations. It is to these issues that we turn in the following chapters.

REFERENCES

1 *The (Maud) Report of the Committee on Management of Local Government* (1967) HMSO
2 The (Bains) Report of the Study Group on Local Authority Management Structures (1972) *The New Local Authorities – Management and Structure*, HMSO
3 R. Greenwood, C. R. Hinings and S. Ranson (1974) 'Inside the local authorities', in K. Jones (ed.), *The Yearbook of Social Policy 1973*, Routledge and Kegan Paul
4 R. Greenwood, M. A. Lomer, C. R. Hinings and S. Ranson (1975) *The Organisation of Local Authorities in England and Wales: 1967–1975*, Discussion Paper series L, no. 5, Institute of Local Government Studies, Birmingham University

5 T. Mobbs (1983) *Local Government Policymaking Handbook*, Institute of Local Government Studies, Birmingham University

6 J. D. Stewart (1971) *Management in Local Government*, Charles Knight

7 T. Eddison (1973) *Local Government: Management and Corporate Planning*, Leonard Hill

8 R. Greenwood, C. R. Hinings and S. Ranson (1976) *The Politics of the Budgetary Process in English Local Government*, Institute of Local Government Studies, Birmingham University

9 R. Greenwood, K. Walsh, C. R. Hinings and S. Ranson (1980) *Patterns of Management in Local Government*, Martin Robertson

10 M. Bradley (1982) *The Co-ordination of Services for Children Under Five*, NFER-Nelson

11 DHSS and Welsh Office (1979) *Patients First: A Consultative Paper on the Structure and Management of the NHS*, HMSO

12 DHSS (1980) *Health Services Development: Structure and Management*, Circular HC(80)8/LAC(80)3, DHSS

13 Comparisons with the national pattern of joint planning machinery are drawn from a national survey of English AHAs conducted in January 1982 and attracting a 79% response rate. G. Wistow and S. Fuller (1983) *Joint Planning in Perspective*, National Association of Health Authorities

14 *Ibid.*

15 Social Services Committee (1980) *Second Report, Session 1979–80, Perinatal and Neonatal Mortality*, HMSO

16 *Op. cit.* (reference 11)

17 DHSS (1977) *Joint Care Planning: Health and Local Authorities*, Circular HC(77)17/LAC(77)10, DHSS

18 *Op. cit.* (reference 11)

19 For an analysis of the impact of restructuring on the formal machinery for collaboration, see G. Wistow and S. Fuller (1986) *Collaboration Since Restructuring: the 1984 Survey of Joint Planning and Joint Finance*, National Association of Health Authorities

20 *Op. cit.* (reference 13)

21 ACC, NCVO and AMA (1981) *Working Together*, Bedford Square Press, p. 27

22 *Ibid.*

23 DHSS/DES (1976) *Coordination of Local Authority Services for Children Under Five*, DHSS/DES Letter LASSL(76)5

24 DHSS/DES (1978) *Coordination of Services for Children Under Five*, DHSS/DES Letter LASSL(78)1

8 ~ *Barriers and opportunities*

The findings presented in the last chapter indicate a high failure rate in coordinating social policy. This means that, for example, whatever else Riverton was good at it was not coordination for elderly people and children under five. Yet this is within a locality where the selection criteria should have allowed advantage of organisational coterminosity. Compare this with Greenshire where, on complexity alone, we might have predicted difficulty in organising interaction and consequently little output. However, despite measured interaction of a commensurately low level, some considerable output was recorded and, from our interview materials, a positive attitude towards joint planning monitored.

These puzzles are what we set out to comprehend in this and the two succeeding chapters. Having mentioned failure, however, it is only failure of degree and as depicted from one point of view: from around the 'optimistic' perspective. This proposes a preponderance of joint plans and policies emerging from within the three arenas. Some of these products were present, yet the overall result for output is of isolated, albeit numerous, projects and alterations to practice. The comprehensive and coherent qualities associated with a strategic overview were difficult to locate. In order to understand this relative failure we need to look back to some of the questions which guided the initial research.

Barriers to and opportunities for coordination

Our analytic framework provided some indicators of where attention might be directed. At the outset we considered some of the sceptical challenges to the expectation of success in coordination. Drawing upon a range of disciplines and diverse literatures, we constructed a set of questions which were counterposed against those emanating from a very 'optimistic' tradition. These were presented in chapter 2.

Thus it was suggested that characteristics of localities such as resource experiences, demographic and other service pressures, would carry some weight in affecting local coordinative environments. What the effects might be were uncertain: would the presence of more or fewer resources matter, and in what way? Turning to less tangible aspects, the implicit assumptions of the 'optimistic' approach which viewed behavioural factors as irrelevant or unimportant were questioned. Was it not likely in the social policy field, as in others, that key individuals might be capable of disrupting or forestalling coordination, or that others might emerge who could lead a JASP type exercise?

Moreover, might the probability of interaction be associated with perceptions of the likely benefits to emerge and of the likely costs to be incurred? Just what were these commodities in the social policy coordination game, and how significant were they in structuring interaction?

By this means coordination was rendered problematic, the odds seemingly stacked against it. If it occurred we might want to mark this up as a real achievement, a success. And as a success, to be as closely analysed as the faults or failures derived from taking the optimistic view.

Our approach was to seek the *barriers* to coordination, to try to identify where altruism faltered and sectional self-interest took over, and to understand why bilateralism might predominate and a systems-wide perspective remain undeveloped.

Going further we sought the *opportunities* for policy coordination, those seized and those unenacted. Was coterminosity really a prime enabling factor? Does resource scarcity engender distance rather than the mutual sharing of skills, resources and facilities? Moreover, we wanted to explore those situations in localities, arenas or tracers which marked reversals: why given similar conditions would a barrier be identified in one situation yet overcome in another, or an opportunity be created and seized in one arena, yet remain dormant in others?

The emphasis in this chapter is on those factors promoting and those inhibiting coordination, those that were implicated in success, and those that implied failure. Because of the patterns and variations both within and between localities, it is apparent that the answers would neither be straightforward nor unidimensional. Indeed, we would be looking for *combinations of factors*, at their interplay and interrelationship: to do this a dynamic element is introduced. This is provided by costs and benefits and their ability to act as local incentives or disincentives to coordination. These questions are taken up in the next chapter. Following that we review some of the main puzzles posed by the findings on local coordination, and place alongside them combinations of barriers, opportunities, costs and benefits. That discussion will take us further into an understanding of rationality and politics, to allow us to begin to draw together the tension provided by the politics of rationality and the rationality of politics, to coalesce the 'optimistic' and 'pessimistic' traditions.

PEOPLE IN STRUCTURES

The 'optimistic' tradition concedes little to the impact on coordination of individuals and individual differences. Behavioural and motivational elements are broadly ignored within a self-less vision of interaction, typified in the call for altruism and self or organisational sacrifice. Yet what if this is not the case? In the first section we explore inter-personal relations, and in the second we look at a group of actors who took a keen interest in coordination and who strove by one means or another to make it work.

Interpersonal relations: the impact of personality

Poor relations between key actors were an important factor inhibiting coordination, particularly when the difficulties were between chief officers or manifested by them in their managerial style. For example, allowing little delegation and tolerance of subordinate initiative:

The director is very autocratic and finds it very difficult to accept what coordination implies, that any comprehensive plan involves arguing things out and getting an agreed plan. Partly because of that people have found ways of achieving things through the back door, working through the informal network rather than the formal.

Similarly disruptive was the 'prima donna' mentality, exhibited by those convinced of always being able to go it alone without partners and without the hindrance of planning jointly. Personality difficulties and poor inter-personal relations were more difficult to overcome within smaller and more compact localities. In wider settings there was greater possibility of a flight into informality or of absorbing, by-passing or being more selective in the choice of partners. Where relations and personalities were compatible, power struggles could be set to one side and ritualised posturing avoided. Opportunities opened up:

I am sure personalities come into it. I don't know if you can organise for it, but if you get senior officers who click it makes a difference. Maybe it doesn't make any difference to what happens, but it certainly does to the speed at which it happens.

Expediting coordination, exercising formal and informal selectivity and operating across agency and professional boundaries were all features of a group of actors we termed *tacticians*.

Acting tactically

Tacticians personalised coordination. They were able to see themselves in relation to other actors' structures, problems and outcomes in coordination. They acted self-consciously. For them coordination was a long-term and complex game: 'like multi-dimensional chess' where they had to:

Get involved in politicing, fixing the ideas, creating a framework in which people can work together. Part of the success is knowing where the boundaries are, getting people sat down and then the barriers crumble.

Acknowledging barriers and circumventing them or breaking them down was an important part of their craft, as was perceiving openings:

This is an entrepreneur thing. I am not being cavalier, it's about opportunism – if that's the right word – the ability to see an opportunity and take it, mobilise resources and get on with it.

Acting tactically required the ability to wait, watch, learn and, importantly, *plan* intervention:

To be able to collaborate you have to know the other organisation and its system, their services, the key people, the influential people, to know where to plug in. You have to gain their commitment before anything is brought out into the open. You have to be in a position where you could run things in their organisation, have that level of understanding before you can collaborate effectively.

This form of mutual learning and timing was matched by understanding the crucial interplay of formal and informal machinery, and how these aided the search for benefits:

You need to know people personally to be effective in coordination. Firstly, to be able to talk to them about issues outside of meetings. To be able to raise things informally. Secondly, you have to have some idea of what might be of benefit to them.

By anticipating benefits for others from some as yet unrevealed interaction, tacticians were able to capitalise within exchange relations by presenting coordination as a positive sum game. This avoided the possibility that others would withdraw in the event of a zero sum proposition.

The substantive nature of these costs and benefits are identified in the next chapter. Here we can just underline the fact that a tactician's skill involved identifying not only what the benefits were to their own agency, but what the *others'* benefits might be. Also, to point out to others that they held resources when often they were unaware of their value to *ego's* organisation.

Tactical positions

Tacticians tended not to be at, although were not absent from, the very top levels of their organisations. They were more likely to be found in second or third tier positions, centrally located and involved in policy development, yet still keyed in through line responsibility to the difficulties presented at an operational level for single service running and the potential advantages to be squeezed out of a joint approach.

Effective tacticians were hence very rare in formal liaison roles, at the periphery of their organisations: such roles might make them active in another agency but often marginal within their own. Under these conditions coordination was hived off as a special activity, whereas the most successful tacticians combined routine intra-agency management with inter-agency flair and expertise.

Often tacticians exhibited anomalous or unconventional career skills, not possessing the professional qualification of their parent agency, and seemingly less bound by the normal and accepted channels of action. This often brought them into conflict with superiors within their own agency and increased the risks in acting in others'.

Tacticians were found within Central Planning Units, often acting as self-proclaimed reticulists,[1] within service departments, and also, interestingly, within the voluntary sector.

What they shared and often recognised in each other, was an ability to locate problem areas in policy development and the position to mediate between a top-down and bottom-up approach to policy formation. Sensing the up–down thrust they moved horizontally into collateral agencies in any of the three arenas in an active attempt to *solve problems*.

These problems were not just associated with policy, service management or delivery, but almost invariably with meeting client need. This was the 'why of planning', the distant objective and one they wished to reach in a hurry. They were motivated by need and impatient with many conventional answers:

I am always aware of the tensions between the radical element which is about change and the bureaucratic element which is concerned with not upsetting precedent. It should be about effectiveness.

Tacticians, seemingly steeped in the craft of coordination, therefore borrowed liberally, within the welfare context, from the need-based paradigm of the 'optimistic' position. They were also acutely aware of need and service interdependencies. This arose not from an abstract systems-wide perspective, but from an immersion in practicality: having identified the barriers they selectively worked for opportunities.

PROFESSIONAL DEFENSIVENESS, ADMINISTRATIVE DOMAINS AND STATUS DIFFERENCES

The 'optimistic' tradition presents coordination as selfless and without a professional, administrative or status base. It focuses upon the ends of coordination and more appropriate ways of meeting client need, rather than where coordination starts from: actors located within agencies, agencies with a history of accumulated professional power, areas of administration control and status to be protected. To what extent are these sublimated, disregarded or significant in movements toward a joint approach?

The securement of administrative domains[2] and moves toward their extension were formidable barriers to coordination. Stepping outside an autonomous zone of activity was presented as a dangerous move, 'that you lose control of the little bit you are able to determine'.

Aside from control difficulties agencies remarked upon the strangeness of others; 'their procedures and ways of working are not the same as ours', and:

There are great disparities between the two types of staff in terms of vastly different conditions of service and different ethos because of their training which leads to problems of working together. They start off with very different assumptions so it is very difficult to dovetail them together.

Education and social services, and health and social services were most likely to exhibit these administrative asymmetries. It was less so with housing and social services, because of a long history of separate development, either through choice or structure.

Although a barrier in these instances, there were examples of others seeing coordination as an opportunity to extend their administrative domains. These were the Central Planning Units whose entries into inter-departmental or collaborative affairs were resisted, especially when they concerned the autonomy of spending departments to formulate policy, even joint policy, or set priorities. To escape outright rejection centrally based actors adopted the tactic of being 'servants of coordination', of supporting, if not initiating, joint meetings and filling an administrative vacuum uncontested by others.

Professional defensiveness
Professional defensiveness[3] reinforced domain defence. This was most strongly manifested for the under-fives tracer and relations between education and social services, and between education and the voluntary sector.

Education perceived and promoted itself as 'more professional' than others, with its own very large and undisputed professional territory 'areas of overlap about the edges only'. Coordination was not central but peripheral to the main concerns of the teaching professions.

Youthful social services and their rapid growth were cast as indicators of 'empire building', and unfavourably contrasted with teaching:

Education has been running a service since 1870 and is very well established with clear policy lines and they know where they are going and how. Social Services for the under-fives are very new, post-war and there is no clear view of what they are trying to achieve. You get a pipsqueak service coming along and saying 'part of that belongs to us because it's got social problems'. Welding that together will be immeasurably difficult.

And difficult it was, with educationalists preferring 'pre-school' to 'under-fives' and stressing the disturbance and disruption to nursery education proposed by 'social problem' children and demands that nursery teachers change their location of operation.

From social services' perspective education was more central to their agency concerns, particularly as an element in the fullness of children's development. Unilateralism not only deprived the most disadvantaged children in day nurseries, it denied social services access to 'under-used educational plant'.

It was only where social services were prepared to censor certain plans and maintain low-key debate with education departments, or where other factors overpowered professional control, that defensiveness was not a major barrier.

In strict relations between education and social services it was very difficult for even astute tacticians to present coordination as anything more than zero sum. However, these barriers meant social services searching for opportunities and alliances in different areas, most notably with the voluntary sector. It was also possible where social services and education preferred not to raise fundamental differences between them, to jointly direct their attention toward the non-statutory sector. This was the case in Portshire and Greenshire. In the metropolitan areas education remained defensive and could not countenance anyone working with under-fives 'without formal training'.

Some similar antipathies were manifest in relations between health and social services professionals. These were, however, diluted by virtue of the fact that the collaborative arena tended to be under-populated by consultants and practising social workers. The difficulties between health and social services or other local authority functions were of a different order.

Status differences

In relations between health and local authority services, notions of status were important barriers. The high-skill, high-tech arena of health professionals, and the clear articulation of a health service administration was contrasted with the undifferentiated and 'amateurish' efforts of social services:

I can't see the Area Administrator accepting a social worker as an equal, or anyone in social services however high you get up the hierarchy.

Social services often reflected back on the limited autonomy they possessed compared to consultants and educationalists.

The status barrier was also a reflection of *professional power*[4] and the ability to define and confine the management of a client group to within particular parameters: medical and educational models of the client were more firmly etched and expressed than those associated with social services.

Professional and administrative domains reinforced and acted in concert as barriers. They were also realised in the grammar of status differentials. Their impact on different policy conceptions and policy paradigms are considered later.

SERVICE STOCKS AND FLOWS

Professionals and administrators also directed attention toward maintaining services themselves: the stocks of nursery units, elderly persons' homes, health visitors, and care assistants etc. Attention was further directed toward the management of clientele into, through and out of existing service units and the potential flow of new units.

Consideration of this aspect of 'people processing organisations'[5] is no less significant in promoting or impeding coordination than the ideologies of carers and administrators. This perspective derives from questioning the neutrality of service stocks and flows suggested by the rational tradition. This assumes that welfare capital and the production of welfare will not hinder the working of enabling structures or inhibit the growth of organisational altruism.

Service systems for children under five

For children under five, a high investment in statutory provision in relation to demand produced a focus on securing inputs, particularly in nursery education. With demographic decline the response was to seek and secure pre-school children via single service options, rather than allowing excess capacity to be used by the voluntary sector, or to redeploy resources in non-educational settings. Competitors to statutory provision were not encouraged.

Where service stock levels were low, statutory attention for under-fives was directed towards the private and voluntary sector and most likely to provide the opportunities for coordination. This was because there was little to defend, and everything to gain by enabling non-statutory alternatives to receive professional support and advice. Children who had been through such alternatives were then available to feed into the primary education sector, suitably socialised.

Service systems for elderly people

Within these systems, overall diminishing service levels in relation to need and demand promoted the search for substitute or complementary resources. The shift was toward community care solutions and an emphasis upon support within domestic settings. The service gap between housing and social services narrowed in some instances.

Similarly the separation between health and local authority provision diminished, with a blurring of the boundary between social and medical care such that joint planning and joint management became an increasing priority and agenda topic, if not a reality. Increasing frailty within residential homes and sheltered housing promoted a willingness to consider medical support and intervention.

In parallel the proportion of elderly people in acute beds reinforced the claims of geriatricians, para-medicals and social services staff in returning people to the community.

Service system pressures were beginning to tease out the framework of inter-dependency between services. What was often lacking was any systemic policy framework: negotiations took place bilaterally to solve immediate system problems, rather than facing, in 'optimistic' style, the overall problems of developing a comprehensive and coherent service for elderly people.

STRUCTURAL COMPLEXITY AND SCALE

The 'optimistic' tradition is exemplified by the issue of structural complexity, the creation of coterminosity, and the planned organisation of service boundaries so as to minimise multiple overlaps. Ensuring coterminosity was seen as a neat mechanism for enabling policy coordination, a tendency most strongly marked in the NHS reorganisation of 1974. However, what happens in practice, can there be an easy technical solution to the historical accidents of administrative formation and reformation?

Our evidence would suggest that this is at best a simplification. We have already seen that there was no clear relationship between complexity scores and machinery totals. Low complexity does not automatically lead to the establishment of machinery, certainly not to its productivity.

From a locality with low complexity:

We have our own education department and coterminous health authority, health district boundary, which provides an incredible opportunity to plan together. There are no barriers at that level.

Low complexity was matched by low machinery levels and low output. Technically everything was set up to go, yet practically hardly anything of a joint nature occurred; the opportunity was not seized.

By contrast, in a much more complex and structurally complicated locality, getting around mismatched boundaries was seen as a very practical and negotiable problem:

In principle a lack of coterminosity is a problem; in practice so long as you know what the boundaries are, and you have good will, you can get around this.

The key to the structural complexity variable would seem to lie in the extent to which it opens up opportunities and provides the space for tactical activity:

I don't think that structure facilitates collaboration, but you have got to have some sort of structure to oil the wheels, some sort of enabling policy, an umbrella mechanism, a means of drawing in education, the most powerful and the hardest to engage with. I think it helps this happy accident that our structure fits in as a useful way of bringing people together at different levels. It is a useful focus, a framework within which you can work.

The preponderance of machinery in the collaborative arena is testimony to the efficacy of coterminosity, but only when backed up by central mandate and the incentives presented by joint finance. In both the corporate and inter-sector arenas even when the opportunity was created it was not necessarily grasped because of the impact of other barriers. Agencies then tended to take the line of least organisational resistance and opted for lower cost options or wholesale avoidance.

A contributing barrier was constituted by asymmetries of scale between organisations. This militated against smaller agencies being able to attract the attention of their more powerful neighbours:

Social services remains miniscule in relation to health and to education. The education service has 120 schools, social services is in the small odds and ends category of their administration. It's the same for the health service, we are a flea on an elephant's back.

POLITICIANS AND POLITICS

We have reviewed the influence exercised by professions and the administrative elites; this section considers the role of political power and political ideology in coordinative arenas. These might be considered as 'irrational' or disruptive features intruding upon the even flow of policy analysis. However, questioning such smooth progress allows us to review their role as barriers or indeed whether they create conditions whereby coordination is enhanced.

We begin with the role of politicians, or members generally (of health authorities but also elected and nominated members in non-statutory settings), and then move to a discussion of ideology. Ideology is relevant because of the different political parties represented in our localities, their different histories of political control and the variety of changes in majority groups over the period of research.

Politicians

Politicians as a class rarely if ever set their faces fully against coordination: it was an important part of their rhetorical armoury, easy and cheap to employ and difficult to resist as an abstract exhortation. As at the centre, however, the ideal was not always translated into action or transformed into a command.

This was the key element for officers, for even if not an order, officers attempted to measure and gauge commitment. They sought the strength behind the word. Without perceiving political commitment to coordination, action was inhibited:

I think you have got to be committed to a thing for it to work. At the beginning no lead was given by politicians as to what should be achieved. That tends to make the work of officers a little bit blander than it need be. If politicians say where we've got to go, then we have got to cut through the barriers – the officers aren't going to do it because they might get cut themselves. The officers may take the coward's way out, but that's reality.

Member commitment was essential in relations with other authorities, in backing and supporting officer initiatives, which could not be subject to unilateral directive. Within the corporate arena barriers posed by departmental divides or professional antagonism were more susceptible to political fiat. This brings us to a second factor in the promotion and inhibition of coordination.

Political style and political life
Political backing for coordination was related to the political style of members within an authority, the extent and nature of their contact with officers, their involvement in policy arenas and the means of fashioning political careers.

There were obvious differences, for example, between elected and nominated members, the latter in health authorities or on the steering groups of voluntary agencies. In health settings a hierarchical authority structure for the transmission of policy, the presence of powerful professions and more transient contact between officers and members lessened the impact of politicians on either intra- or inter-agency coordination. Role ambiguity and role tension negated the influence on coordination of members within voluntary agencies or within their own councils on voluntary matters.

Within local authorities where key members were consistently involved in policy issues and the minutiae of departmental life there was a high probability of officers being aware of political priorities and where commitment should be enacted. This tendency was particularly marked where there was a strong lead from a comprehensive manifesto and a programme for implementation and review. This did not necessarily lead to the creation of coordination. Or again, there were examples of high levels of coordination within authorities with only cursory member overview and a sketchy manifesto. Other factors came into play.

Not least was the culture of the authority and the relationship between those chairing service committees and the power politics within majority groups. These would often reinforce sectional divides if not create them in the first instance. An outcome from this division is related below:

One [chairman] was obsessed with getting people out of elderly persons' homes, the papers were full of his wanting to get 10% out. But he hadn't thought about where they were to go, and because we have no sheltered housing policy and he was not chair of the housing committee ... two years later he is chair of the housing committee and he's got his sheltered housing and the chair of social services is not interested. The units have been built and virtually none of the residents are from EPHs. It's ships that pass in the night or it's like just missing a train, but if you run fast enough behind you might just catch it.

Such a sustained but dramatically flawed conception of coordination was not the norm. A major barrier was the different time perspectives as between officers and members:

Politicians are very much short-term animals. They go for something which they can grasp and deliver to people in a short space of time.

This draws upon politicians' assessment of the value of their investment in coordination. Member interest was depicted as essentially unreliable and 'freakish', with coordination as 'unexciting' or perhaps even more damaging that it was not seen as 'political activity at all in the way that party politics are waged'. Coordination was consigned to political inactivity and the politically inactive. Under such conditions harnessing short-term political aspirations to long-term coordination required delicate skill.

Political values and ideology

Political commitment created opportunities for coordination. The development of commitment was dependent upon broader political values and ideology associated with different political positions. Within a Conservative ideology that allowed little place for the concept of social need *per se* and saw little relevance in social policy issues, and so joint policies were by definition largely non-existent.

At the other end of the political spectrum a Labour ideology created opportunities by its espousal of a clear inter-relationship between economic and social policy spheres and the firm definition of service interdependencies.

We must look at social policy as a whole and not each service in isolation ... the question is not what policy are we going to have this year in education, but what policy are we going to have this year for children, what policy are we going to have this year for elderly or disabled people.

This stance has operated successfully within the corporate arena, but was not extended to the collaborative or inter-sectoral arenas. In these two, ideological variations made their biggest impact.

Within Labour authorities a strong tradition of prior local government control of health services died hard. The NHS was variously castigated as undemocratic and lacking in legitimacy. Such a posture inhibited officer action, particularly where community benefits might be derived from an expansion of health and local authority community services at the expense of a hospital dominated sector, whilst politically it was wholly unacceptable that any hospital should be run down or eventually closed.

Conservative authorities similarly retained some memory of control of community services but were less inclined to present these as barriers especially with their allegiance to central governmental policies and initiatives. For them the NHS represented needless bureaucracy and repositories of professional and union power. They would collaborate if somewhat uneasily and in expectation of conflict.

The non-statutory sector marked clear differences. Within paternalistic Labour authorities the position was, 'if a job needs doing then the Council will do it and do it properly'. This made coordination highly problematic. It certainly ruled out coordination, as opposed to control, of the private sector. Amongst other authorities the voluntary sector was supported by both the left and the right – the latter as an evocation of independence and self-help with intervention aimed at stabilising a substitute for statutory services. The only dangers were over-involvement and fears that voluntary agencies might be stifled by local government bureaucracy or contaminated by public sector attitudes and modes of organisation. In these extreme instances little attention was paid toward encouraging voluntary organisations and joint policies, but great claims made for volunteers.

For the 'new left' in local government voluntary and self-help groups were supported. They represented an alternative political power base within communities and a radicalising force in decentralisation: such groups were repositories of consumer and community interest as against the elitism of welfare bureaucracies. Often a clear distinction was made between traditional voluntary organisations and those more recently active, such as voluntary housing associations and tenant collectives. For their part the voluntary agencies were clearly aware of both the advantages of close political affiliation and grant aiding, and the disadvantages of being funded and allied to one political grouping.

Political ideology was also significant in creating barriers and opportunities in relation to the tracers. For elderly people, aversion to private care inhibited comprehensive policy analysis, not dissimilar in effect to a Conservative laissez-faire ideology. For children under five childminding was less contentious in relation to profit, but a matter for regulation in Conservative authorities, and for this plus questions of the role of women as carers in Labour authorities. The political concern for women's issues in these localities was not always matched within the officer structure, with resultant difficulties in service and policy development.

RESOURCE ENVIRONMENTS

The localities were chosen to provide a range of resource environments: from those organisations with a high resource base to those with low stocks; those moving into relative scarcity after sustained growth, and those with a consistent record of expenditure constraint. We also covered resource asymmetries where, for example, the local authority was likely to be constrained in the future whereas the health authority was expected to gain from RAWP redistribution.

This selection pattern was chosen to answer some of the key questions in coordination; both the 'optimistic' and the 'pessimistic' traditions accord significance to resource positions.

The rational planning tradition acknowledged the place of opportunities when there was a relative diminution of resource levels in relation to expanding demand. This was firmly at the centre of the JASP programme amongst government departments: in order to achieve social policy goals of the late 1970s and beyond, departments would need coordination to achieve maximum policy effect. This tradition portrays advantages in pooling resources for a client group, and of reducing service overlaps and cutting out duplication of effort.

Whilst accepting the logic of low resource bases and diminished flows, questions were posed about the interrelationship between resource positions. Thus, would situations where two agencies mutually experience resource scarcity promote and sustain interaction for mutual benefit? Or would asymmetrical positions, with the threat of power-dependence, create defensiveness? The 'pessimistic' tradition reintroduces an interactive element and poses a more problematic view of the likely success of resources in creating coordination.

A range of responses: triumphalism and defensiveness
A general answer to the resource equation is that where localities had been characterised by historically high or low resource bases, barriers were raised to coordination. Conversely, this can be expressed in terms of a range where the outer edges mark the limits of coordinative opportunity:

I think people collaborate best if they are reasonably humble; if neither side has got much money they use what little they have got to maximum effectiveness. You have to be fairly secure to avoid the twin pitfalls of triumphalism and defensiveness.

This is a symmetrical position with neither party overly well endowed or impoverished.

The *triumphalist* camp operated on the basis of an ability to generate and secure funds internally without recourse to external sources.

Between about the early seventies and 1978 there was tremendous expansion, everything was go and you didn't have to worry too much about what others were doing, there was plenty for everyone to get on with.

Unilateral development was the order of the day. Growth was achieved within organisational budgets. Any notion of resource incentives to coordination was slight.

Where there was little for anyone *defensiveness* and resource consolidation and protection were an important organisational goal.

Collaboration is very much a fringe activity and during shortages departments are drawn into the mainstream of activities. There is less chance of collaboration.

Where a rational sentiment might be expected to prevail, low growth and low base, the opportunity was rarely seized even if the logic was clearly appreciated:

We know we ought to be pooling resources and we do give lip service to it. But when it gets down to looking at it in practical terms we tend to draw the boundaries instead.

Again, resource incentives were negated if they imposed future penalties. Within both the unilaterally expansive and constrained positions coordination was unlikely: either the wealthier partner displayed little interest, or the less well-endowed feared take-over.

Between the barriers

Between plenitude and scarcity lay opportunities for coordination, especially when these were symmetrically aligned between agencies. Where there had been a recent slowing down of growth or there had been constraint over time, the search for additional resources promoted interaction:

Hopefully financial constraints will push us into doing what good professional practice would suggest anyway. If it hadn't been for financial constraint it might have been that we would have carried on ploughing our own furrows and building up our own services. It may be that the opportunity will come, it might give us an opportunity of coming together because we've got no other option.

In those localities and amongst agencies which had experienced resource constraint by virtue of ideology and market compression objectives, planning for expansion had long since been replaced by planning for contraction and allowed the development of planning skills and planning models which placed emphasis upon maximising resource gains through coordination. A key element in this was the ability to provide some additional funding as an incentive to collateral agencies, or for the agency itself to pick up the resultant costs of utilising 'funny money': coordination was not achieved solely on the basis of the rationality of jointly meeting need.

Resource environments were also significant for the voluntary sector. An authority which sought expenditure compression at all costs could mean an impoverished voluntary sector. An expansive local authority could fund an active and growing voluntary sector. Whether either of these occurred depended upon the translation of ideology into resource policies on grant aiding.

The human factor

For a resource environment to have a particular effect upon coordination it must be interpreted by local actors as having relevant qualities. This was not always the case. Partly this had to do with an inability or incapacity to monitor resources and changes in resource flows which might create opportunities. For example, one of the local authorities had been in receipt of real growth albeit low over some time. Within the authority it was not perceived or experienced as such, but as a continuation of retrenchment with no scope for coordinative possibilities.

In a situation defined as one of unrelieved scarcity or unabated growth it was difficult to change tack and alter policy practices and processes. Within a situation of defined scarcity, forward planning was replaced by crisis management and absorption in everyday detail. Morale was lowered and time horizons shortened. Joint planning was perceived as a luxury:

I'd love to sit for three hours but I haven't the time. It might be productive in the long run, but I live for in the short run.

With the possibility of cuts in the near future and little possibility of securing the time and space to engage in more rational and measured analysis, the potential for officers to be creative and engage in risk taking with other agencies was severely curtailed.

In well-resourced agencies service problems and resource difficulties had historically been resolved by increasing expenditure. The on-set of retrenchment, however, left them without the intellectual or managerial resources to solve new problems and a period of uncertainty and the loss of constancy resulted:

So much of what we are doing now in our corporate thinking is really new and revolves around the last couple of years and the economic depression. Nobody has much experience since the war of working within the present financial climate and rules are being made up as we go along almost. You'd be amazed how things were done in the past.

A time lag between the beginning of recession and the growth of adaptation and the formalisation of new responses had been experienced in certain localities much earlier than others. There actors were able to identify the increased demand for intellectual and planning input for solving the problems of reconciling reduced resources with expanding need.

Standstill planning and non-expansionist planning means losing the assumption that if we spend we can find the right solution. My motto – and this may be surprising – is this: looking at a big problem apart from need and professional issues, I would say that imagination has not kept pace with resources.

If opportunities created through resource conditions were to be seized then there had to be a clearer re-working of the inverse relationship between diminishing resources and expanding cognitive skills and planning.

PLANNING MATTERS: CAPACITY AND PHILOSOPHY

As we have already noted, there was a significant lack of planning capacity within the localities. It was also the case that where capacity was most needed it was probably least likely to be present: within poorly resourced authorities, planning personnel were a scarce resource and detailed information gathering an unaffordable luxury. The likelihood of capitalising upon resource opportunities was limited.

As important a barrier as low capacity in planning resources were differences in philosophy and the practice of planning. It was noticeable that the health service had the strongest sense of a planning identity, albeit one as part of a national planning system. Largely, health service planning was organised and legitimated around the application and manipulation of norms and numbers (perhaps typified by the 'black box' methodology and magic of the 'balance of care' model).[6] This clashed with the less formalised and very much more bottom-up approach of local authorities. Rigid adherence to bed number planning, 'if you think beds, beds are funded and attract X numbers of doctors and nurses and so on', conflicted with community and service needs identified by housing and social services. The distinction was also between a capital led planning framework and the revenue domination of much local authority thinking.

The health service philosophy resulted in a plethora of highly structured and potentially inflexible plans and programmes. The local authority pattern was considerably more disjointed and nowhere near as programmatic within our localities. It was more likely to be research based and dislocated from the policy making process. This lack of gearing was reflected in the absence of local authority planners from the collaborative arena. When they were juxtaposed, either in direct confrontation or more routinely during the perusal of plans after routine exchange, the difference in perspectives induced stereotypical and inflammatory responses:

They [the NHS] think if you produce enough paper and put in enough figures, out pops the solution.

The social services approach to planning is containable not just on the back of a postcard but on the back of a postage stamp!

Such feelings made a constructive dialogue on coordination problematic and certainly inhibited the possibility of rational analysis producing a measure of consensus.

Similar differences in planning philosophy and practice were noted between the various departments of local authorities, for instance between the housing need paradigm as measured by housing waiting lists, and social services definitions of need which was client and age related. Social services' measures of the housing needs of elderly people could not be reconciled easily with the traditional housing need measure of position on a waiting list.

Education measured pre-school groups and characteristics of individual pupils rather than age groups and family or community indicators. Such differences, however, opened up the possibility for the exchange of infor-mation, and the use of information as commodities in bargaining relation-ships. These might include information on the numbers of disabled and elderly persons registered – and registerability – collected by social services but of value to housing in the formulation of HIPs bids.

Social services research capacity could also be used as a resource to interest potential coordinative partners, for example: examining and assessing levels of dependency within sheltered housing schemes. Social services' experience of managing and measuring frailty within residential and domiciliary settings could be made available to health and housing.

Underlying the reactive model of social services planning was the relative *turbulence* of their budgetary environment compared to the stability of that experienced by health authorities. Yearly budgeting and fiscal uncertainty made investment in a structured planning programme extremely difficult for local authorities and voluntary agencies. To this uncertainty was added differences in planning cycles and planning timetables between health and local authorities. If coordination were to proceed, the barriers posed by these mis-matches had to be overcome.

POLICY CONGRUENCE

The 'optimistic' tradition assumes that for there to be progress in coordi-nation agencies will share certain values and have some interests in common concerning policies for care groups and the likely benefits to clients of a joint approach. It assumes that there will be a measure of consensus on the nature of problems and their solutions. Was this actually the case, or were there wide discrepancies in what could be described as *policy stances* which would create barriers to coordination?

From the 'pessimistic' tradition dissensus would not necessarily pose a problem: interaction would be avoided or the possibility of negotiation raised.

Where there was disagreement over basic and fundamental elements of policy stances such as the definition of community care, or the constitution of a client group, then major barriers to coordination were in place.

Elderly people

Where a health authority associated the term 'community care' with residential provision outside of a hospital setting and social services defined the term as services which enabled people to live at home, clashes were inevitable. This was particularly the case when the health authority wished to 'pull out the plug' on blocked acute resources, and transfer people rapidly to local authority residential care, whereas the local authority preferred to 'turn off the tap' of demand pressure on hospital beds.

Similar barriers were identified in conflicting perspectives between social services and housing in relation to the role of sheltered housing in the care of elderly people. Social service authorities tended to take the position that sheltered accommodation was for frail elderly people moving on from ordinary housing. Housing authorities perceived this as a transfer of the burden of care posed by restrictions in the number of Part III and hospital places.

Sheltered housing ought to be for people who need a bit of support, but essentially they should be independent.

It was only where there was a gradual convergence of policy stances between housing and social services, with some dilution of the housing need paradigm and amelioration of housing management difficulties, that opportunities for coordination were realised.

We are conscious we cannot stick rigidly to the 'good neighbour' definition. The role of wardens has changed as there is more longevity and people grow older, and as old people's homes are not really what people want.

This represented a change from the situation where it was remarked that one 'needed to be an Olympic athlete to currently qualify for sheltered housing'.

Children under five

Incongruent policy stances for this tracer posed serious barriers to effective coordination between agencies. This was most noticeable between education and social services, although the differences between them and voluntary organisations stressing 'play' and parental involvement created further divergence.

The polarisation of education and social care stances meant that attempts to develop even joint projects, let alone joint policies, were highly unlikely. Commitment to different policy stances by the statutory agencies rarely led to effective integration, but rather to a division of responsibility if not total separation. In policy terms this meant an age-based divide, social services managing zero to two year olds, and education three to five year olds. In project terms it meant either the movement of children between facilities, or the division of space and of labour within a single development. An alternative scenario to this end-on coordination was a joint decision to focus the statutory gaze upon the non-statutory sector. It was largely here that opportunities were perceived.

BROAD BARRIERS AND OPEN OPPORTUNITIES

The discussion of policy congruence and incongruence completes our review of the major elements promoting and inhibiting coordination. It is not an exhaustive list, but it does provide the main components of what we might term the *primary coordinative environment*. Any prospective attempt at a joint approach must, on the grounds of our work, come to terms with features of this environment.

The passage from rational beginnings to the production of output entails negotiating a vista of potential barriers and being able to exploit a range of opportunities. This coordinative orienteering marks the beginning of the politics of rationality. Conversely, we can begin to appreciate from a 'pessimistic' position the logic of power and influence and the rationality of politics.

Both themes enable local coordinative environments to be perceived as *structured environments*. The task of our final chapter will be to show how the basic building blocks of these local environments can potentially be rearranged and reordered, with a major responsibility for setting the boundaries of interaction and the local rules of the game residing with central government departments. Hence coordination can be made more or less difficult if the dynamics of structure are attended to.

Before moving onto the dynamic element we can briefly review the *significance* of particular barriers and opportunities: the centrality or marginality, coverage and scale of the impediments or facilitators of coordination. Which were the broadest barriers, and the most open opportunities?

Behaviour elements
Some elements inimical to coordination were essentially behavioural: disruptive or difficult personalities; professional defensiveness, domain claim and status differentials; and divergent planning philosophies. In terms of incidence none were widespread in any locality or arena. They could be transient and to some degree avoided, or subject to change by replacement of

personnel. Their presence or absence could not be predicted without invoking other more significant barriers. In isolation none of them were sufficient to fully sabotage coordination. Acting in parallel or in *combination*, as we see later, their influence could be powerful.

Similar significance must be placed upon *the role of tacticians* and their skill in perceiving opportunities or circumnavigating barriers. Tacticians were not exactly a populous species amongst our local actors, and indeed were rare enough to qualify as anomalies. Rarely did they constitute a formal social group, although the most active did attempt to establish relationships through which their actions would have most impact and hence constituted a form of social organisation.

Structural elements

Behavioural elements were less significant in forming the terrain of local coordinative environments than others such as: resource bases and flows; service stocks and flows; political factors; complexity and scale; planning factors and policy issues.

These structural elements could be either a major barrier or significant opportunity: they exhibited a duality whereas the behavioural elements were unitary in nature. Moreover, the significance of structural elements is accentuated by the value they added to behavioural notions. For example, domain claims were more loudly expressed the greater the perceived threat to resources implied by coordination.

Beyond duality and a conditional impact on behaviour, each was singly important. The resource element was widespread and the most commented upon feature, matched only by the impact of local political factors. The influence of service stocks was more peripheral and related to the details of negotiative activity. Complexity and scale were important background features but not wholly intrusive. The influence of planning matters and policy issues was less widespread.

However, these elements could compensate for each other, or indeed negate each other, depending upon their arrangement and relative strength in structuring coordination. This points to understanding their interplay. Before we do so, however, we now move to another feature of the *political economy of coordination*:[7] costs, benefits and incentives.

REFERENCES

1 J. K. Friend, J. M. Power and C. J. L. Yewlett (1974) *Public Planning: The Inter-Corporate Dimension*, Tavistock

2 S. Levine, P. White and B. D. Paul (1963) 'Community inter-organisational problems in providing medical care and social services', *American Journal of Public Health*, vol. 53, no. 8, pp. 1183–95; S.M. Schmidt and T.A. Kochan (1977) 'Inter-organisational relationships: patterns and motivations', *Administrative Science Quarterly*, vol. 17, no. 3, pp. 371–81; J.J. Molnar (1978) 'Comparative organisational properties and interorganisational interdependence', *Sociology and Social Research*, vol. 63, no. 1, pp. 24–8

3 K. Gyarmati (1975) 'The doctrine of the professions', *International Social Science Journal*, vol. 27, no. 4, pp. 629–54

4 T.J. Johnson (1972) *Professions and Power*, Macmillan

5 Hassenfeld (1972) 'People processing organisations', *American Sociological Review*, vol. 37

6 D. Boldy *et al.* (1980) 'Planning the balance of care', in D. Boldy (ed.) *Operational Research Applied to the Health Services*, London: Croom Helm; A.G. McDonald (1974) 'Balance of care: some mathematical models of the National Health Service', *British Medical Bulletin*, vol. 30, no. 3; G. H. Mooney, 'Planning for balance of care of the elderly', *Scottish Journal of Political Economy*, vol. 25, pp. 144–64

7 K. J. Benson (1975) 'The inter-organisational network as a political economy', *Administrative Science Quarterly*, vol. 20, pp. 229–79

9 ~ Costs, benefits and incentives

It has been argued that the perception and adjustment of particular costs and benefits provides the explanatory element which accounts for the differential impact of apparently similar barriers and opportunities within and between localities, tracers and arenas. Barriers and opportunities, identified in the previous chapter, appear less as determinants than as predisposing factors which variously impede or facilitate coordination.

As we have suggested at the end of the previous chapter, barriers and opportunities constitute a primary coordinative environment. They refer to those features which together form a basic context to interaction. Variations existed between the localities' primary environments as a consequence of our initial selection criteria. A *secondary level* of environmental variables is concerned with the less tangible features which relate more to process than to structural conditions. It is in relation to these process factors that cost and benefit considerations arise.

The rational planning approach to coordination takes little account of costs and benefits. The broadly based 'pessimistic' tradition which we identified pays such variables considerably more attention. The extensive literature of exchange theory which embraces bargaining and negotiation alongside power dependency conceptualisations, has such variables at its core. We constructed a number of 'common sense' questions around such theoretical bases. If, as this tradition would suggest, interaction is based upon the exchange or extraction of valued resources, then we might expect such interaction to be greatest when mutual benefits are likely, and least when no benefits are apparent to either party. In between these extreme symmetrical positions we might expect interaction to vary according to how the costs and benefits appear to each party.

The 'optimistic' approach to coordination and collaboration makes the assumption that the end result will be a maximising of client benefit. The 'common sense' opposition might accept this as an objective or an end, but it questions that the means towards this will be a cost-free exercise. It seems highly likely that the process of coordination will generate costs – and the nature of barriers in coordination discussed previously has begun to indicate the character of some of these. The same logic might also be applied to the benefit side of the equation: interaction might be more likely to occur when benefits are on offer not solely in terms of a vague notion of client benefit, but also including other valued properties.

We began our research, therefore, with a sharpened awareness of the probable significance of cost and benefit variables. We challenged the assumptions of the rational planning approach in which the different dimensions of interaction are treated as essentially similar, and we suggested that in practice costs and benefits might impinge differentially at the level of: the individual actor; sectional; agency and other interests. Furthermore, it seemed likely that these could be mutually antithetical: exhorbitant costs at individual or sectional levels might nullify broader potential benefits. Conversely, when the benefits of a broader nature appeared great, cost considerations falling on agencies and individuals might possibly be altruistically discounted against objectives of maximising client welfare.

The introduction of cost and benefit considerations then provides the *dynamic to the process of coordination*, and emphasises the *interactive* element. Neither cost nor benefit factors are objectively valuable, but depend upon assumptive worlds.[1] As with barriers and opportunities, some of these were more readily apparent than others. Costs – and benefits – are of obvious relevance in the resource context. Other dimensions were less apparent, and this reinforces the centrality of actors' perceptions in shaping the impact of costs and benefits. In the same way that barriers and opportunities often blurred at the edges and were conditional on other factors (a barrier in one situation might be perceived as an opportunity in another), so costs and benefits had areas of overlap. In the resource context such a characteristic was best illustrated by the 'mixed blessing' nature of joint finance.

Few actors systematically viewed the process of coordination – across all levels – through a cost-benefit framework. While many were aware of such features in the more obvious and structural areas (such as those arising from resource factors; domain control and the investment of time and energy), few could recognise more subtle processes and fewer still were able to engage in a strategic manipulation of the net balance of costs and benefits for participants.

Often actors perceived only benefits or costs, and failed to see their inter relationship. Those few who did operate in such a way were chiefly those we have termed 'tacticians'. Such actors were playing the coordinative 'game' for all it was worth. This game had rules (open to limited adjustment and re-negotiation), the number and nature of the players was often restricted, the stakes could be high, and it was conducted over a highly extended time scale.

Any potential arena of coordination could produce a complex web of barriers and opportunities, costs and benefits. The net outcome – a decision to proceed with interaction and the pursuit of particular objectives, or not – reflected a series of trade-offs and cost-benefit equations producing positive, negative or zero sum conditions.

COSTS

Individual and personal

The assumption that interaction may not be a cost-free exercise applied to the level of the individual as much as to that of the section or agency. The capacity of particular individuals, and of personality variables to variously shape barriers and opportunities has been explored. The construction of barriers at the level of the individual – an unwillingness to interact with other agencies – might be an indicator of actual or anticipated costs. What form did such personal costs assume in practice, and how salient were they?

The costs associated with individuals' potential involvement in coordination activities provide some further insight into variations and similarities of experience within and between agencies, tracers and localities. The costs for some individuals are prohibitive. For others, they are unavoidable, and, for certain posts and responsibilities, inherent. For some of these incumbents, however, if there were alternative routes around such processes, they would have been seized. As one joint finance administrator protested:

I would if I could. Believe me, there are easier ways of earning your bread and butter.

The inter-personal dimension

Some costs might be carried at a number of levels: administrative and time costs for example were reported both by individual actors and by their parent sections and agencies. However, there were also the more specifically personal costs reported by some actors in terms of psychological and inter-personal considerations.

In at least one locality 'disturbance costs' were identified. For example, in the collaborative arena while the principle of coordination was paid considerable lip service, in practice it was marginal to in-house concerns. For most health service personnel collaboration was 'neither understood nor appreciated', and was viewed at best as a 'fruitless activity' of benefit only to the local authority:

Within health services management there are probably only three or four – less than the fingers of one hand – people who are even interested in collaboration. For the majority it is foreign territory of strange customs, language and culture . . . They do not know the ins and outs, the give and take, they have to be goaded and led.

Such 'strangeness' was disquieting; disruptive of routine and the familiar:

It upsets their planning, their tidiness, and provides them with things they can't fully comprehend. And that disturbs them.

The marginality of collaboration to most mainstream service activity was accompanied by an awareness in some instances that 'the dictionary definition of collaboration is "plotting deviously with the enemy" '. Elsewhere there were further allusions to the slightly underhand nature of the activity. One local authority liaison officer located within an AHA was viewed by the SSD as 'our spy in the camp'.

Statutory/non-statutory interaction

The costs of crossing boundaries and disregarding conventional demarcations were potentially greatest for the non-statutory sector. For these bodies – often very concerned with the need to retain their independence – visible interaction with the statutory sector could entail 'being seen to be a turncoat on your principles by your parent organisation', or as 'a Trojan horse in reverse'. Such considerations often produced a reluctance to become 'too closely involved'.

For the statutory agencies, interaction could again entail personal and individual costs – albeit of a different nature. The *risk of exposure* was evident in some situations, and as a cost consideration had an inhibiting influence upon inter-sectoral relations and interaction. A sense of 'inappropriate' business in the presence of outsiders often circumscribed both agendas and discussions in inter-sectoral forums.

Some costs of operating multi-lateral forums were experienced in the increased administrative burden occasioned by scope and scale, and in the technical difficulties of managing large groups. However, the more subtle, psychological considerations were of equal or greater force. Thus, the risk of revealing 'family secrets' in the presence of these more 'distant relatives' could be a major constraint. Anxieties about the public washing of dirty linen added to a general discomfort with these outsiders, and to worries and tensions over policy ownership and domain encroachment.

The statutory/non-statutory interface typically lacked any dynamic. While officers met in and around these forums and continued their discussions elsewhere, this was the only place where the two worlds usually met. A consequent lack of informality and familiarity put non-statutory actors at a considerable disadvantage. It was remarked that, 'in short, they do not know the rules of the game'.

The dangers of allowing the uninitiated to participate in the game were apparent. It was recognised, for example, that it was 'often easier to negotiate trade-offs outside of the JCPT because of all the attendant camp followers there'. Participants unfamiliar with the local 'case law' and 'tricks of the trade' were apt to challenge process and decisions, and to generally disturb proceedings and inhibit a 'free and frank discussion between departments' by 'asking silly questions'.

The exclusion of members from certain forums was explained in the same terms. Members might have been interested in these issues, but their presence inhibited officers. Open government could sometimes be a nuisance 'to the extent that things are held up', and there was often a preference for discussion 'behind closed doors'.

Boundary crossing: classification and contamination[2]

In other arenas the costs of being seen to consort across boundaries were perceived in career terms. For example, one social services actor who was prepared to venture across boundaries and forge alliances with the housing department encountered the resistance of his director who took the view that 'John Smith spends far more energy than I like in Fulborough House – working the market.'

The risks attached to leaving the security of a home port and sallying forth into the unknown from which there may be no return were similarly noted at the centre–local interface. A civil servant on secondment to a senior position in a health district had shown a very clear awareness of the possible career consequences of such a move:

I would not have touched the job if it had not been on secondment. I didn't want to leave the civil service. I was very much in two minds about it. The custom now is that one period of secondment is unusual, and two I would guess is breaking completely new ground, and I didn't want to prejudice my civil service career.

Indeed, being in 'two minds' was reported to us in the sense of his former colleagues questioning his sanity – 'you must be mad'.

The threat to mainstream career development reflected the marginality of collaboration and coordination activity. Such endeavour was irregular, its main participants highly visible, anomalous – and, at times, ostracised. Typically, the threat of the non-routine and the unfamiliar was dealt with in the downgrading of collaboration to a few poorly supported posts. The loneliness of such endeavour was frequently remarked upon.

Supplication and prostration

A further aspect of individual and personal costs was sometimes identified in the 'costs of supplication'. These underlined the power-dependency element of the interactive process. If some currency of equivalence is a prerequisite of sustained inter-agency interaction, the inability to reciprocate in kind may be perceived as a cost. Such a situation skews the essential nature of exchange relations; casting one or other partner always in the role of supplicant, or always as bestower, distorts the distribution of costs and benefits. Such imbalances were identified at times between social services and housing agencies, and between social services and education. For example:

We tend to take out of housing resources which they might value holding, and our contribution is very rarely something that they would value. We are the takers and housing are the providers.

The sense of 'always asking for something' was clearly a cost for some actors. Unreciprocated 'begging for help' could create and reinforce power-dependency relations and so constrain interaction and potential benefit.

Resource costs

Both the 'optimistic' approach to coordination and the 'pessimistic' tradition are sensitive to the likely significance of resources under certain conditions. The barriers and opportunities posed by particular resource situations, and by changes in such conditions, have been described previously. Questioning this we assumed that the availability of special monies to fund coordination and collaboration might make the activity more likely (and might be expected to be especially attractive to poorly resourced agencies). Likewise, it seemed reasonable to expect that when coordination suggested heavy demands upon resources, it would be less likely to develop – particularly in the context of scarcity and retrenchment.

The availability of '*funny monies*' meant that our interest was directed largely towards the collaborative arena where such resource mechanisms were well established. The perception of resource costs or benefits depended to a great extent on the particular time scale adopted. In the short to medium term, *joint finance* was generally viewed in positive terms and operated as an incentive. However, with joint finance programmes reaching maturity in all localities, the longer term consequences were of growing concern, and an awareness of financial commitment increasingly dominant.

In the collaborative arena financial costs of interaction were borne primarily at an agency level. For most local authorities (and that largely meant the social services departments) the allure of joint finance palled with impending tapering requirements and the prospect of increased revenue commitments. A typical observation was that:

Joint finance is a marvellous idea but picking up the tab at the end of five or seven years is the sting in the tail.

In some localities the SSD's awareness of 'commitments writ large' had 'forced second rate decisions'. While elsewhere, the costs of further commitment were so prohibitive that the prognosis for future joint planning was wholly pessimistic.

There will be no more joint planning because local authority commitment is the problem at the moment. At the end of the day if it means any more resources it won't happen. Usually the problem is over staffing and revenue – so joint funding won't help that.

Avoidance strategies to reduce or remove such costs were systematically developed in some localities. In at least one locality, joint finance was deliberately used only 'for things which can be easily disposed of', and similar 'contrivances'. This introduced further costs in the souring of health authority and social services relations, with increasing suspicions within the AHA that joint finance was being abused in underwriting local authority indiscretion.

While such cavalier attitudes to joint finance were less advanced elsewhere, some manipulation was widespread. Joint finance was typically used in ways which would return the maximum benefit, while causing the least damage to overall budgets (such as through revenue commitment).

A further potential cost arising from a preoccupation with the input side of the equation was that of reduced quality of service output. The speed of spending joint finance was frequently the major – or sole – criterion of 'success' in joint planning. The consequences of particular schemes were typically 'not thought through' nor evaluated. Joint finance was said to have been explicitly used 'to hustle through joint planning'. Certainly the spending of joint finance could not be viewed as a proxy of the development of joint planning or strategic coordination.

Administrative and time costs

To the extent that interaction and coordination activities may be time consuming and administratively tedious, we advanced the assumption that certain 'costs' would emerge for participants. We might further expect that such costs would fall more heavily on some than on others: the maintenance of machinery demands servicing. We might also suppose that this administrative task would appear as a greater burden and an onerous chore within those settings in which resource and other variables allowed little slack for the performance of seemingly non-essential work.

The cost of coordination in terms of the associated administrative and time demands was certainly one of the most consistently voiced complaints. This was true both between localities, and across agencies, tracers and arenas. What form did such costs take?

On one level there were the costs of actually operating the machinery, that is:

in the actual time spent, and in getting together reasonably highly paid senior officers.

The resentment of this time investment and its perception as a cost was greatest where machinery was generally viewed as ineffectual. A distinction was made between 'talking shops' and 'doing shops'. Talk without action was dispiriting in the longer term, and 'talking shop' was a pejorative term for certain machinery – most often in relation to the JCC and JCPT.

Interestingly the boredom factor has been identified as important at the central government level. This concerned the activities of the CPRS in general, and apropos JASP in particular: 'They like meeting to take decisions rather than to deliberate. The JASP committee was essentially a deliberative forum and never really reached the decision-making stage.'[3]

Similar costs were also apparent in relation to the development of semi-formal and informal networks. If anything, such 'networking' was even more demanding of time and effort.

Time is the biggest cost, if you can call that a cost. I've spent hours wooing housing and health ... I'm putting time into the consultant geriatrician at the moment, supporting him in his battles with the other consultants, going over two or three times a week. Things can be made to work, but it's time, time and time.

The perception of time investment as a cost could indicate the marginality of the activity to mainstream work, as perceived by others. The costs of 'time taken away from the basic regular work of the department' were the guilt feelings 'about taking time off'. Guilt might be reduced by minimal or tokenistic participation, and the following remarks were typical:

I have often not attended [the JCPT] because there seemed to be more important and immediate tasks on my desk here.

Lack of time is the big thing in all the departments; people tend to feel guilty – even now they tend to see coordination as meeting, not working.

Other factors also intensified the potential costs of coordination time and administration. *Scope and scale of interaction* were especially important. The operation of coordinative processes could be considerably more demanding on resources in such situations. Within large shire counties, for example, the costs and aggravations of drawing together scattered district council representatives for a JCC could be overwhelming. The resulting 'huge meetings' were generally seen 'as expensive and useless'.

The aggravation of these processes indeed points to a further dimension of administrative costs in the 'frustration of not getting anywhere' or, at the least, getting there very slowly and tediously:

Sometimes I wish you could make the decisions quickly. By the time you have consulted with everybody weeks have gone by ... more and more people are involved.

Moreover, such costs are likely to escalate over time: 'having set up a network you have to put work into maintaining it'.

Loss of domain

Within the 'pessimistic' perspective on coordination, domain was a further area which was thought to be of relevance to actors' and agencies' perceptions of the likely or possible costs of interaction. If we make the assumption that altruism is not generally a guiding precept of organisational life, and that agencies are basically self-interested (self-preservation being a primary motivation), it follows that activity which threatens professional domains and identities will (logically) be viewed negatively and avoided.

The literature of organisational theory posits that agencies seek to maximise the supply and control of valued resources. A crucial resource for the people processing organisations of the welfare world is clients. If control over either the supply or management of clients is challenged by interaction with outside agencies, domain defensiveness might be expected to emerge. The operation of such defensiveness has indeed been cited as a barrier to interaction. The repercussions of that barrier, and the extent to which it proved impenetrable or might be circumnavigated, is illuminated now in an examination of some of the costs which agencies identified.

The anticipation of domain loss clearly frustrated interaction in some aspects of the corporate arena, and reduced the likelihood of joint endeavour:

In the local authority there are a lot of mini-empires that are continually being squashed. But how can you sacrifice what autonomy you have when dealing with outside organisations?

Such a perspective suggested that successful interaction between statutory and non-statutory agencies was even less likely. Within the corporate arena the cost of losing empires had sometimes to be tolerated – or submitted to (particularly where Corporate Planning Units were active) – in which case it seems likely that agencies would cling more tightly to remaining autonomy in interactions in which they did have greater control.

The loss of domain was not only a loss in terms of autonomy in a given area. Other considerations were identified in '*the costs of compromise*'. Compromises were evident in relation to attempts to unify opposing priorities and differing policy paradigms. Compromise threatened service purity or integrity, and at the level of the individual could be a humbling experience. In well resourced localities such considerations weighed more heavily on the 'prima donna chief officers' than did the more tangible costs which might be more readily absorbed.

There are the costs of compromise. We are not particularly worried about administrative or time costs – not when it is for something which is anyway a high priority.

These costs, the issues of 'do people really want to compromise and share control? Because that is what it means', were particularly apparent in *combined working endeavours.*

Combined working between education and social services departments for children under five, for example, illustrates some of these costs. In some localities this manifested itself in the education department's view that sharing the under-fives domain was a second rate option compared to full control.

We have noted the defensiveness of education authorities in many of the localities as a barrier. Rigid professional demarcations were probably encountered more often with education agencies than with any other. In most instances an awareness of the costs of compromise and a 'paranoia' concerning the effects of a dilution of service integrity outweighed any consideration of wider benefit.

Similar concerns were evident in the collaborative arena where joint working carried potential costs both for individuals and agencies in a loss of power and status:

It is essential that someone says that they are prepared to allow their resources to be used on a joint basis. A big problem is the number of beds. The difference between a local authority administrator and a geriatrician is that for the latter beds are everything. Consultants' power and status rest on the number of beds they have got, and they jealously guard them.

BENEFITS

The previous section has outlined the major dimensions of the costs of coordination. To look at costs in isolation, however, is to consider only the debit side of the equation. The significance of costs, whether they were major or marginal, prohibitive or merely an irritant, indicates the role of benefits in shaping the final calculus. Costs and benefits were rarely polarised, rather they formed a complex dialectic.

The net assessment of positive, negative or zero sum conditions was especially dependent on perceptual variables, and on the particular time scale of reference. In many instances costs appeared as foreground and immediate considerations, while benefits were often deferred over a considerable period. This factor again underlines the scarcity of a coordinative mentality at work: for most actors and agencies it was the pressing business of today which dominated concerns. A longer term perspective, and a willingness to take risks in planning for distant returns was largely restricted to the 'tacticians'.

The 'optimistic' approach to coordination assumes that an awareness of the interconnection of client needs will promote interaction across fragmented agency boundaries, and the development of rational comprehensive (coordinated) planning. Such a perspective assumes the dominance of organisational altruism: the expectation of enhanced client benefit from more appropriate service packages is the sole motivation for agencies and actors. However, we have already seen that the road to such an end is strewn with obstacles and with costs. Under such conditions organisational altruism would appear wholly irrational.

A more pessimistic view gives rise to the assumption that the end result will depend much more deliberately upon the calculation of both costs *and* benefits at each stage of the interactive process.

This section examines some of the main dimensions of benefits which were identified, and which parallel – or mirror – the delineation of costs. The interactive nature of the cost/benefit dialectic is also developed. The chapter concludes with a section which assesses the relative weight and importance of the variables which have been presented.

Individual and personal

We have seen that the price of interaction for some individuals was very high. The personal costs of loneliness and marginality could be overwhelming. Nonetheless, our common sense perspective led us to expect, and the evidence from the bureaumetry confirmed, that interaction *did* sometimes occur. This leads us to suppose that personal and individual *benefits* could also sometimes be extracted, or be attractive to certain personalities.

As one respondent pointed out, whether benefits are perceived 'as an advantage to the organisation, or to the client, depends on how you regard it'. Similarly, benefits to individuals, sections and agencies intertwined and overlapped.

Generalised benefits of interaction which were appreciated on both individual and agency levels concerned improved understandings and enhanced relations. Meeting and talking together – even if limited and ritualised – might be better than not meeting and not talking.

The joint planning mechanisms have forced everybody to look at everybody else in new ways, which has meant that sets of relationships have improved by and large. We have been forced into contact with people who otherwise we would not select as people we would want to make contact with. The more easy interchange of people, ideas and facilities is a real benefit.

For some actors collaboration and coordination were a way of life: the reticulists and the entrepreneurs. Some of these were cast in such roles by training and appointment, others by fortuiosity and necessity, who moulded the role to suit their own objectives. Some of these individuals were able to extract personal benefits through such activity. For example, the *reduction of marginality* through the performance of valued liaison activities, and the absorption of others' administrative costs, was one possibility. As one corporate planner remarked:

Others don't like doing it. For the rest of their lives they are health service managers; social services or education managers. Much of their joint work is peripheral to their main task. They are more than happy to have someone neutral to do the job.

Mutual benefits were apparent in this area: in addition to providing the tacticians with a legitimate role, the activity relieved other actors of some of the potential costs of coordination – at least in terms of administration. This is explored more fully in the section on resources.

While for some tacticians marginality might be reduced, for others the activity entailed greater costs; the classic dilemma of the double agent who 'belongs' in neither camp.

The establishment of a *reputation*, and even of notoriety, was perceived as a benefit of interaction in some localities and arenas. Certain individuals clearly relished their 'maverick' image, while the attainment of 'success' and the recognition of good practice also had a wide appeal to both officers and members. In one locality, for example, the excitement of working for a 'renegade' authority which 'thinks years ahead of its time' was accompanied by a more restrained pride in an earlier nationally publicised partnership between chief officers in housing and social services.

If collaboration and coordination were generally marginal activities, and those individuals most closely involved in such work were typically marked and set apart, there were certain exceptions to this rule. In another locality reputational benefits were clearly recognised in the under-fives field. More-over, a 'culture of coordination' was identified which encouraged such endeavours and made them a positive feature of career enhancement:

[Collaboration and coordination] is seen here as very much the thing to do, and you are successful if you do it successfully . . . Apart from feeling that you are doing a better job, there are the rewards of external publicity, a little bit of kudos. There is an undoubted intellectual climate favouring collaboration.

The final comment is particularly significant; it begins to suggest the intellectual demands of coordination – which further reduces the likelihood of its incidence. In this locality the under-fives field had been claimed as one of several areas of 'joint enterprise' between the education and social services departments. High visibility coordinative endeavour – acclaimed both locally and nationally – provided both intrinsic and political benefits, which were particularly relished by senior staff in both departments. The authority had been cited as an example of 'good practice' on more than one occasion, and had attracted the personal interest of representatives from the DES, DHSS and the Home Office. Visits by such persons had been received as 'a great political reward'.

This section has examined some of the dimensions of personal and individual benefits. As we pointed out at the beginning of the section, there was considerable overlap between benefits which ostensibly flowed to the individual actor, the agency or to the client. In terms of personal satisfactions, many actors clearly derived benefit from the sense that their activity enhanced client welfare, and maximised their agency's objectives. Some of these further dimensions of personal benefit will continue to be drawn out in the following sections.

Resources

The resource costs inherent in joint investments and joint working have been presented, but clearly this is not the whole picture. The 'mixed blessing' nature of joint resource pools (most notably of joint finance) has also been previously indicated. Benefits in both practical, and less tangible, forms were on limited offer via joint finance. As a source of additional resources (and often the *only* growth increment to SSDs' budgets) joint finance typically had an incentive effect – at least in the short term.

If joint finance was not a 'provider of goodies' in anything other than an opportunistic and ad-hoc mode, nonetheless, most actors' accounts of collaboration stressed the wider benefits which were consequent to agencies being 'forced together' by the due process of joint finance. The need to meet in order to discuss joint finance arrangements and proposals typically brought the wider benefit of increasing mutual understanding and empathy for the problems and resource dilemmas confronting other agencies. 'Scapegoat and adversary positions' were at least reduced. The following observation is typical. It epitomises the nature of the benefits of joint finance, and their limited quality.

Joint finance has given joint planning teeth, though it has caused problems and also had benefits ... The advantage is a simple one: it has enabled us to give effect to some aspects of joint planning, it has allowed it to take off.

A further comment illustrates the limited nature of the benefits which joint finance offered, serving essentially as a catalyst to existing aspirations or practices, rather than as a source of great innovation:

Joint finance may *just* have got things to be provided earlier, but it has not persuaded them to do things they would not have been doing anyway.

Consideration of the benefits variable in the resource area provides some additional insight into the manipulation of elements which on first sight appeared as limiting and absolute structural features. In practice, the resource environment is malleable and conditional rather than absolute (albeit within certain fairly rigid parameters). Its flexibility was most apparent in the deliberate construction of certain resource benefits. One such area where this was evident was that of cost dispersal.

Cost dispersal

The dispersal of organisational costs – at both administrative and financial levels – was a clear benefit of interaction in some localities and within particular arenas, and in some instances was pursued as a deliberate strategy of service development.

As we have indicated in the previous section which considered personal benefits, the capacity to absorb a proportion of other agencies' administrative and aggravation costs through servicing of the collaborative and coordinative machinery, could provide an acceptable role for the otherwise resented Central Policy Units.

But what of the dispersal of more tangible costs, of those which could make significant demands on over-committed budgets? The strategic development of dispersal techniques was not commonplace. However, in localities and situations in which the tacticians were peculiarly aware of the distribution of costs and benefits, this was certainly in evidence.

In one such locality the development of home-based community care programmes consolidated resource and care considerations through entre- preneurial opportunism. The dispersal of cost was vital to the claim for the programme's cost-effectiveness, and therefore 'the more I can put on the housing revenue account, the better'. Similar dispersal of costs was achieved through social security resources:

I can sell adult foster care as being more cost-effective. It is, but there are hidden costs. I get more out of social security, so the real cost is probably the same as it is for residential care, but the mere fact that the cost is dispersed makes it easier.

The benefits of such action were highly tangible: providing access to housing units and reducing expenditure for the SSD. Less tangible benefits were also reported: in addition to personal satisfactions and an enhanced reputation for successful operation, there were said to be improved levels of confidence and trust between housing and social services.

Assumptions about the process of coordination led us to suppose that interaction would be greatest (or most likely) when mutual benefits were perceived. Exchange theory and power-dependency perspectives treat the apparently unequal positions of donor and recipient as crucial. In practice these positions were not always so clearly differentiated.

Reciprocal benefits need not be of the same kind, nor indeed of apparent equivalence. In the instance of cost dispersal described above, the housing department also perceived benefits from cooperation. The kudos which attached to developing special needs provision proved highly attractive. Compared to the very practical and financially valuable benefits which were returned to the SSD, such a benefit appeared vague and of lesser worth, nonetheless:

The special needs bit was very tangible to them. What appealed was the joint element. We stated throughout our reports that any successes were due to the joint nature and the cooperation we had received from housing. That was very important to housing, they get a lot of flak. It was quite important for them to achieve something – on both a personal and organisational level.

Other examples of deliberate cost dispersal were encountered elsewhere. Once again these were initiated by the SSD in an attempt 'to engineer a switch between residential and community services'. Mutual benefits were again evident: social service resource flows and direct service pressures were eased and policy paradigms promoted, whilst simultaneously assisting the district councils to expand their HIPs bids for special needs provisions (via linked Part III and sheltered housing developments; extra care sheltered housing and district housing officers for elderly people).

The above examples indicate a tactical and interactive pursuit of the benefits of cost dispersal. Elsewhere, other instances revealed processes of cost dispersal by default. Thus the largely unchecked mushrooming of private residential care for the elderly effectively dispersed the costs of care onto social security funds, while reducing visible service and demand pressures on Part III provisions.

The dispersal of costs was closely related to the *sharing of responsibility*. This theme is explored more fully in the following section. The examples above concerned attempts by SSDs to disperse both costs and responsibility increasingly onto housing departments. These approaches were not always successful. The resistance of such ploys in other circumstances was indicative both of the failure to recognise commensurate benefits, and of the strength of barriers posed by conflicting policy and service paradigms.

Cost dispersal and sharing of responsibility was also apparent as a benefit of interaction around the under-fives tracer. The inclusion of the voluntary sector generally fitted into an opportunistic mode of interaction. The offer of 'a place in the sun and a foot in the system' was typically grasped by voluntary agencies. For those making the offer it was of pragmatic value. The resources and additional capacity which the organised voluntary sector could provide was particularly welcome at a time of retrenchment, and with little prospect for the development of unilateral statutory services. For the most part there was little doubt that if and when the resource environment became more favourable, the 'usefulness' of the voluntary agencies would take a poor second place to the expansion of the more prestigious nursery education programme.

This overview has highlighted the range of experience in the recognition and seizure of resource benefits. It is clear that resources were very broadly defined, and went far beyond the strictly financial concerns. Moreover, a financial benefit for one partner need not necessarily be matched by a similar kind of benefit for another. In this context a resource is anything which is valued and sought after by the agency in question.

Diffusing responsibility: taking the blame and sharing the glory

We began to suggest above that a diffusion of responsibility – a 'sharing of blame' – was often a benefit which was closely related to that of cost dispersal. Our 'pessimistic' perspective would lead us to expect interest in absolving agencies of sole or major service responsibilities to be greatest when resource and service stocks and flows are under pressure, and likely to remain so for the foreseeable future.

For agencies *in extremis* we might expect that the benefits of spreading the burden will outweigh cost considerations around service integrity and professional exclusiveness. Such considerations may be sacrificed on the altar of necessity – at least in the short term. Prolonged and continuing constraint may reverse perceptions of costs and benefits. The benefit or advantage of professional exclusiveness in times of plenitude may emerge as an unaffordable luxury and, indeed, a millstone in less favourable conditions.

This perspective also begins to indicate a *distinction between ends and means in coordination*. Clearly, if the above factors are acknowledged, then coordination may be pursued for a number of reasons. Among these reasons may be included such concerns as enhanced client well-being; more integrated and rationalised service delivery etc. In other words, those factors which provide the *raison d'être* for the pursuit of coordination within the 'optimistic' tradition. However, if such objectives are pursued only when they are in alignment with other objectives and interests (individual, sectional or agency), while the end result (coordination) may be the same, the means towards it will be radically different.

The apparent presence of a systems-wide perspective – the acknowledgement of crucial interdependencies and overlaps 'with collateral helping agencies' – may emerge less from the 'optimistic' approach than from an essentially opportunistic outwardly directive policy and planning orientation. The recognition of opportunities for coordination could indicate less of an attempt to achieve the goals which the 'optimistic' model would advocate, so much as the retreat from a position of major to subsidiary responsibility. Within this latter approach interaction is both pragmatic and selective, albeit legitimated by appeal to the positive values attached to coordinative endeavour and perceived good practice.

Where service pressures (particularly around the elderly tracer) were instrumental in forcing awareness of service inter-dependencies, the potential benefits of cost and responsibility sharing were evident. The pragmatic approach to coordination in this vein was succinctly expressed by one social services actor:

> making other agencies offers they can ill afford to refuse. We go in for joint decisions, then everyone takes the blame and shares in the glory.

In contrast to responsibility sharing (and cost dispersal) by neglect (or non-interactive adjustment) such as we pointed out in relation to the mushrooming growth of private residential care in some areas, the approach highlighted here was characterised by interactive entrepreneurial zeal.

We have argued that the intensifying of service pressures provided a fillip in some situations to attempts to diffuse responsibilities and spread costs more widely. These service pressures were greatest at the health and social services interface, and at the inter-sector juncture. In some instances the 'silting up' of the acute hospital sector by inappropriately placed elderly patients similarly forced a greater awareness for the health service of the opportunities and likely benefits of interaction and inclusions. A stress upon the 'most crucial interdependence ... between the health services provided for the elderly and those provided by local authorities' was one attempt to operationalise this. The failure of most health authorities to implement such objectives indicated the strength of barriers which impeded this, and most of all – the paramount cost considerations which deflected local authority interest.

Client benefit

The 'pessimistic' tradition which informed much of our analysis presented a largely economistic model of human behaviour. Nonetheless, we have indicated at various points where there were factors relating to individual psychology and motivations which would not seem – on first sight – to be easily accommodated by a cost-benefit taxonomy. We have further indicated, however, that objectives such as client benefit need not be antipathetic to this perspective. While the 'optimistic' perspective requires the demonstration of organisational altruism, the 'pessimistic' perspective would assume the inclusion of client benefit within (rather than outside of) any cost-benefit calculus.

Was client welfare an important consideration in the judgement of costs and benefits? In certain localities political ideologies and a commitment to public service (often expressed as civic pride) were paramount in shaping perceptions of benefits and the greater good. In others, professional ideology was similarly important in sharpening the focus on client benefit.

We have a lot of people who care about the borough rather than their own status or promotion. There are lots of people who think about the borough first.

Would we say that such a commitment was altruistic? It may be argued that altruism entails a deliberate discounting of cost, but it is clear that the pursuit of client benefit need not be inimical (or costly) to other interests. There were inherent rewards and personal satisfactions reported by those adherents to a service philosophy. This was expressed in one locality as a 'rather masturbatory' benefit:

They like to feel that they are doing good for people, whether they want it or not. The need to achieve something which is intellectually proper and which is caring is a powerful motive in social service departments.

A powerful motive indeed, as the history of social philanthropy testifies.

While for some individuals 'client benefit' was a vague and generalised concept, for others it was highly specific. Tacticians typically viewed the coordination world through a perspective which balanced off short and long term interests. It was largely among these activists that any awareness of longer term strategy and planning was located. A commitment to maximising client well-being in this context entailed the patience and confidence to implement gradual change within long term objectives.

For actors and agencies who did not perceive the collaboration and coordination arenas in broader cost-benefit terms, a singular commitment to the clients' best interests provided the leitmotiv for this activity and interaction.

Even where actors *did* perceive both costs and benefits, certain cost considerations might be discounted in an attempt to secure broader service benefits. In one locality, for example, the SSD was willing to surrender claim to the under-fives domain if necessary:

I would not have cared if the nurseries had gone over to education . . . in fact, that might be what needs to happen, they should be responsible for all care for under-fives . . . I really don't care what happens so long as the service is provided.

Similar considerations were sometimes evident in the collaborative arena. In general there was a high degree of tolerance of many local authorities' manipulation of joint finance and collaborative techniques. While health authority personnel usually felt strongly that this was wrong, and a gross mis-use of health service resources, a commitment to the principles of joint planning made wide allowances for these transgressions:

We could always have said no to their schemes, but we have problems with carry forward . . . I nonetheless feel that this is better than nothing. It would not be worth the suffering to clients/patients to stop schemes going ahead.

COSTS AND BENEFITS: A SUMMATION

The foregoing has presented some analysis of the nature of costs and benefits consequent upon actual or anticipated coordinative interaction. This overview has further outlined the experience of costs and/or benefits for individuals, sections and agencies. We are left with a general picture of the reasons for success and failure, but we need to go further than this broad-brush impressionistic image and fill in some of the finer detail.

We move now to consider the *relative weight* of those factors we have presented. How widespread was the experience of particular costs and benefits, and how important was it? Which costs were of central and overwhelming force, and which were more marginal and manageable; which were long standing and which more transient?

Similarly, which benefits were of most worth, and most likely to sway participants, and which were 'small beer' of little significance? Through the complex weave of individual localities' experiences can we now discern an underlying pattern and common precepts?

Inter-personal and individual costs
While inter-personal and individual costs tended to contribute to a general accretion of costs, other more major factors were of greater independent force. Many of the costs experienced at the level of the individual were conditional on perceptions: certainly not all actors would have articulated coordination as 'disturbing'; perceived the 'risks' of boundary crossing, or the costs of prostration. Even for those who did, such concerns were rarely of sufficient strength to wholly dictate the course of action. Nonetheless, cumulatively these cost factors could be considerable.

Resources
Resource considerations were probably the most crucial of costs. The attractiveness of joint finance (and of other 'funny monies') in the short to

medium term faded with the growing prospect of revenue commitment. Even in historically well-resourced localities, an indifference to either the costs or benefits on offer from joint resource pools was receding.

Movement towards the experience of relative resource scarcity sharpened an awareness of the 'opportunity costs in developing anything which we put forward in shrinking resource conditions'. This, in common with all the localities: resource pressures and the experience of absolute or relative retrenchment coloured assessments of 'gaining additional resources through interaction'.

Some areas of resource costs weighed more heavily than others. Administrative and planning resources, and the organisational slack necessary to accommodate these, were usually the first to be reduced in times of stringency. *Nowhere* were the administrative and time costs of coordination irrelevant. While they were of lesser significance in relatively affluent localities, in those experiencing the bite of retrenchment they were of paramount importance.

Domain loss

Domain issues were a further area of *major* costs. However much the principles of coordination were paid lip service, there was widespread dislike of surrendering autonomy. Of course there were some exceptions to this, and at times other considerations overrode domain concerns. In general, joint working (combined centres, joint user establishments etc.) proved the ultimate test for domain cost awareness, which few passed.

The cost and benefit dialectic

We noted previously that costs and benefits formed a dialectical relationship. We might say that resource concerns and domain issues were the most significant costs reported in terms of their incidence and coverage, their centrality, and duration. The precise impact of many of the other variables depended to a large extent upon a more complex interplay of factors. This amalgam includes barrier and opportunity variables, but for the moment let us consider the cost, benefit and incentive factors alone. An accretion of costs – which independently may appear to be marginal and irritating – can, in combination, and in the absence of particular and sufficient benefits, direct a very different course.

The difficulties in operating the coordination machinery have been examined. This machinery could be costly in both time and administration; its operation could be tedious and frustrating. The 'talking shops' and 'doing shops' distinction is pertinent. While basic joint planning machinery is a statutory requirement of all localities, the establishment of extra-ordinary machinery is not, and its incidence suggests the operation of particular cost-benefit calculations. The promise of resources, and the hope of service development, could provide sufficient lure to off-set the additional operational aggravations.

The perception of benefits generally was less vivid than that of costs. As was the case with opportunities, for benefits to be apparent required individuals and agencies to be actively seeking them. Benefits, both in resource and other terms, *were* on offer, but in general they had to be found and quarried out. Other than the very broad and widespread benefits such as in 'improved understandings' and 'enhanced informal relationships', benefits did not simply drop on participants in quite the same way that costs might do.

Tacticians were the risk takers and the deliberate game players. A bargaining and exchange framework directed their interactions. Typically adopting very much longer time horizons than most of their peers, they were better able to perceive and assess both costs and benefits. They were, moreover, adept at adjusting the relative weight of these factors: able to find ways around particular difficulties, reduce areas of cost, and enhance potential benefits. The highly proactive approaches to cost dispersal and responsibility sharing illustrate this mode particularly well. Experience in this area developed skills in anticipating others' needs and aspirations, and in presenting them with appropriate packages too good to refuse.

While resource benefits were important everywhere to a lesser or greater extent, the impact of other benefits was highly variable. The *failure* to recognise others' needs or to accept that such benefits could be adequate was sufficient to block potential exchanges and areas of interaction. For some, the perceived costs of 'being always the receiver' were blind to the benefits which potentially existed for the donor.

Perhaps our 'pessimistic' starting point assumed an overly economistic approach to the calculation of costs and benefits. Certainly we were surprised at the force of concerns over client benefit. Even among the most zealous entrepreneurs and opportunists, the best interests of the client were often uppermost.

Packaging and gift wrapping: active triangulation
Success in interaction and attempts at coordination were most likely when a number of factors fell – or were manoeuvred – into positive alignment. Thus, if client benefit could be achieved simultaneously with the pursuit of particular service and policy paradigms, and further return the benefit of easing service pressures and providing new resources, this was likely to offer a highly attractive package. Conversely, the opposite was true: where all, or many, dimensions of cost appeared great, and with little prospect of beneficial

outcome for most participants, productive interaction was increasingly unlikely.

To assess the likelihood of coordination occurring and to delineate those factors which are of the least and greatest force, is to presume a particular mode of interaction. We are talking mainly of the non-routine. In general, participation in standard machinery and process did not demand such an approach. We have seen that this participation could be (and often was) routinised and tokenistic. To move beyond this point is to begin to weigh up the costs and benefits of so doing. To reach this point there are certain pre requisites. These have been discussed in the context of barriers and opportunities, but it is particularly worth reiterating the importance of a 'systems-wide perspective' (the capacity to view things 'in the round'). In the absence of this a one-dimensional perspective fails to perceive certain factors crucial to the cost-benefit calculus which may be far more complex.

REFERENCES

1 K. Young (1977) 'Values in the policy process', *Policy and Politics*, vol. 5, pp. 1–22
2 M. Douglas (1973) *Rules and Meanings*, Penguin
3 P. Hennessy, S. Morrison and R. Townsend (1985) *Routine Punctuated by Orgies: The Central Policy Review Staff 1970–83*, Strathclyde Papers on Government and Politics, no. 31

10 ~ *Understanding coordination*

The two preceding chapters have prepared the way for a return to the major puzzles and paradoxes generated by the empirical data presented in chapter 7. The central question to be addressed is what were the reasons for 'failure' in terms of the rational, comprehensive and synoptic (i.e. 'optimistic') approach to coordination.

Alongside this, the examples of limited but perhaps unexpected 'success' likewise demand explanation. Why should coordination apparently succeed in one arena, or for a particular tracer and in certain localities and yet not in others? What were the crucial factors?

We have identified a range of variables within the barriers, opportunities, costs and benefits taxonomy. We have seen that the barriers to coordination were formidable, the costs potentially great. Yet we have also found opportunities being sought out and benefits realised, apparently against all odds.

The attempt at weighting the relative strength of barrier, opportunity, cost and benefit variables begins to indicate the explanatory force of particular *combinations of factors* rather than of discrete variables. If we can reach the point at which these combinations can be specified, we can also approach the issue of whether such conditions can be deliberately replicated: can the prerequisites for successful coordination be constructed? These issues are addressed in the final chapter.

Progress toward unpacking the puzzles and the development of the analytic framework suggests the complexity of explanations. The puzzles themselves were far from simple, basically they were of three types: those that were apparent *between arenas*, those *between the tracers*, and others *between localities*.

Neither the puzzles nor their solution (or illumination) are self-contained. Gross variations between localities might be partially explained by one set of factors, but these would neglect broader questions of variation and degrees of success and failure *within* each locality: what then explains the differential development of various arenas and of the tracers?

PUZZLES AND PARADOXES: (I) ARENAS

As we saw in chapter 7, puzzles might be identified in terms both of machinery and of output. The *collaborative arena* featured the highest overall volume of machinery, while the *corporate arena* featured the least, and client group machinery in particular was virtually absent from this arena. In all arenas outputs were most likely to assume the form of individual projects or practices, rather than plans or comprehensive strategies.

Perhaps a more fundamental question that needs to be answered is that of whether differences in machinery levels really made any significant contribution to the product of coordination. Also, why should collaboration produce more machinery than the corporate arena? And, what were the relationships – if any – between machinery levels and output and informal activity? Is it possible to proceed with coordination without an overlay of formal mechanisms; conversely, is it possible to do so solely through informal processes?

A further question would ask why none of the arenas – whether formally or informally organised – were an effective vehicle for policy coordination at a strategic level. What combination of barriers and opportunities, costs, and benefits produced this largely negative finding, and do we have examples, however limited, of the beginnings of a strategic approach, and what were the factors associated with this?

Considering the tracers together, total output was greater in the collaborative arena than in the corporate, and the highest output of all was from the inter-sector arena. The volume of informal output was very similar between all arenas, while machinery output varied enormously, with the inter-sector arena producing almost twice as much as the corporate one.

Combined explanations by arena

Machinery levels

Why should the collaborative arena have featured almost twice as much machinery as the corporate one, and conversely, why should the corporate arena have featured the least of all?

We have seen that formidable barriers to the development of machinery existed, and furthermore that the operation and maintenance of machinery entailed widespread administrative, time and aggravation costs (*nowhere* were these costs insignificant).

In localities with significant reliance upon formal machinery, administrative costs were obviously multiplied, especially where this machinery was of a free-standing and unlimited nature. Machinery can be made more productive by time and task limitation, and establishing a 'problem-solving' focus, rather than an endless and open commitment to continue meeting.

If the costs of operating machinery form part of the explanation for the differential development and productivity of the arenas, further light may be shed by also considering the benefits side of the equation.

There were obviously some wider benefits involved in a long-term round of interaction, for example the gains to informal relations such as have been previously noted. However, it may be appropriate that these informal benefits are built upon – in the longer term – by the establishment of problem-solving machinery after an induction period. These may be particularly relevant for relations between authorities where the opportunities for informal interaction are more limited. Within the corporate arena these might be superfluous, given the everyday opportunities for interaction.

Corporate and collaborative arenas
Machinery levels within the collaborative arena can be considered to be *inflated* by the opportunities posed through the incentive of joint finance, and central government political will expressed in mandatory form. The amount of variation in output, however, indicates the extent to which enabling structures were not sufficient to override barriers and costs posed by resource positions, and planning structures.

The lower machinery levels in the corporate arena are indicative of the *deflationary* impact of the barriers and costs posed by a lack of local political will, the strength of professional demarcations and domains, and the limited appeal of joint policies. In resource terms there were very few readily apparent incentives to interaction. The likelihood of mutual benefits being realised was substantially reduced in a situation in which agencies were potentially competing for shares of the same resources.

One consequence of this was the reinforcement of domain defensiveness and budget protection. Such incentives as were present were more difficult to identify by the actors concerned, and required greater tactical skill. For example, the information resources and technical skills of complementary services. These had to be sought out or staked out far more deliberately before departments would either acknowledge their value or realise their presence.

Having noted this deflationary characteristic it is interesting that the history of corporate endeavour was not characterised by any incentives other than client outcomes. The limited power of such an incentive (which cannot be disregarded as a motivating factor even for the most astute tacticians) has not produced the expected strategic gains, particularly for children under five.

Nonetheless, we have seen that there *were* some examples of apparent success and notable output from the corporate arena. Such examples, however, confirm rather than contradict, the centrality of particular benefits. Thus where potential resource pools were perceived, incentives to interaction might nullify certain cost factors. For example, in Fulborough, home-based community care programmes were facilitated by the opportunistic securement of social security funds; while in Greenshire additional resources were procured under the special needs provisions of the HIPs allocations.

Informal processes

The similarities in informal output across arenas is of particular interest. For the corporate arena this output was slightly greater than that produced directly by machinery. This indicates that the barriers and costs to formal interaction can be avoided or reduced by movement into the informal. In this instance informal activity was a substitute for formal machinery processes, and one which was not notably successful, certainly not at a strategic level. The most that informal processes could produce was alterations to practice and some limited projects. Without political commitment or chief officer support, informal activity produces covert bottom-up outputs.

Within the collaborative and inter-sector arenas formal machinery was necessary even to begin the establishment of informal processes: the development of informal benefits through mutual learning were complementary to and largely dependent on the formal.

A major question arises as to whether it is possible to proceed with either machinery, or with sole reliance upon informal processes. Firstly, the paucity of product from either suggests that neither alone is sufficient. Secondly, there are important gains to be made by seeing them as complementary activities, and least is gained in coordination when there is enforced substitution of the informal for the formal because of the combined costs of the latter. The construction of local coordinative environments must therefore take account of incentives to informal interaction and not just the creation of formal machinery.

Informal output in general was often the product of 'behind the scenes' operations of tacticians, and we have noted the incidence of tacticians both within central planning units, within service departments and within some parts of the voluntary sector. The space available for tactical manoeuvre could be severely restricted by rigid professional demarcations. We have observed that such positions were at times displayed between education and social services, and between health and social services professionals, where the preservation of *operational* autonomy was at the cost of rejecting possibilities for *strategic* joint planning. The 'tribalism' of some departments in certain localities was a clear constraint on coordinated output.

Professional bigotry and status differentials were, as we remarked above, similarly present in the collaborative arena. Why was output not similarly encumbered there? In practice terms, true joint planning remained fairly scarce.

At the practitioner level, status clashes between consultants and various social services actors would have been virtually unavoidable. At a planning level, however, the collaborative arena benefited from the highly developed planning and administrative roles within the health service. The strangeness of the 'foreign territory' of collaboration for most health service practitioners was substantially reduced by the strategic operations of those few who were prepared to step into this other world, learn its customs, language and culture, and generally operate as the 'go-between'.

A further puzzle was identified in the nature of outputs. In general outputs were more likely to be largely ad-hoc projects or practices. Differences were however apparent between the arenas.

From the inter-sector arena a higher proportion of output tended towards practices rather than projects (or indeed policies). We have seen that project-inclined output was most likely in an environment in which resource structures encouraged such one-off developments. Except where special funding might be secured, the emergence of practices – or the modification of existing procedures – was a more likely outcome. Joint finance, we know, skewed the development of collaboration. Success in spending joint finance allocations often said little about successful collaboration *per se*. It is noteworthy that those localities which registered most collaborative machinery output had the least *informal* activity and output.

Different patterns of output between the arenas were further related to differences in *type* of machinery. The high level of overall output for the inter-sector arena is accounted for largely by the large number of practices and projects which were achieved under various ear-marked budgets (urban programme funds, joint finance, Section 11 monies etc.).

There was no example of a comprehensive policy being developed between the sectors, and this was a highly remote possibility. Interaction between the sectors was more inclined to be issue-specific or 'problem-solving' in orientation. The lack of any substantial planning capacity, planning tradition or style, and the absence even of any clearly defined policies within most voluntary agencies, militated against strategic interaction in any sphere. The inability to take a broad view or adopt a systems-wide perspective was underlined in the very low volume of cross-tracer machinery in this arena. While both the corporate and collaborative arenas featured *more* cross-tracer than tracer-specific machinery, quite the reverse was the case in the inter-sector arena.

PUZZLES AND PARADOXES: (II) TRACERS

In many ways tracer and arena puzzles and explanations overlap, and the distinction between them is artificial. In some respects the arena delineation matched that of tracer definition; we know that the collaborative arena was concerned primarily with the elderly tracer, while the corporate arena produced almost twice as much output for the under-fives as for the elderly. The most prolific arena of all – the inter-sector one – was similarly biased towards output for the under-fives. How are we to account for this?

The history of planning initiatives for elderly people and children under five were channelled through different arenas. It is perhaps therefore not wholly surprising that most output for the elderly tracer was located in the collaborative arena with only a residue within the corporate arena, whereas the under-fives were placed by central exhortation as the concern of the corporate augmented by the inter-sector arena. What is interesting is the relative failure of the corporate arena for either tracer.

Again what was common to the tracers was the lack of comprehensive and strategic plans: output centred on projects and practices. The major puzzle of the tracers is why for each there is any success and failure, and whether comparison between the tracers provides relevant material for the future structuring of coordination.

Combinations by tracer

Children under five
For children under five the corporate arena brought together the professional protagonists of education and social services worlds. The barriers posed by incongruent policy stances when combined with the difficulties associated with a declining child population and hence the search for clientele meant there was very little room for the manipulation and search for benefits.

When this was in a situation of mutual resource scarcity or relative abundance coordination between departments was rarely apparent. Either each funded their own unilateral services for children or were wholly intimidated by the prospect of take-over. Professional definitions reflected these underlying resource tendencies.

If to these were added political barriers, of politicians not wishing nor considering the possibilities of supporting coordination, it was even more unlikely to occur. This combination describes the situation which we have observed in Fulborough and Riverton, for example. However, where political will was strongly expressed in terms of comprehensive and systems-wide policy perspectives it was sufficient to override professional and service flow issues. Adding the availability of extra resources for joint activity went some way toward ensuring positive outcomes. This combination was in evidence in Woodtown.

In the above complexity was low and it was a relatively cost-free exercise to organise machinery. The fact that such machinery was – under the conditions depicted – unable to produce coordinated outcomes, beyond largely practices and small projects, was indicative of the salience of other significant combinations.

Amongst these were those where service stocks were low, where the costs of professional sacrifice were avoided by a joint decision to focus upon the thriving and articulate non-statutory sector. Also, where the resource situation had been constrained for some considerable time with the result that only by looking for low-cost and substitute services could any development occur.

The barriers of statutory domains were obviated by a focus directed outside of the local authority. They were able to tap into the resources and energy thus available without having to address their internal difficulties. Moreover, the political framework was amenable to such an interpretation.

Where ideology proscribed the intensive development of the private and voluntary sector, such a coordinated expansion was unthinkable and impractical for officers to engage in. In Greenshire and Portshire such barriers were non-existent and, indeed, the general political climate favoured the initiative of officers in such developments to the extent that in Portshire at least coordination was of high personal and career benefit.

Under such conditions of positive reinforcement for joint initiatives, whether for agency or individual benefit, tacticians were an emergent and influential force. Within Greenshire this was on an unregulated and largely charismatic basis, whereas in Portshire individual actors saw this as a normal progression and a normal feature of career development within their chosen service. Such was the pervasiveness of tactical activity that the voluntary sector also operated in like mode, to the extent that there was an interchange of personnel with movement from voluntary positions to joint liaison and development positions within the local authority.

This combination of political sanction, systems-wide perspective, and recognition of the prohibitive costs of corporate interaction meant that the opportunities for coordination in the non-statutory arena were quickly seized.

An incentive for this direction was the availability of joint finance for joint projects and joint workers, and sufficient priority and influence directed toward exploiting resources elsewhere associated with collaborative planning. In this the local authority and non-statutory partners made most of the running and were prepared to recast their definitions of service development and policies to fit in with health concerns. Nothing was lost by allowing the health service some input to parenting, child development and health education.

Indeed, such input positively strengthened the credibility of non-statutory activity by aligning it with even more powerful professional concerns. There were therefore clear benefits for the majority of partners, with only the health service feeling aggrieved that perhaps their involvement was being sought purely for the resources they could sanction through joint finance.

A further factor in this positive sum game was that without the non-statutory development there would have been none at all. This would have left the statutory partners either presiding over dwindling domains, or in open conflict for each other's resources. Where there still remained an outside chance of diverting resources, and no political will for coordination, education and social services met in head on collision.

It was also different from the elderly tracer because of a built in through-put in the service system, whereas for the elderly the reverse was largely the case. Here engendering through-put and managing dependency created opportunities for interaction.

Elderly people
As noted above, through-put issues provided opportunities for engaging in coordination, affecting housing and social services and these two in relation to the health service provision of long-stay places. Very rarely were the opportunities created seized in anything other than a bilateral mode. Systems-wide thinking was present but broad strategic concerns were not translated into coherent joint action. It was only where through-put problems combined with demand pressures and resource constraint that the benefits of coordination were in any way sufficient to promote interaction. This was further conditional on the insights and dexterity of tacticians able to think through and around barriers and apparent costs.

The scope for achieving successful coordination with the non-statutory sector was very much less in relation to the elderly tracer than for children under five. The principal protagonist voluntary agencies for each tracer were of a fundamentally different kind.

Those for children under five (mainly PPA) were concerned with practical policy and service development, both alongside and independently of statutory services. For elderly people the main agent was Age Concern, a very much more traditional voluntary body in which policy concerns were more residual. The private residential care sector was of increasing significance for elderly people in many of our localities. Interaction had, however, been largely confined to the requirements of registration and regulation. While some localities were more inclined to make use of facilities thus available, nowhere had a planned or strategic approach been attempted. The political sensitivity of this area was a prominent consideration.

Some of the projected costs and putative barriers for coordination in policies for elderly people were organised around professional defensiveness and professional aggrandisement. By moving into lower cost areas of interaction, such as those between housing and social services for example, or between social services and voluntary agencies, coordination was more likely.

This was certainly the case in Greenshire which achieved notable and isolated success in the development of community care of elderly people. The complementary resources and service stocks of sheltered housing units and the domiciliary skills, residential resources and long-standing expertise of the social services provided a basis for exchange relations. This was a symmetrical exchange of benefits which both sides appreciated.

Relations between health and social services were often prejudiced by a narrow focus upon their respective residential resources which were seen as close substitutes or competitors, rather than complements. The potential complementary nature of domiciliary support services in aiding hospital through-put and medical expertise and nursing skills in Part III settings were rarely the basis for exchange. Although systems-wide planning could be constructed on the basis of these interdependencies, this was rarely the case because of the extensive time period before which agency benefits would accrue and the professional costs of joint working within a unilaterally controlled setting.

SYNTHESIS AND RECOMBINATION

The synthesis of arena and tracer puzzles is lodged in the localities themselves. The arena and tracer recombinations give substance to the relatively abstract catalogue of barrier, opportunity, cost and benefit variables. Slicing across this amalgam, however, the locality strata adds form to substance.

When success or failure might have been predicted on the prima-facie evidence of arena and tracer combinations, the particular features of localities and their idiosyncratic mediation of variables provide the dynamic. Local characteristics then, are the joker or 'wild' card in the pack: the catalyst to success or the extinguisher of potential.

We turn now to consider how these features variously combined within the localities; we can see both the parameters of largely external coordinative environments, together with the fluidity injected by internal and assumptive environments.

The localities revisited

Portshire

For both tracers resource and service levels created potential opportunities. Domain issues were largely neutralised by the positive combinations of benefits achieved by movement into the inter-sector arena. Such activity had political support, and was endorsed by all participants to the extent that it was congruent with perceptions of costs and benefits.

This latter dimension, however, explains the differential 'success' around the tracers. Combinations of costs and benefits aggregated differentially around children under five and elderly people. The barriers to interaction posed by domain defence, and the costs therefore inherent in coordination, were reduced in relation to children under five by benefits which could outweigh these – at least in the short to medium term – in a pragmatic compromise.

For the elderly tracer both barriers and costs were significantly greater than in relation to the under-fives. While the under-fives policy field offered opportunities for visible (and prestigious) but largely cost-free interaction, any similar developments for elderly people would have been far more costly. The attraction and potential incentive of cost and responsibility sharing was present for both tracers, but in the case of elderly people would have required greater administrative and financial investment. Such costs were judged to outweigh possible benefits, and any interaction was defensive rather than proactive (off-loading rather than sharing).

Greenshire
For children under five Greenshire presented a very similar picture to Portshire, i.e. the barriers of professional domain defensiveness (and the consequent costs of domain loss) were outweighed by the perceived advantages of inter-sector activity, and the particular benefit of being seen to be active in a field where resources constrained any independent action.

For elderly people, perceptions of unacceptable costs of collaboration were too great to facilitate service pressures offering any opportunity for both the SSD and health authority. Barriers to interaction in the corporate arena (not least structural complexity) were, however, turned to advantage by tactical manoeuvring. Informally negotiated solutions were able to meet the needs of clients and offer benefits to the mutual satisfaction of both housing and social services.

Cliffshire
Considerable barriers to interaction around the elderly tracer existed in the absence of basic value consensus or shared policy paradigms. The polarised positions of health and social services skewed perceptions of costs and benefits. While considerable resource and service pressures could have provided the incentive and opportunity for interaction, professional and finance considerations effectively blocked any such development – both

between health and social services, and between social services and housing. For housing authorities, for example, pressures on sheltered accommodation could have been eased by the development of more Part III accommodation. For the SSD, however, this could offer no basis for negotiation while it was seen to contradict objectives of community based care.

For children under five barriers in terms of status differentials and absence of consensus proved too great to allow potential resource benefits to be realised other than in an ad-hoc manner. Joint budgets did, on occasion, succeed in drawing together disparate interests (aided by influential member commitment).

Woodtown

Within Woodtown major barriers to effective coordination were posed by high resource inputs and service stock levels. If nothing else, the health and local authorities would have been able to develop relatively independently. However, a major countervailing force to unilateralism in policies for elderly people, was the pivotal position that was represented by political power and commitment. This was expressed as both public duty to meet social need and a clear understanding of the interdependence of separately administered services.

The combination of political awareness and will to achieve better services for elderly people transformed the coordinative environment: providing clear benefits to officers to engage in coordination; and an overriding of administrative, domain and professional costs. It also joined with the pressures created within the housing service system and that within social services. The availability of corporate machinery was utilised to realise political commitment.

For children under five political support for a joint approach was muted and the traditional professional and departmental hostility between education and social services meant few incentives for interaction.

Riverton

By contrast in this locality barriers and opportunities, costs and benefits all combined to ensure there were virtually no incentives to coordination. Low resources and inadequate service stocks, allied with and fuelled professional and domain defensiveness, and exacerbated status differentials. Even at the margin, the costs of collaboration were far outweighed by an inability to secure medium term resources to fund future development.

The political component of resource compression at all costs was an overriding barrier in any attempts at a joint approach.

Fulborough

Within this inner London locality general resource plenitude had both facilitated the development of high levels of unilaterally based services in the past, and reduced the value of potential benefits offered by coordination and combined services.

In addition the costs of compromise implied in joint action were strenuously resisted. This was aided by an entrenched tradition of departmental separatism, and the absence of any political corporate will.

Moreover, at a formal level of interaction from within a relatively small group of actors personality clashes between individual chief officers mitigated against effective interaction, only allowing lower placed individuals to engage in short range opportunistic incursions across departmental and domain boundaries. This was particularly the case for the elderly tracer where the overt dependency of social services on housing resources, with little perception of housing's needs, obstructed a constructive dialogue.

In terms of children under five, the statutory authorities perceived coordination as a marginal and costly activity that held few benefits in the long term. The political distance of the ILEA from local service concerns meant that coordination was conducted by largely professional interests, with considerable dissensus.

Templeborough

Structural complexity was not a key feature in Templeborough. Within a small, coterminous outer London authority it was the presence of barriers posed by status and domain issues, particularly for children under five, that dominated the corporate and inter-sector arenas.

Despite a clear systems-wide perspective on the part of the social services, and an awareness of the system benefit that would accrue to clients from a joint approach, this foundered on the strength of the educational claim to manage and run their own service system, without interference or contamination. There were very clear expressions of divergence in policy stances, which in the absence of any directive political influence, left the field to the conflicting professions and antagonistic departments. The voluntary sector was insufficiently strong to mediate.

In such a situation, even the broadest altruism of the social services in being prepared to cede the entire service to education was treated with, if not mistrust, a definite lack of enthusiasm.

For elderly people, social services were again clearly aware of the opportunity for collaboration created by current and future demand levels: no agency could hope to succeed alone, and in terms of community care, social services would act in a residual role. The burden was being spread but at a clear cost to the resources and service definitions of other agencies and authorities. This was either largely resisted or ignored, apart from a number of informal agreements which were not tied in to either official machinery or expressed more generally in formal policy statements.

REFLECTIONS AND CONCLUSIONS

These combinations have clarified the general conclusion reached earlier that systematic rational planning is an infrequent occurrence within and across the localities. Whatever the abstract appeal of such a sensible package, within the everyday environment faced by local actors it is considered to be of relevance, but often struggles to survive in the face of barriers posed by particular combinations of structural and behavioural variables.

In general terms neither the 'optimistic' tradition nor its more 'pessimistic' analogue is wholly adequate in covering the range of locality detail.

Broadly, the notion of organisational altruism is unfounded as a generalised concept, but it is effective as a motivating agent – especially when combined with some element of single agency and individual benefit. The latter might be in career terms or the sheer ability to do something in a bureaucratic organisation which rarely achieves much: coordination can be valued precisely because it creates a new fluid and potentially malleable structure.

This is what distinguishes the actors within Greenshire, Fulborough and Templeborough from their counterparts in, for example, Riverton. In the latter only short term costs and benefits were a consideration. Also, there was little indication of longer term benefits for clients, a perspective reinforced by the prevailing political ideology.

Similarly, it is easy to dismiss the appeal of the 'optimistic' tradition if it is inextricably linked to the notion of a systems-wide perspective.

In terms of the tracers this was often not grounded in a comprehensive joint analytical task, although this was on occasion an activity engaged in on a unilateral basis.

Either agencies had inadequate planning capacities to sustain such an activity, or they could not generate the necessary information to underpin systems-wide planning. In some instances the intellectual equipment to manage this task was either absent or deflected by other interests and managerial responsibilities. However, the most important reason for the failure to establish purely rational systems-wide planning was the dangers presented in terms of the redistribution of financial resources, the reorganisation of domains and the gulf it had to bridge in terms of different values attaching to the planning activity itself, or to the future shape of services.

There were, however, instances in which a movement toward a partial understanding of the inter relationship of service systems was forthcoming. This was largely not as a result of analytic rationality, but of political rationality. In Woodtown, for example, political ideology was crucial in establishing a positive cost-benefit equation in favour of coordination, even if conservative interests of profession and specialism prevailed in curtailing joint output.

In localities such as Greenshire the political persuasion of members had long been accommodated, services were expanded and coordination sought as a means of achieving cost-effectiveness and cost-dispersal compatible with a politically restricted resource position.

From both traditions it is then possible to abstract certain elements conducive to achieving coordination: there must be some focus on organisational altruism and meeting need; an awareness of service interdependency however partial; and the importance of securing and aligning with political support.

In addition the 'optimistic' tradition presumes a high degree of consensus between agencies on the need for planning, the content of policy and the shape of future services. Much of this consensus was found to be lacking within the localities.

Yet where coordination did take place consensus was a feature of success. Not in the pluralist fashion implicit in the 'optimistic' tradition, but as a result of the assessment and negotiation of mutual benefits. Consensus is an achieved and constructed quality, rather than an automatic precursor of thinking about coordination.

In summary, the 'pessimistic' tradition is useful in charting the barriers and opportunities, costs and benefits associated with the attempts by local actors to achieve coordination. Indeed, it is the particular skill of certain actors in being able to monitor and reflect upon the process that accounts for some of the more successful coordinative endeavours. Machinery is made to work and informal processes treated with the delicacy and importance they deserve. An appreciation of costs and benefits at this level has considerable explanatory power.

However, the strengths of the 'pessimistic' tradition require supplementing by aspects of the 'optimistic' approach in order to complete the explanation.

Having described and understood the reasons for success and failure of coordination in terms of different aspects of both traditions, it is possible to construct different packages of variables such that coordination may be achievable or at least attempted. Certainly it will be possible to provide prescriptions for analysing local environments and suggesting that 'coordination is not worth the candle' in certain instances. Whereas in others, with some attention to the balance of costs and benefits, it may be possible to overcome barriers and capitalise upon opportunities via the introduction of selective incentives.

11 ∼ Towards a new model of social planning

In this chapter, as in chapter 4, we explore a paradox. This is that coordination is both problematic and necessary. It is problematic because, in practice, it turns out to be extremely difficult to achieve as we have seen in the preceding chapters. It is necessary because it is an essential for managing the ever-increasing complexity of society. From this flows the manic-depressive cycle of the policy debate about coordination with fits of enthusiasm yielding to bursts of disillusion. When we launched out on this study, the cycle was in its depressive stage: coordination was out of fashion. However, as noted in the preface, by the time we had completed it, the cycle was once again in its manic phase: Mrs Thatcher's Conservative government had embraced the rhetoric of coordination.

If enthusiasm is not once again to give way to disillusion, it is essential to be clear about why the reality of coordination always appears to fall short of expectations and why achievement always seems to lag behind rhetoric. If coordination is indeed necessary (and all governments, sooner or later, seem to find it so), how can rhetoric and achievement be brought into line?

To answer this question, we examine our findings in the light of the two competing models of social planning which tend to shape all discussions of coordination, explicitly so in the case of the academic literature and implicitly so in the case of the men and women engaged in the day-to-day business of policy design and delivery. These are what we called, in our opening chapters, the 'optimistic' and the 'pessimistic' models. Each makes very different assumptions about the desirability and feasibility of coordination. The former sees coordination as an essential part of a collective, rational approach to policy-making, with an emphasis on comprehensive analysis and the design of appropriate machinery. The latter sees coordination as not only redundant but doomed, in so far as it cannot be planned or mandated by governments since the policy process consists of individuals and organisations bargaining in the political market place. The former explains the manic stage of the policy cycle; the latter explains the depressive phase.

If we are to break out of the cycle, we may therefore also have to re-think the underlying models. In fact, to summarise the theme of this chapter, neither captures the full complexity of the world of policy making although both generate important insights. Accordingly, we put forward a somewhat different model of social action – the *planned bargaining model* – to serve as a framework for thinking both about policy coordination and the wider context of government policies and institutions. From this model, which explains our findings more satisfactorily than either of the two dominant ones, we then derive some prescriptions for promoting policy coordination designed to lessen the gap between expectations and achievements.

EXPLANATIONS AND CONTRADICTIONS

The evidence we have accumulated from our empirical studies overwhelmingly points in one direction: to the lack of fit between practice on the ground and the propositions derived from the 'optimistic' model. This message emerges no less strongly from our studies at the centre than from those at the local level. The failure of the Joint Approach to Social Policy in the 1970s and the demise of the Central Policy Review Staff in the 1980s sit squarely alongside the local experience of national initiatives to improve coordination and suggest a common conclusion. Social policy coordination in the rational mode has been tried and has failed, or not attempted at all. Thus the approach at the heart of the thinking and prescriptions of successive governments has produced few obvious or tangible returns for all the aspirations, time and effort invested in it.

Where there is coordination, as between government departments, it tends to be defensive in character: designed, that is, to protect existing organisational interests rather than to produce policies cutting across those interests. Where a machinery of coordination has been developed its productivity is – as our locality studies demonstrate – at best, uncertain and at worst, poor. The preconditions assumed by the 'optimistic' model – consensus about objectives, analytical capacity, systems-wide perspectives and organisational altruism – are all in short supply, if to varying degrees. All our evidence suggests further that the model over-predicts consensus and organisational altruism; consensus is hard won and altruism is comparatively rare. Divergences on the choice of means tend to be embedded in professional and organisational paradigms while divergences on priorities are embedded in the competition for resources.

This is not to imply that our research produced a totally Hobbesian picture of organisational life. It did throw up examples of the preconditions required by the 'optimistic' model, such as systems-wide perspectives and organisational altruism, just as it provided some instances of successful outputs as the result of coordination and collaboration between organisations. But all these were conspicuous by their rarity. What defeats the 'optimistic' model is the infrequent *concurrence* of all these preconditions in two or more organisations or professions rather than the total absence of all – or any – of them. Given a limited supply of each (and no guarantee that it will be distributed symmetrically among the organisations or professions engaged in any policy arena), the laws of probability are against coordination through collaborative planning.

Nor does this interpretation seem to be contingent on the harsh economic environment in which our study took place. On the one hand, scarcity of resources and perceptions of unmet needs do create a heightened awareness of the desirability of coordinated action, just as they deepen regret at failures to achieve it. On the other hand, however, they also tend to increase the competition for resources and to predispose actors towards defensiveness. The special nature of the economic environment which creates a willingness to engage in collaboration therefore also contributes to the comparative low probability of coordinated outputs. Conversely, economic plenty might well weaken the pressures to engage in coordination, even while lowering the costs of so doing.

So our study would seem to lead to a conclusion that is wholly unremarkable and very much in line with previous case studies which have found social planning to fall far short of the 'optimistic' model's assumptions. Like our predecessors, we found inter-agency arenas to be largely characterised by limited and conditional interaction rather than by frequent and free relationships; by attempts to resolve existing problems rather than to anticipate future ones; and by relatively small scale and isolated examples of 'ad-hocery' and opportunism rather than coherent and consistent implementation within some grand design. More specifically, the potential gains of coordination for clients or systems had to compete, as an over-arching agency objective, against such organisational imperatives as budget maximisation, maintaining autonomy and professional self-interest. And while those who stand to gain from the successful outcomes of coordination usually are a diffuse and unorganised constituency, those who stand to gain from the maintenance of the status quo are by definition concentrated and organised. So, more often than not, there was no contest worthy of the name. In other words, our findings would seem to compel us to embrace the 'pessimistic' model of social action as a more accurate predictor of behaviour within and between organisations than the 'optimistic' one.

Where does this leave us? Are we to conclude that coordination has proved to be not only the holy grail of administration for the many but also a poisoned chalice for those few who have been persistent or reckless enough to drink from it? Should we recommend that government departments and social welfare agencies abandon the illusion that coordination is possible and concentrate upon the management of affairs within their own jurisdictions? Alternatively, should we expose coordination as a substitute for policy – as a comforting slogan in which politicians and civil servants take refuge when they are bereft of substantive proposals or are reluctant to take hard decisions – especially those which require the re-allocation of responsibilities between powerful agencies and professional groups?

Before drawing such a nihilistic conclusion, however, it may be sensible to put the 'pessimistic' model on the rack. Again, our research provides a warning against embracing it without reservation. Our findings suggest that the 'optimistic' model's taken-for-granted assumption of an unlimited supply of organisational altruism, as well as consensus about both ends and means, is excessively naive but they also indicate that the 'pessimistic' model's assumption that organisational life is dominated by the pursuit of self-interest is excessively narrow. So, for example, the latter does not account for our finding that coordination was widely perceived to be desirable, nor for our (admittedly few) success stories. In short, the 'pessimistic' model tends to over-explain.

The reason why it does so stems from a central weakness in the model. This is its failure to place the process of interaction, of bargaining and negotiation between organisational actors, within the wider political and social environment which determines the rules of the game. Just because coordination cannot be imposed by government or mandated through the creation of machinery but can only be the product of spontaneous interaction, it does not follow that the behaviour of the organisational actors is independent of the structure within which they operate. In the case of the social services – whether public or private – this is a structure created by governments. If the metaphor of the market is illuminating to the extent that it stresses the importance of trading and bargaining by organisational actors, it is misleading to the extent that it ignores the fact that this is a regulated market created by public policies which help to shape the attitudes of those participating in it.

Hence, perhaps, the evidence thrown up by our study in support of at least some of the assumptions of the 'optimistic' model. A value commitment to the well-being of clients, or to the public good more broadly conceived and transcending departmental or organisational interests, emerged strongly in parts of central government and in some of our locality studies. Systems-wide perspectives and organisational altruism are a reality, contrary to the predictions of the 'pessimistic' model. Professional, bureaucratic and political behaviour is therefore best understood as a complex and variable mixture of self-regarding and other-regarding activity, of rational calculation and routine response. A basic philosophy of service does retain a hold in the social policy field, and provides some degree of support for the 'optimistic' model. In turn, the particular composition of the mixture will – at any point in time – be influenced by political culture, the prevailing political ideology and by sociali- sation. Moreover, this is a dynamic, learning process. The rules of the game, and the value of the currency used in trading, will change over time. If the great weakness of the 'optimistic' model is that it only identifies one source of learn- ing – rational analysis – the great weakness of the 'pessimistic' model is that it ignores the factors external to any particular policy arena which may influence the learning process: for example, the use of authority to shape people's per- ceptions of their own interests and legitimate objectives. Lastly, the 'pessi- mistic' model presents a problem in logic. Its strength lies in its descriptive power, in its ability to explain the failure of attempts by governments to impose a top-down pattern and machinery of coordination. In this respect, despite the reservations made, it undoubtedly offers a more convincing description of reality than the 'optimistic' model. However, in moving from description to prescription, it conflates the 'is' with the 'ought'. If we allow the descriptive power of the 'pessimistic' model to dictate policy prescription, we therefore become trapped within the limitations of organisational behaviour which it identifies. The present, by implication, dictates the future.

Conversely, the 'optimistic' model imposes a vision of the future on the present. It assumes that descriptive reality will fall into line with its prescriptive aspirations. To the extent that this merely remains a presumption, it explains why the 'optimistic' model seems to be discredited. However, its strength (and enduring appeal despite recurrent disillusion) lies precisely in the fact that it holds out the *possibility* of improvement. It does not condemn us to the tread- mill of the *status quo*. Unlike the 'pessimistic' model it offers the hope that the future may be different from the present. Because all governments – whatever their ideology – share this hope they come sooner or later to discover the importance of policy coordination in pursuit of their own vision of the future.

In the next section, we therefore examine whether it is possible to combine the descriptive insights of the 'pessimistic' model with the appeal of the 'optimistic' model. In doing so we advance a new model of social planning. This starts from the assumption that for as long as governments promulgate policies, there will be a perceived need for policy coordination but that success depends on recognising and working within the constraints rather than ignoring them.

THE PLANNED BARGAINING MODEL

In moving towards sketching out a new model of social planning, it is important to be clear just why the two dominant models came up with such very opposed descriptions and prescriptions. The reason lies in their very different perspectives. The 'optimistic' model starts with the problems of governance in complex modern societies, and addresses the question of how these could best be solved. The 'pessimistic' model starts with the problems of implementing government policies, and addresses the question of why in practice there is such a wide divergence between aims and achievements. The former is an architectural approach. The latter is a social anthropologist's approach. It studies the people who come to inhabit the building and – as a result – queries the attempt of the architect to impose a pattern of living and behaviour.

Our model seeks to bring these two perspectives together. We have called it a 'planned bargaining' model, in that it starts from the assumption that, inescapably, government is all about the creation of institutional architecture but that the design itself needs to incorporate the insights generated by studies of how people actually behave. In short, in line with our findings, we assume that architecture affects the way in which people behave, but that it does not dictate their activities: that it can create opportunities – a new sense of what is possible – even though it cannot impose a pattern of living. If the ultimate logic of the top-down perspective is central autocracy, the ultimate logic of the bottom-up perspective is anarchy at the periphery: hence the need for a synthesis.

So our model starts from the assumption (which it shares with the 'optimistic' one) that it is the proper role of governments to create a framework for strategic planning, in which coordination will have a part to play. But it further assumes (in common with the 'pessimistic' model) that the implementation of such a strategy is problematic and liable to be distorted or frustrated by organisational self-interest, local bargaining and so on. From this follows the crucial characteristic of our 'planned bargaining' model, which is the insistence that the design of the strategic framework must be such as to take account of the incentives and interests of those in the policy arena. Rationality, in this model, is multi-dimensional, and pluralistic. It seeks to incorporate not only the rationality of the central policy actors – the philosopher kings, as it were, in search of some over-arching national policy objective – but the rationalities of the individual organisational actors pulling in different directions. It aims to regulate the political market of interaction, bargaining and negotiation, not to abolish it. In doing so, it recognises – in line with the findings of our study – that organisational behaviour is not something set in concrete but is affected by the environment in which it takes place.

Let us now apply this model to the particular case of coordination. First, the model recognises that coordination is not a self-evident good. It involves costs and benefits to the organisational actors, as stressed in the previous chapters, and those who carry the costs do not necessarily reap the benefits. An unwillingness to waste time and energy in crossing organisational boundaries may be entirely appropriate – and rational – if there is good work to be done on one's own patch and the outcomes are more predictable than are those of coordinated action. From this follows the model's second presumption: that if coordination is thought to be desirable, the strategic framework must be such as to limit the costs and raise the benefits to the organisational actors involved. For, thirdly and crucially, the model assumes that coordination will be the product of autonomous organisational actors not of institutional structure and machinery. Appropriate structure and machinery may be a necessary condition for systematic as distinct from occasional coordination; it is certainly not a sufficient condition, as our findings clearly show. It is only if there are appropriate signals and incentives to the individual organisational actors that the machinery will spring to life.

From these general propositions about coordination follow some specific prescriptions. The first task of a strategic framework is to avoid *disabling* coordinative endeavour: to avoid sending our contradictory or confusing signals to the organisational actors. There must be compatibility between 'high' and 'low' politics. So, for example, if different policy streams at the level of central government are incompatible – if public expenditure policies pull in the opposite direction from service policies – then it is unrealistic to expect the organisational actors at the periphery to coordinate their activities. The second task of a strategic framework is to create the *enabling* structures required to allow coordination to take place: for example, machinery which lowers the costs of participation to the organisational actors involved. The third task of a strategic framework is to encourage the development of an *organisational culture* which sustains coordinative endeavour and a *reward structure* which provides appropriate incentives.

These prescriptions follow from the findings of our research, which suggest that the key features of successful coordination and collaboration are:
a strong value predisposition towards system-wide thinking and other-regarding behaviour, as well as the structural forms and analytical capacities identified in the 'optimistic' model;
uninterrupted and possibly prolonged opportunities for interaction across boundaries in order to permit learning about divergent paradigms, practices, constraints and competences – as a basis for the development of trust and a soundly-based system-wide perspective;
external catalysts to such learning – including powerful representation of the client's interests and needs, as well as resource pressures which nonetheless permit opportunities for the pursuit of 'positive sum' coordination;
the consistent exercise of political and administrative authority in support

of system-wide thinking, policy analysis and collaborative action;
the provision of other incentives, including resource incentives, to bargaining and collaborative behaviour – as an alternative to a complete
dependence on altruistic behaviour.

The model thus seeks to combine the top-down formal approach to
coordination with the bottom-up spontaneous interaction approach. It recognises that individual organisational actors – the reticulists, entrepreneurs and
brokers whose activities we have described in previous chapters – have an
important role to play. Our fieldwork identified many examples of coordination being pursued successfully through informal processes: some 40% of
all the outputs logged were produced in this way. And the case for
emphasising the importance of organisational cultures and reward structures
is precisely that these should be designed so as to encourage this kind of
activity. But our model also recognises that formal machinery apparently
produces more outputs, and over a shorter period of time, than informal
mechanisms. Once again we conclude, therefore, that the conditions required
for promoting coordination can only be met by the combination of encouragement for policy entrepreneurs and formal machinery, for paying equal
attention to the motives of individual organisational actors and the structure
of the environment which shapes their activities.

The proposed 'planned bargaining' model does not offer an easy route or
short-cut to successful coordination. On the contrary, it makes more
stringent demands on the policy-system than either of the other two models.
For its prescriptions depend on consistency and coherence across
time and, above all, political commitment: as the history of the Joint Approach
to Social Policy shows most clearly, in the absence of sustained political
commitment, institutional structures quickly become ancient monuments of
interest only to academic tourists. Structures and processes which cut across
professional and departmental boundaries at the highest level are necessary if
political and administrative support for policy coordination is to be systematic
rather than spasmodic. And such support has to be systematic and sustained if
the environment in which individual or organisational actors operate is to be
changed so as to modify their perceptions and definitions of their self-interest
in a way calculated to improve the prospects of policy coordination. In the
next, and final section, we therefore discuss some specific ways in which the
newly rediscovered enthusiasm for coordination could be harnessed to such a
long-term endeavour.

FROM RHETORIC TO ACTION

The new enthusiasm for coordination tends to be expressed in the language
and concepts of the 1960s. It is hortatory in character. It stresses structural

change and formal machinery. It uses the rhetoric of the 'optimistic' model, with its culture of coordination. In this there is a central irony. For the new enthusiasm is the product of a government which in other contexts, repudiates the language and concepts of the 1960s. It is a government which uses the rhetoric of the 'pessimistic' model, with its culture of enterprise. It stresses individual initiative rather than collective endeavour. Does this mean that the invocation of coordination will inevitably be no more than rhetorical rhubarb? Or can the new enterprise culture, with its emphasis on individual innovators, be harnessed to the traditional coordination culture, with its emphasis on altruism, rational analysis and a systems-wide approach? Our model suggests that the concept of coordination can indeed be rescued from rhetoric, and that the two cultures can be mutually reinforcing if the appropriate framework is created. Specifically, it also suggests the following strategies:

1. Creating reward structures for coordination
At present reward structures in both central and local government tend to reinforce organisational loyalties: promotion and knighthoods go to those men and women who have successfully pursued a mainstream career. Policy entre-preneurs, by contrast, operate at the margins of their organisations. They tend to be marginal, vulnerable and expendable – and may not even be employed in the public sector. If the aim is to encourage a culture of coordination, then this has to be reflected in the reward structure: promotion and knighthoods must go to those who are prepared to take risks by cutting across organisational boundaries.

2. Creating crocks of gold for coordination
If personnel policies can create incentives for individuals to engage in coordinative activities, similarly incentives are needed for organisations. The joint finance scheme for health and social services to engage in collaborative projects provides both an example and a warning. It provides an example in so far as it provides special, ear-marked funds for projects which must be agreed by two different organisations and thus, in theory, also provides an incentive to coordination. It provides a warning in so far as it does not have adequate safeguards against collusive behaviour and thus, in practice, allows both organisations to use the funds to do what they would have liked to do anyway. This suggests that the allocation of such 'crocks of gold' should be contingent on evidence of coordination in the production of proposed projects, rather than being merely a hopeful distribution of funds on the assumption that coordination will follow.

3. Creating a system for evaluating coordination
Coordination is not an end in itself, but a means for achieving certain objectives: notably the more efficient and effective use of resources. This

implies, in turn, that every ministerial circular or initiative calling for coordination should also specify what the objectives are (following the example of the Financial Management Initiative). If there were such account- ability for the production of specified outputs (and our own research suggests that outputs *can* be measured) there would be less risk of the rhetoric of coordination becoming merely a substitute for action, and machinery becom- ing a substitute for performance.

In putting forward these strategies, we are not suggesting that there are any cook-book recipes for successful coordination. What we are suggesting is something both more limited and more ambitious. This is that it is possible to institutionalise a commitment to coordination and, by so doing, gradually create the climate, value-system and incentives which will persuade indi- vidual and organisational actors to adapt their behaviour accordingly. The end is change in the behaviour of the actors; institutions are only the means. The perspective is essentially long-term. Our approach sees coordination not as an instant policy-fix for specific problems but as a way of thinking about social policy. And it offers, we believe, the only way of breaking out of the manic-depressive cycle of excessive expectations being followed by excessive disillusion.

INDEX

Abel-Smith, Brian, 80, 91
administrative domains
  as barriers to coordination, 214
administrative machinery
  in central government, 124–8
  in the collaborative arena, 180–4, 196–206
  in the corporate arena, 166–70
  and costs, 233, 237–9
  in the inter-sector arena, 191–6, 197–206
  study of, 155–8
Age Concern, 188, 189, 190, 195, 196, 260
AHAs (Area Health Authorities) 16
  in Cliffshire, 148–9
  and the collaborative arena, 177–8
  in Fulborough, 153–4
  in Greenshire, 149
  and NHS restructuring, 184
  in Portshire, 150
  in Riverton, 151–2
  in Templeborough, 154–5
  in Woodtown, 152–3
  see also health services; National Health
    Service
Aitken, M., 40
Allison, G. T., 35
altruism
  organisational, 33–4, 43, 44, 45, 136, 239,
    241, 248, 265, 268, 270
  and social policy, 18
Amery, Leopold, 7

Bachrach, P., 43–4
Bains Report (1972), 15–16, 159
Baratz, M. S., 43–4
bargaining: and policy coordination, 137
barriers to coordination, 108–15, 209–30,
    231, 259
behavioural elements: and barriers to
    coordination, 228–9
benefits of coordination, 240–6
  and costs, 231–3; of operating machinery,
    254
Bentham, Jeremy, 4, 9
Berrill, Sir Kenneth, 80, 89, 90, 91
Booth, T. A., 53
Bradley, M., 61, 167

Cabinet
  and the Haldane Report, 8–9
  and policy coordination, 27, 75
  and policy ownership, 110
  Social Services Committee, 71–2, 73, 100
Care in Action (DHSS), 20, 52, 55, 60
Care in the Community (DHSS), 124
Carr, Robert, 78
Castle, Barbara, 54, 66, 80, 84, 87, 88, 89,
    98, 103
central government
  and local authorities, 85–7, 113
  and policy coordination, 106–38
  reorganisation of: White Paper on, 17
  see also government departments
Central Planning Units, 213, 214
Central Policy Units, 244
centralisation, 26; see also decentralisation
Chadwick, Edwin, 6–7, 12, 18
Challis, L., 56
childminding, 56, 58, 149, 151, 170, 221
children under five
  administrative machinery for, 199
  and barriers to coordination, 214–15,
    258
  and central government policy, 140
  in Cliffshire, 148, 149, 263
  in the collaboration arena, 176, 177–80
  in the corporate arena, 166–71
  and cost dispersal, 245–6
  in Fulborough, 154, 264
  in Greenshire, 149, 262
  and the inter-sector arena, 193–6
  machinery and output for, 201–6
  and policy congruence, 227–8
  and policy coordination, 107, 152–70,
    258–60
  as policy tracers, 47, 48–9, 55–6
  and political ideology, 221
  in Portshire, 147, 150, 262
  in Riverton, 147, 150, 151
  service systems for, 216
  in Templeborough, 154, 155
  in Woodtown, 152, 263
CHOG (Chief Housing Officers Group),
    163

277